# Lecture Notes in Computer Science 13569

More information about this series at https://link.springer.com/bookseries/558

Lin Gan · Yu Wang · Wei Xue ·
Thomas Chau (Eds.)

# Applied Reconfigurable Computing

## Architectures, Tools, and Applications

18th International Symposium, ARC 2022
Virtual Event, September 19–20, 2022
Proceedings

 Springer

*Editors*
Lin Gan
Tsinghua University
Beijing, China

Wei Xue
Tsinghua University
Beijing, China

Yu Wang
Tsinghua University
Beijing, China

Thomas Chau
Samsung AI Center
Cambridge, UK

ISSN 0302-9743          ISSN 1611-3349 (electronic)
Lecture Notes in Computer Science
ISBN 978-3-031-19982-0          ISBN 978-3-031-19983-7 (eBook)
https://doi.org/10.1007/978-3-031-19983-7

This Springer imprint is published by the registered company Springer Nature Switzerland AG
The registered company address is: Gewerbestrasse 11, 6330 Cham, Switzerland

# Preface

The 18th International Symposium on Applied Reconfigurable Computing (ARC 2022) was organized by the Tsinghua University, China, during September 19–20, 2022. With consideration of the COVID-19 pandemic situation, the event was held in a hybrid mode.

As with previous years, the ARC 2022 edition covered a broad spectrum of applications of reconfigurable computing, including numerical application, machine learning, communication, architecture, etc. This year's symposium program included 13 regular contributions selected from a total of 16 submissions. The selection process was very competitive with each submission having at least four reviews in an open peer review process. The strong technical program also included keynote talks and workshops that covered both academical and industrial breakthroughs.

This year's successful program was made possible by the contribution of many talented individuals. First and foremost, we would like to thank all the authors who responded to our call for papers and the members of the Program Committee and the additional external reviewers who, with their opinion and expertise, ensured a program of the highest quality. Last but not the least, we would like to thank the steering committee and staff from Springer who ensured that publicity and web interactivity remained engaging and responsive.

Thank you all.

September 2022

Yu Wang<br>
Wei Xue<br>
Thomas Chau<br>
Lin Gan

# Organization

## General Chair

Yu Wang                          Tsinghua University, China

## Program Committee Chairs

Wei Xue                          Tsinghua University, China
Thomas Chau                      Samsung AI Center, UK

## Local Chairs

Lin Gan                          Tsinghua University, China
Mengxue Qi                       Tsinghua University, China

## Proceeding Chair

Yun Liang                        Peking University, China

## Journal Special Issues

Zhao Liu                         NSCC-Wuxi, China

## Finance and Sponsor Chair

Yan Zhang                        Tsinghua University, China

## Web Chair

Shuo Li                          Tsinghua University, China

## Program Committee

Qiang Liu                        Tianjin University, China
Zhilei Chai                      Jiangnan University, China
Dimitrios Soudris                National Technical University of Athens, Greece
Diana Goehringer                 TU Dresden, Germany
Tomasz Kryjak                    AGH University of Science and Technology,
                                   Poland

| | |
|---|---|
| Antonio Carlos Schneider Beck | Universidade Federal do Rio Grande do Sul, Brazil |
| Kyprianos Papadimitriou | Technical University of Crete, Greece |
| Michael Huebner | Brandenburg University of Technology Cottbus, Germany |
| George Theodoridis | University of Patras, Greece |
| Krzysztof Kepa | GE Global Research, USA |
| Marek Gorgon | AGH University of Science and Technology, Poland |
| Georgios Keramidas | Aristotle University of Thessaloniki/Think Silicon S.A., Greece |
| Kimon Karras | Think Silicon S.A., Greece |
| João M. P. Cardoso | University of Porto, Portugal |
| Roberto Giorgi | University of Siena, Italy |
| Yuichiro Shibata | Nagasaki University, Japan |
| Jesús Barba | University of Castilla-La Mancha, Spain |
| Giorgos Dimitrakopoulos | Democritus University of Thrace, Greece |
| Yukinori Sato | Toyohashi University of Technology, Japan |
| Christian Hochberger | TU Darmstadt, Germany |
| Daniel Chillet | CAIRN-IRISA/ENSSAT, France |
| Antonio Miele | Politecnico di Milano, Italy |
| Andrés Otero | Universidad Politécnica de Madrid, Spain |
| Monica Pereira | Universidade Federal do Rio Grande do Norte, Brazil |
| Steven Derrien | Université de Rennes 1, France |
| João CanasFerreira | University of Porto, Portugal |
| Takefumi Miyoshi | e-trees.Japan, Inc., Japan |
| Ricardo Ferreira | Universidade Federal de Viçosa, Brazil |
| Angeliki Kritikakou | IRISA, University of Rennes 1/Inria, France |
| Ray Cheung | City University of Hong Kong, China |
| João Bispo | University of Porto/INESC TEC, Portugal |
| Chao Wang | University of Science and Technology of China, China |
| Mihalis Psarakis | University of Piraeus, Greece |
| Pedro C. Diniz | University of Porto, Portugal |
| Thilo Pionteck | Otto-von-Guericke Universitat Magdeburg, Germany |
| Cathal Mccabe | Xilinx, USA |
| Andreas Koch | TU Darmstadt, Germany |
| Zachary Baker | Los Alamos National Laboratory, USA |
| Hayden Kwok-Hayso | University of Hong Kong, China |
| Hideharu Amano | Keio University, Japan |

| Apostolos Fournaris | Technological Educational Institute of Western Greece, Greece |
| Jim Harkin | University of Ulster, UK |
| Horácio Neto | INESC-ID/IST, University of Lisbon, Portugal |

# Contents

100% Visibility at MHz Speed: Efficient Soft Scan-Chain Insertion
on AMD/Xilinx FPGAs ................................................. 1
  *Hossein Omidian, Eddie Hung, and Dinesh Gaitonde*

FPGA-Accelerated Tersoff Multi-body Potential for Molecular Dynamics
Simulations .......................................................... 17
  *Ming Yuan, Qiang Liu, Quan Deng, Shengye Xiang, Lin Gan,*
  *Jinzhe Yang, Xiaohui Duan, Haohuan Fu, and Guangwen Yang*

A Runtime Programmable Accelerator for Convolutional and Multilayer
Perceptron Neural Networks on FPGA ................................. 32
  *Ehsan Kabir, Arpan Poudel, Zeyad Aklah, Miaoqing Huang,*
  *and David Andrews*

A Multi-FPGA Scalable Framework for Deep Reinforcement Learning
Through Neuroevolution .............................................. 47
  *Javier Laserna, Andrés Otero, and Eduardo de la Torre*

Development Progress of SWLBM a Framework Based on Lattice
Boltzmann Method for Fluid Dynamics Simulation ...................... 62
  *Chu Xuesen, He Xiang, Li Fang, Liu Zhao, and Yang Guangwen*

Entropy-Based Early-Exit in a FPGA-Based Low-Precision Neural
Network ............................................................. 72
  *Minxuan Kong and Jose Luis Nunez-Yanez*

FPGA-Extended General Purpose Computer Architecture ................. 87
  *Philippos Papaphilippou and Myrtle Shah*

Multi-spectral In-Vivo FPGA-Based Surgical Imaging .................. 103
  *Majed Alsharari, Lorenzo Niemitz, Simon Sorensen, Roger Woods,*
  *Ray Burke, Stefan Andersson Engels, Carlos Reaño, and Son T. Mai*

Hardware-Aware Optimizations for Deep Learning Inference on Edge
Devices ............................................................. 118
  *Markus Rognlien, Zhiqiang Que, Jose G. F. Coutinho, and Wayne Luk*

IPEC: Open-Source Design Automation for Inter-Processing Element
Communication ...................................................... 134
  *David Volz, Christoph Spang, and Andreas Koch*

xii    Contents

Light-Weight Permutation Generator for Efficient Convolutional Neural
Network Data Augmentation ........................................... 150
    Bowen P. Y. Kwan, Ce Guo, Wayne Luk, and Peiyong Jiang

Real-Time Embedded Object Tracking with Discriminative Correlation
Filters Using Convolutional Features ................................... 166
    Michal Danilowicz and Tomasz Kryjak

VenOS: A Virtualization Framework for Multiple Tenant Accommodation
on Reconfigurable Platforms ........................................... 181
    Panagiotis Miliadis, Dimitris Theodoropoulos,
    Dionisios N. Pnevmatikatos, and Nectarios Koziris

**Author Index** ........................................................ 197

# 100% Visibility at MHz Speed: Efficient Soft Scan-Chain Insertion on AMD/Xilinx FPGAs

Hossein Omidian$^{(\boxtimes)}$, Eddie Hung, and Dinesh Gaitonde

AMD, San Jose, USA
hosseino@gmail.com

**Abstract.** FPGA-based prototyping has become an increasingly important part of the overall integrated circuit design and verification flow, providing the ability to test an integrated circuit running at (near) speed with realistic inputs and outputs. The reconfigurable aspect of FPGA technology makes them suitable for hardware emulation and prototyping, plus their nature of having over-provisioned resources — inherently necessary to support the late-binding of a wide range of applications — allows support for 'out-of-band' functionality such as debug. It is imperative that as much visibility into the inner state of the circuit is accessible in order for debugging to be effective. Full visibility for functional debug can be achieved by building a soft scan-chain out of LUTs and flip-flops, or by using hardened device readback capabilities that use the configuration network to exfiltrate circuit state. In this paper, we show how soft scan-chains can be efficiently and intelligently inserted to give 100% visibility into all user flip-flops of a design and demonstrate how performing parallel scan dumps can be more than 10x faster (reaching 1 MHz) than hardened readback when evaluated on industrial emulation designs in excess of 200K flip-flops.

**Keywords:** Emulation · Prototyping · Debug · Scan chain · Readback

## 1 Introduction

Since the cost of fabricating a custom ASIC is so time-consuming and expensive after which changes (for example, to fix a design error or to insert some debug infrastructure) are not always possible, reconfigurable technology such as FPGA is widely used in this area. FPGAs are inherently flexible devices that are composed of programmable logic cells, memory and interconnect. This allows them to be customized and used in a broad range of applications including ASIC prototyping and hardware emulation [1].

A problem common to ASIC and FPGA technology is the lack of on-chip visibility for diagnosing erroneous behaviour. In ASICs, such errors can be caused by (a) fabrication defects or (b) functional bugs. Fabrication defects are caused by the imperfect nature of silicon fabrication process whereby, for example, a metal wire or a transistor is randomly manufactured incorrectly. To identify

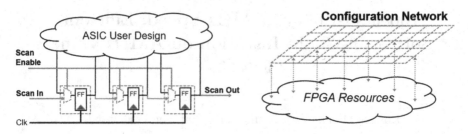

**Fig. 1.** *(left)* ASIC scan flops (scan-mux and regular flop) arranged into a chain. *(right)* Hardened FPGA config. network allowing both write and read back.

these cases, ASICs often employ 'scan flops' in place of regular flip-flops to enable manufacturing tests. A scan-flop behaves just as a regular flip-flop but with the optional capability (achieved using a scan mux) that new values can instead be sequentially shifted in and existing values shifted out when arranged into a scan-chain as shown in Fig. 1. The utility of a scan-chain is that post-fabrication, a known test pattern can be shifted into all flip-flops of a design, the clock advanced to capture the next state computed by the device, and then this newly captured state can be shifted out and compared with a known golden value. Deviations from this golden value would indicate a manufacturing failure.

After manufacturing tests, these same ASIC scan-chains can be reused to investigate *functional bugs* by following the same shift out method: halt the design at the clock cycle of interest and proceed to shift out all values on the scan-chain to gain a complete picture of all design state to aid debugging.

In contrast, even though FPGAs may suffer from the same issue of fabrication defects, their reconfigurable nature provide alternate ways to perform manufacturing tests without the overhead of hardened scan-chains as for ASICs. An unavoidable overhead that FPGAs do have to pay, however, is that of a configuration network. The purpose of this network is to transport all of the configuration necessary to implement a user design, such as all LUT contents, flip-flop initialization values, interconnect switch states, etc. to all locations of the device. Some FPGA vendors, such as Xilinx, allow this same configuration infrastructure to be re-purposed as a method of extracting user-state to aid in the investigation of functional bugs, in the same way as ASIC scan-chains. We refer to this FPGA capability as 'hardened readback'.

Hardened readback for functional debug shares the same limitations as for ASIC scan-chains: the design must be halted during the shift out procedure, for a length of time proportional to that necessary to perform configuration readback of all used flip-flop resources in the design or to unload the longest ASIC scan-chain. In this work, we show how the use of multiple soft scan-chains (i.e. scan-chains created out of regular LUT logic) can be used to dramatically reduce this overhead for functional debug; our main contributions are:

1. An approach for the efficient insertion of multiple soft scan-chains capable of acquiring 100% visibility into all flip-flops of a user design while still allowing such designs to continue operating in excess of 1 MHz while a typical emulation design operates between 1 to 10 KHz.

2. Integration of our techniques into a production quality and fully timing-driven commercial FPGA toolflow, one mindful of real-world considerations such as hold time requirements, clock skew, etc.
3. Robust evaluation on 29 industrial emulation designs containing multiple clock domains and more than 200,000 user flops, finding a 10x speedup over a hardened readback solution.

The remainder of the paper is organized as follows: Sect. 2 explains background and related studies. Section 3 describes the proposed approach of inserting soft scan-chains into a user's design. Section 4 provides experimental results and comparison of our approach with hardened readback. Finally, Sect. 5 concludes the paper.

## 1.1 Related Work

The novelty of our work is not in using soft-logic to implement scan functionality. Prior work from Wheeler et al. [2] examined the application of ASIC-style scan-flops (as per Fig. 1) to *replace* existing flip-flops (as opposed to our proposal of *shadowing* existing flops) to allow design state to be both observed as well as modified (where our shadow approach is unable to modify). The cost of this prior work is a reported 20% reduction in Fmax during normal operation, a 2.3x increase in LUT count, and the need to halt the design during the scan out procedure. Wheeler et al. state that is an acceptable overhead during development since this handicap is removed for the final production design. In contrast, our approach focuses on this development phase and we show that there is no Fmax degradation when scan functionality is not used, a temporary Fmax slowdown during scan-out, and no effect on the size of FPGA required, when evaluated on industrial designs from the emulation domain.

Work from Tiwari and Tomko [3] explores the use of soft scan-chains to implement software-like "watch-point" functionality to detect when specific values appear on predetermined internal signals, after which the clock can be halted and the state of the design examined. Here, scan-chain functionality is used to update watch-point values efficiently. However, both prior works [2,3] do consider using FPGA device readback to reduce the area overhead and for providing observability respectively, recognizing as we do, that readback is a slow operation.

## 2   Background

When a hardware design does not behave as expected, debugging is required to find the root cause of this erroneous behaviour. Key to the effectiveness of the functional debugging process is the visibility that the designer has into the internal signals of their circuit. Using software simulation, unlimited visibility is available but the speed at which large complex designs can be simulated is often many orders of magnitude slower than their target frequency. With real silicon, this frequency gap is significantly narrowed on FPGAs and may even be eliminated on ASICs, but the tradeoff is that visibility becomes severely limited. To overcome this limited visibility, designers must repurpose existing or insert new infrastructure to expose internal signal activity. There are two main categories for visibility infrastructure: scan-based and trace-based.

As described in Sect. 1, ASICs are often built with scan-chain capabilities to test that the silicon was manufactured correctly. Post manufacturing test, such functionality can be repurposed for debug. As long as the design can be halted at precisely the clock cycle of interest, by unloading all values of the scan-chain a designer can determine of all flip-flops in the design (and consequently, all intermediate combinatorial signals too). Equivalently, the same concept can be applied to FPGAs that support a hardened readback capability once the design is halted, its configuration network can instead be repurposed to read/scan out all flip-flop state. The design can then be advanced to the next state by single-stepping the clock, and further scan dumps performed to understand how the design evolves over time.

The disadvantage of a traditional scan-based approach is the time required to dump its contents. For FPGA technology, the max frequency of a user design with full readback $Fmax_{D-with-RB}$ is proportional to the number of flip-flop values that need to be dumped $NF_{user}$, the efficiency of hardware readback $Eff$, as well as output bandwidth of the configuration controller (on Xilinx devices, this is referred to as ICAP [4], $BW_{(ICAP)}$):

$$Fmax_{D-with-RB} \propto Eff \cdot \frac{BW_{ICAP}}{NF_{user}} \qquad (1)$$

$Eff$ here is a $(0, 1]$ scaling factor that reflects the overhead of using hardened readback. In Xilinx UltraScale+ devices, the configuration network operates at a frame granularity where each frame contains 2,976 bits of configuration data that must be atomically written or read [5]. Using hardened readback to extract the value of just one flip-flop value requires the entire frame to be read back, leading to an efficiency of 0.00034. The efficiency is improved, up to a limit, when multiple user flops that happen to be placed into the same frame are read back.

Trace-based approaches require the insertion of trace buffers and supporting logic to non-intrusively record a small subset of signal activity into on-chip memory [6]. The advantage of this method is that a design-under-trace need not to be halted in order to gain visibility, as well as being able to capture behaviour of the circuit over time without single stepping the clock. However, the disadvantages of trace infrastructure is that it does occupy precious on-chip memory and logic resources which can limit the amount of information that can be traced — both in terms of the number of signals that can be traced in parallel (corresponding to the width of the trace memory) as well as how many cycles of history can be captured (the depth of the trace memory).

Recent work by Attia and Betz [7] has demonstrated a compelling need to export the entire state of the design — that stored in user flip-flops as well as

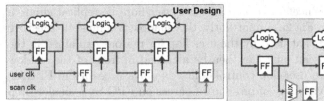

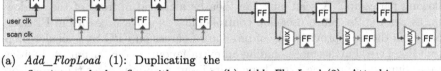

(a) *Add_FlopLoad* (1): Duplicating the user-flop into a shadow-flop with separate clock.

(b) *Add_FlopLoad* (2): Attaching a scan-mux to the shadow-flop input.

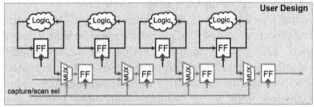

(c) *Add_ScanChain*: Forming a chain of scan-mux to shadow-flop connections.

**Fig. 2.** Two-step scan-chain insertion: *Add_FlopLoad* followed by *Add_ScanChain*.

RAM contents — so that a faulty subset of the design already executing in an FPGA can be migrated into the much-slower (but more familiar and productive) software simulator to continue debug. To achieve this, they use Xilinx's hardened readback [4] capabilities, making it closer to the scan-based approach than a trace-based one.

In this work, we propose that a soft scan-chain approach be used to overcome the performance penalty incurred by continuously applying a hardened readback solution, yet without restricting the visibility available to a designer as would be necessary with a trace-based approach.

## 3 Soft Scan-Chain Methodology

The implementation and requirements of a soft FPGA scan-chain are very different to those in ASICs. Firstly, ASIC scan flops are typically highly optimized macro cells that can be used as drop-in replacements to regular flop cells with only a small area impact. For an FPGA, it is not practical to make all customers pay this area cost (along with even more area to expose the additional pins to the routing network) for a feature that many would not need, especially since manufacturing test is a FPGA vendor responsibility. Secondly, since an FPGA scan-chain is not used for manufacturing test there also does not exist the requirement to load new values into user-flops.

***Add_FlopLoad:*** Instead, FPGAs can use soft logic resources — lookup tables — to implement the 2:1 scan multiplexer functionality. Rather than add an extra 3-input LUT to every path leading into a flip-flop, we propose that each flop in the user design (henceforth referred to as a *user* flop) be replicated into a *shadow* flop, as shown in Fig 2a. Importantly, this shadow flop must be sensitive to a different clock than that used by the user flop for reasons explained in the following paragraph. A scan-mux can then be attached in front of the shadow flop, as per Fig 2b. Since user-flop controllability is not a necessity in FPGAs, along with the over-provisioning of flip-flop resources on FPGAs, a shadow flop is suitable here. Furthermore, adding an extra fanout to the output of the user flop, as opposed to adding extra logic to its input, also minimizes the impact on compilation quality and runtime. Both the shadow-flop and scan-mux insertion is accomplished in the *Add_FlopLoad* stage of our flow.

After capturing a design's state into shadow flops, all those captured values need to be stored or exported at every user clock cycle so that it may be analyzed or post processed. This can be done connecting the shadow flops into a serial chain (Fig. 2c) similar to a shift register; once the user clock is halted, advancing the scan clock will cause its contents to be dumped out one value at a time. Attaching the shadow flops to an separate scan clock independent from the user design is both necessary so that the scan-chain can be dumped without interfering the user design, and also beneficial since the scan dump procedure can also be safely operated at a higher frequency.

Figure 3a shows a design with 6 flip-flops $FF_1, FF_2, ..., FF_6$ with values $D_1, D_2, ..., D_6$. After each user design clock cycle, the *Capturing_Value* process starts by saving each user flip-flop's value into their respective shadow flops. This step is done by selecting the top input of all scan-muxes. The *Capturing_Values* step was also shown as "Read" in the Fig. 3a waveform. After capturing values into the shadow flops, we move to the *Scan_Dump* mode to send the values out serially.

In the *Scan_Dump* mode, the bottom input for all scan-muxes are selected to enable shift out functionality[1]. As one can see in the waveform from Fig. 3a when scan functionality is desired the user clock period needs to exceed the time necessary to perform a scan dump when operating the scan clock at a different, faster period. Hence, the maximum frequency of a design with continuous scan dumps (Fmax) will be always dependent on the Fmax of the scan-chain as well as the number of scan flops that need to be unloaded.

With $NF_{scan}$ as the number of scan flops on the scan-chain (which in this work is equivalent to the number of user flops $NF_{user}$) Eq. 2 shows the relationship between the Fmax of the slowed user design ($Fmax_{D\_with\_SC}$) and the scan-chain's Fmax ($Fmax_{scan}$).

$$Fmax_{D\_with\_SC} = \frac{Fmax_{scan}}{NF_{scan} + 2} \tag{2}$$

The +2 factor in the denominator represents a cycle to first read (capture) the user flop values into the shadow flops, and a cycle at the end to export the last value in the chain.

---

[1] *Scan_Dump* can be done every cycle or once in while. For this study we focus on capturing and reading back flops every cycle since it covers both cases.

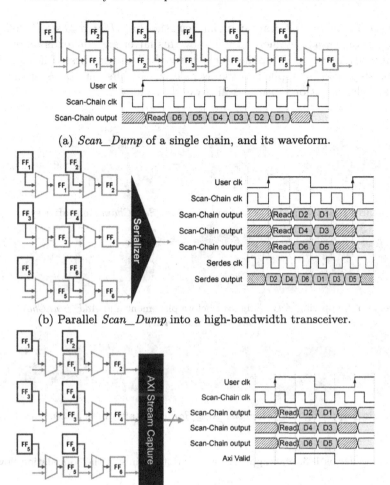

(a) *Scan_Dump* of a single chain, and its waveform.

(b) Parallel *Scan_Dump* into a high-bandwidth transceiver.

(c) Parallel Multiple *Scan_Dump* into an AXI stream.

**Fig. 3.** Single and multiple/parallel *Scan_Dump* in which the scan clock operates at a multiple of the user clock.

To improve the user-design-with-scan Fmax ($Fmax_{D\_with\_SC}$), it is possible to have more than one scan-chain and read out multiple in parallel. In other words, we divide the set of all shadow flops into different scan-chains. Having more than one scan-chain leads us to have less number of flops in each chain ($NF_{scan}$) which leads to a higher $Fmax_{D\_with\_SC}$. Figures 3b and 3c have three scan-chains instead of one, with each containing 1/3 of all flops. This means we can shift out all scan flop values in only 2 cycles instead of 6 cycles, and $Fmax$ can be increased almost 3x.

**When to Insert Scan-Chains:** In our flow, the *Add_FlopLoad* step is followed by *Add_ScanChain*. The method taken by this latter step depends on when in the compilation flow it is applied, which we shall discuss first. Each of these previous steps can be applied to the user design at different stages of the flow: synthesis, placement or routing as illustrated in Fig. 4.

(a) Scenario 1: applying *Add_FlopLoad* and *Add_ScanChain* steps after synthesis.

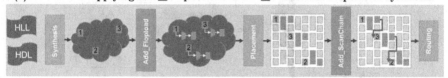

(b) Scenario 2: applying *Add_FlopLoad* before placement and *Add_ScanChain* after. *(proposed approach)*

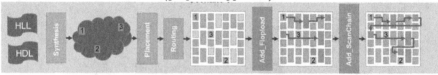

(c) Scenario 3: applying *Add_FlopLoad*, *Add_ScanChain* after both placement and routing.

**Fig. 4.** Scenarios 1–3: scan application at various points of the compilation flow.

Scenario 1: apply both *Add_FlopLoad* and *Add_ScanChain* steps after synthesis and before placement. In this scenario, the place and route tool will have maximum flexibility to find optimum overall placement of the combined design (user design and the scan-chain). Since the placement algorithm places the design considering its routability, finding a performant routing will be more likely. For example, in case of possible routing congestion, the placer might spread out the design throughout the chip to ensure the router can find a high quality routing solution. On the other hand, there are two shortcomings in this approach. First, adding the full scan-chain to the user design before placement will bias the placer to give the user design and the scan-chain equal priority, which may lead to a subpar placement for the user logic. Second, the placer is given exactly one scan-chain ordering, with zero flexibility, which can also lead to a subpar placement for one or more scan-chain connections thus lowering $Fmax_{scan}$ and affecting overall system performance.

Scenario 2: applying *Add_FlopLoad* before placement, letting the tool place the design, and then applying *Add_ScanChain* to the placed result. In this scenario since all the shadow flops are only connected to user flops, the placer is going to place the design without being significantly affected by any scan-chain connections. The placer algorithm will simply see the shadow flops and scan muxes as floating logic attached only to the user flop's output, thus place the user flop as it would do normally and then place the shadow flop at a nearby location. Since *Add_ScanChain* is done after placement, the exact location of each shadow flop is known and this information can be used to find an efficient scan-chain order that minimizes the routing distance between shadow flops.

Scenario 3: performing *Add_FlopLoad* and *Add_ScanChain* both after placement/before routing, into just the FPGA resources left unused by the design. This scenario comes handy when the user design was anchored or floor-planned with a specific criteria. Adding the scan-chain after the placement technically doesn't affect user design's placement and will try to add scan logic into any unused resources left behind. However, finding unused LUT and compatible flip-flop resources near to user flops is far from guaranteed.

Experimentally, we have found that Scenario 2 performs best and is the focus for the remainder of this paper.

**Add_ScanChain**: For Scenarios 2 and 3, *Add_ScanChain* is to be applied post placement. The main goal of this step is to maximize $Fmax_{scan}$ by reducing the total wirelength and worst-case delay of all shadow-flop to scan-mux paths across all connections within and between all scan-chains. Given a placed result where all scan-mux and shadow-flop locations are known, the problem is almost exactly that of the travelling salesman — starting at any shadow flop, determine the order in which all other scan-mux/shadow-flops are to be visited before finishing at a particular input pin, with no flop visited more than once and with the objective of minimizing the total travelled distance (equivalent to routed wirelength, minimizing which will improve the likelihood of finding a legal routing solution). An additional objective on top of the travelling salesman problem is to also minimize the maximum distance between any two flops, as that determines $Fmax_{scan}$.

Despite the (NP) difficulty of optimally solving the travelling salesman variant, experimentally we have found that a simple greedy heuristic was sufficient to achieve high performance. Starting from top-left of the chip, go down and find the nearest shadow flop and connect that to the scan-chain repeating until we hit the bottom of the chip. Then move right by one column and this time move to the top of the chip continuing to connect shadow flops in this way. This zig-zag move continues until all shadow flops are visited. Figure 5 shows an example of adding one scan-chain to 1% of the flops in a design. We picked 1% of flops randomly through out the design; 1% simply to make the figure clearer. The scan-chain is shown in purple color.

Similar to top-down approach, a left-right approach was also implemented. Experimentally, we observed that a top-down approach had slightly better results compared to left-right approach. We believe that top-down is more suitable for columnar FPGA architectures such as those from Xilinx.

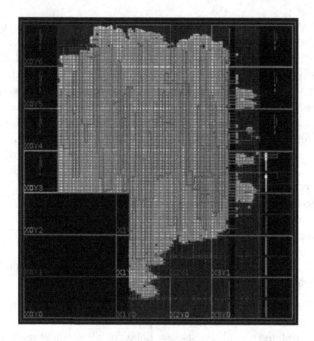

**Fig. 5.** Device view visualizing the connections made by one scan-chain visiting just 1% of the shadow flops in the design, using the top-down approach.

**Partitioning:** So far we have talked about the two main steps for adding scan-chains to a user design and the different scenarios for when to do so. We also talked about the benefits of having more than one scan-chain In the following, we will explain different ways to break a single scan-chain into multiple and explain the tradeoffs in doing so.

As discussed, one dimension that can improve $Fmax_{D\_with\_SC}$ is by increasing the number of scan-chains, thus decreasing the amount of time required to dump their values (in parallel). Partitioning techniques can be used to cut the design into smaller partitions and assign a scan-chain for each partition. Partitioning can be define based on different parameters. One way of partitioning a design is considering the FPGA architecture and partition based off that. For example, Xilinx's latest FPGA devices use Stacked Silicon Interconnect (SSI) technology, which creates high-capacity FPGAs by combining multiple dies called Super Logic Regions (SLRs) [8]. Considering that crossing from one SLR to another incurs a significant wire delay, partitioning can be done along these lines.

Partitioning based on design hierarchy would be another method that generates multiple scan-chains within each hierarchical sub-tree. Under the assumption that the FPGA placer typically tries to place elements within the same hierarchy close to each other, partitioning along hierarchy lines can be beneficial for $Fmax_{scan}$ as well, and especially so for Scenario 1. Moreover, having scan-chains which stay within the same hierarchy can help the eventual post-processing and analysis steps too.

Both approaches were employed in this work.

**Exporting Scan Data:** Lastly, we must consider what to do with data from the scan-dump: sending it off-chip or to another module to do post-processing. We consider two different ways to do it in this study. One approach is using a hardened high speed on-chip serializers such as Xilinx GT transceivers [9] to export this device off-chip. In this approach, $Fmax_{D\_with\_SC}$ is also dependent on the serializer's bandwidth ($BW_{serdes}$) as shown Fig. 3b. Equation 3 captures this new consideration:

$$Fmax_{D\_with\_SC} = \max \left( \frac{Fmax_{scan}}{NF_{scan} + 2} , \frac{BW_{serdes}}{NF_{scan}} \right) \tag{3}$$

Another approach to capture multiple scan-chain outputs is by having a soft logic shim implemented on the FPGA fabric which gathers their outputs, buffers them, and transmits it using the AXI stream protocol. In this study we also implemented a parameterized soft logic shim that our tool flow uses to receive all scan outputs. This soft logic shim uses the AXI Capture module. One shortcoming of this approach however is its area overhead, which scales with the number of parallel scan-chains that exist.

**Trade-off and Optimization:** As discussed before, overall system performance $Fmax_{D\_with\_SC}$ is a function of $Fmax_{scan}$ and the maximum number of shadow flops across all scan-chains. Therefore to improve system performance, it's possible to break down a big scan-chain into multiple smaller ones to reduce the maximum number of shadow flops in any one scan-chain. Although having several scan-chains can increase $Fmax_{D\_with\_SC}$, it also adds complexity to output capturing logic at the end. Moreover, having too many parallel scan-chains unloading at the same time might saturate the off-chip bandwidth. Our scan-chain insertion tool flow explores this problem space to find a trade off between number of parallel chain and the number of shadow flops in each while considering area usage/bandwidth capabilities of export logic. During scan-out, the Fmax of the user design must be slowed to $Fmax_{D\_with\_SC}$ as defined in Eq. 2, which describes the frequency if the state of all user flops is to be scanned out at every cycle. Relaxing this requirement to a complete state dump every $N$ cycles would improve $Fmax_{D\_with\_SC}$ by the same factor – in this mode, software simulation (along with a trace of any external stimulus) could be used to interpolate missing user flop values.

## 4  Experimental Results

Our experiments are carried out using the Xilinx Vivado toolflow (version 2021.2) targeting Xilinx UltraScale+ devices. We have developed a tool that analyzes post-synthesis, post-place or post-route netlist and finds a good tradeoff between area/speed for adding soft scan capability to the user design to enable hardware testing/emulation. Our tool flow explores area/speed tradeoffs to find how many scan-chains should be implemented, how many flops in each scan-chains are needed and how the design needs to be partitioned. After finding a good tradeoff, it applies the *Add_ Flopload* and *Add_ ScanChain* steps described in the previous section. Moreover, the tool determines an appropriate value for $Fmax_{scan}$ (and thus, computing $Fmax_{D\_with\_SC}$) and constrains both clocks accordingly. After adding the soft scan-chain, our tool flow adds all the necessary control units and soft IPs for parallel capture to send the test flops' values off-chip. We examined 29 industrial emulation designs ranging from approximately 100,000 flops to over 200,000 flops. In those 29 designs, we targeted a different numbers of user flops using a different number of scan-chains and let our tool insert the necessary logic and connections.

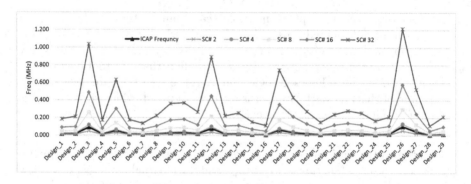

**Fig. 6.** Achievable user design Fmax with full per-cycle visibility — our work using soft-scan-chains being dumped continuously: SC#x ($Fmax_{D\_with\_SC}$); baseline using hardened readback (The ICAP/$Fmax_{D\_with\_RB}$ results presented assume an optimistic but unrealistic value of *Efficiency* = 1 within Eqn. 1, meaning that hardened readback is capable of returning only user flop values. Even though this result is not attainable in current devices, we believe this reflects the upper-bound of what a configuration network based approach is capable of.): ICAP ($Fmax_{D\_with\_RB}$).

Figure 6 shows the $Fmax_{D\_with\_SC}$ for different numbers of scan-chains while continuously dumping out all flop values in the design. To compare with the baseline approach, we also show an optimistic hardened readback approach (See footnote 2) using the ICAP ($Fmax_{D\_with\_RB}$) and the configuration network to do so. As we can see after adding only four scan-chains to the design, $Fmax_{D\_with\_SC}$ exceeds that possible with the ICAP approach. By adding 32 scan-chains, on average the improvement over $Fmax_{D\_with\_RB}$ is 10x.

The bandwidth results for 29 designs in our design suite are shown in Fig. 7. As discussed in the prior section, scan data needs to be transferred off-chip to be analyzed. We considered two approaches in this study to send the design status off-chip; 1) using GT ports and 2) dumping the values into DDR memory. Our tool flow, analyzes the bandwidth needed for sending the data off-chip and

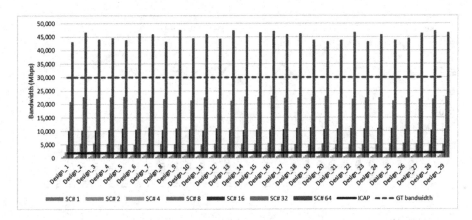

**Fig. 7.** Achievable soft scan/hardened readback (See footnote 2) bandwidth, along with achievable off-chip bandwidth using GT transcievers.

adds the necessary IP to the design. As mentioned, having more scan-chains is desirable to achieve higher $Fmax_{D\_with\_SC}$ but also requires more bandwidth to send the data off-chip. At 64 scan-chains, we exceed the bandwidth available supported by one GT resource. This means the tool flow needs to assign appropriate number of scan-chains to each GT based on the bandwidth. We face a similar limitation for DDR as well. A user needs to consider these limitations and force our tool to partition accordingly. This can be automated and will be addressed in future work.

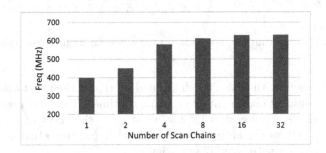

**Fig. 8.** Relationship of $Fmax_{scan}$ and number of scan-chains.

The average $Fmax_{scan}$ results for different numbers of scan-chains is shown in Fig. 8. As we can see, by breaking a big scan-chain into a number of small chains, our tool flow can find a set of shadow flops closer to each other and create chains with lower delay.

Lastly, we added one long scan-chain using our tool flow, once for half of the flops in the design and once for all the flops in the design. We measured the placement and routing runtime and compared it with baseline (with no no scan-chains). We observed that place and route runtime for one long scan-chain is

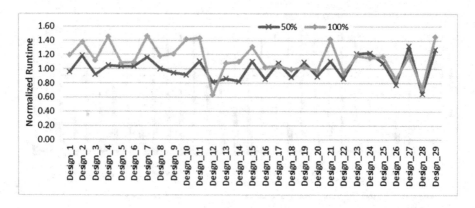

**Fig. 9.** Placement runtime, normalized to runtime for original user design.

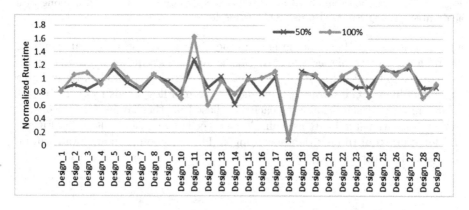

**Fig. 10.** Routing runtime, normalized to runtime for original user design.

higher than having multiple shorter chains and we report the worst case scenario for runtime. Results of placement and routing runtime is shown in Figs. 9 and 10 respectively. As we can see even for the worst case, the effect of adding scan-chains on place and route runtime is acceptable when gaining a 10x improvement for $Fmax_{D\_with\_SC}$ with only 32 scan-chains.

## Conclusion

FPGA prototypes have become an increasingly important part of the overall integrated circuit design and verification flow, providing the ability to test an integrated circuit running at (near) speed with realistic inputs and outputs. This make FPGAs great platforms for hardware emulation and provides visibility into many signals. This paper presents a soft scan-chain methodology for FPGA technology which can be applied to user design to give full and continuous visibility into all flop values, in a way that reduces its Fmax impact drastically compared to a hardened readback approach using the FPGA's built-in config-uration network. Our tool flow analyzes the user design, explores its area/time tradeoffs, and partitions the scan connections into multiple parallel chains auto-matically in order to obtain an efficient solution. We evaluated our tool flow on a production-quality toolflow, using realistic industrial designs, and across a vari-ety of different scan configurations to find the approach with the highest Fmax. Our findings show that by inserting only 32 parallel scan chains, post-placement, we can achieve a 10x higher Fmax compared to the baseline readback approach, allowing 100% visibility into designs able to continue running beyond 1 MHz.

**Future Work:** We plan to extend our work to the AMD/Xilinx Versal FPGA architecture [10] and leverage its high-bandwidth hardened Network-on-Chip (NoC) for on- and off-chip movement of scan data. Also, we plan to add and evaluate an automatic pipeline insertion to improve long connections within scan-chains, improving $Fmax_{scan}$ at the expense of efficiency-loss due to redundant flops, as well as to modify the insertion methodology to be congestion-aware so that routing runtime can be reduced.

A second direction would be to examine Scenario 3 (post routing insertion) in more detail since this scenario provides the benefit of leaving the user design fully untouched — such a concept that may require different algorithms could be explored using the open-source RapidWright framework [11]. Lastly, we intend to investigate how a hybrid implementation of using hardened readback (for reading Block RAM contents as well as any hard-to-reach shadow flops) in combination with our proposed soft scan-chain can lead to an even more efficient solution.

# References

1. Lo, W.Y., Choy, C.S., Chan, C.F.: Hardware emulation board based on FPGAs and programmable interconnections. In: Proceedings of IEEE 5th International Workshop on Rapid System Prototyping, pp. 126–130 (1994)
2. Wheeler, T., Graham, P., Nelson, B., Hutchings, B.: Using design-level scan to improve FPGA design observability and controllability for functional verifica-tion. In: Brebner, G., Woods, R. (eds.) FPL 2001. LNCS, vol. 2147, pp. 483–492. Springer, Heidelberg (2001). https://doi.org/10.1007/3-540-44687-7_50
3. Tiwari, A., Tomko, K.: Scan-chain based watch-points for efficient run-time debug-ging and verification of FPGA designs. In: Proceedings of the ASP-DAC Asia and South Pacific Design Automation Conference, vol. 2003, pp. 705–711 (2003)
4. Xilinx, LogiCORE IP AXI HWICAP (2020). https://docs.xilinx.com/v/u/en-US/pg134-axi-hwicap
5. Xilinx-Inc, UltraScale Architecture Configuration (2022). https://docs.xilinx.com/v/u/en-US/ug570-ultrascale-configuration
6. DNoronha, D.H., Zhao, R., Que, Z., Goeders, J., Luk, W., Wilton, S.: An overlay for rapid FPGA debug of machine learning applications. In: 2019 International Conference on Field-Programmable Technology (ICFPT) (2019)
7. Attia, S., Betz, V.: StateMover: combining simulation and hardware execution for efficient FPGA debugging. In: FPGA 2020: The 2020 ACM/SIGDA International Symposium on FPGA, Seaside, CA, USA, 23–25 February 2020

8. Saban, K.: Xilinx stacked silicon interconnect technology delivers breakthrough FPGA capacity, bandwidth, and power efficiency. Xilinx, White Paper (2011)
9. Xilinx, UltraScale Architecture GTY Transceivers. 2020. https://docs.xilinx.com/v/u/en-US/ug578-ultrascale-gty-transceivers
10. AMD, Versal: The First Adaptive Compute Acceleration Platform (ACAP) (2022)
11. Lavin, C., Kaviani, A.: RapidWright: enabling custom crafted implementations for FPGAs. In: 2018 IEEE 26th Annual International Symposium on Field-Programmable Custom Computing Machines (FCCM), pp. 133–140 (2018)

# FPGA-Accelerated Tersoff Multi-body Potential for Molecular Dynamics Simulations

Ming Yuan[1], Qiang Liu[1], Quan Deng[1], Shengye Xiang[2], Lin Gan[2(✉)],
Jinzhe Yang[3], Xiaohui Duan[2], Haohuan Fu[2,4], and Guangwen Yang[2,4]

[1] Tianjin Key Laboratory of Imaging and Sensing Microelectronic Technology School
of Microelectronics, Tianjin University, Tianjing, China
[2] Department of Computer Science and Technology,
Tsinghua University, Beijing, China
lingan@tsinghua.edu.cn
[3] Imperial College London, London, UK
[4] Zhejiang Lab, Hangzhou, China

**Abstract.** Molecular Dynamics simulation (MD) models the interactions of thousands to millions of particles through the iterative application of fundamental physics, and MD is one of the core methods in High-Performance Computing (HPC). However, the inherent weak scalability problem of force interactions renders MD simulation quite computationally intensive and challenging to scale. To this end, specialized FPGA-based accelerators have been proposed to solve this problem. In this work, we focus on many-body potentials on a single FPGA. Firstly, we proposed an efficient data transfer strategy to eliminate the latency between on-chip and off-chip memory. Then, the fixed-point description of data type is developed for computation to increase the utilization of on-chip resources. At last, a custom pipelined strategy is presented for *Tersoff* to get a better simulation performance. Compared with a floating-point implementation based on NVIDIA 28080ti GPUs, our design based on Xilinx U200 FPGA is 1.2 times better.

**Keywords:** FPGA · Molecular dynamics simulations · Pipeline · Accelerator

## 1 Introduction

Molecular Dynamics (MD) simulations have been widely used in various aspects of life [1] and material sciences [2,3]. They have tremendously succeeded in many application areas during the past several decades. In particular, with the rapid development of the semiconductor industry in recent years, MD simulation, which contains multi-body potential formulations, such as *Tersoff* potential, plays an essential role in the design space of new semiconductor materials [4] such as GaN, CdS, and TIOZ. The results from MD simulations provide helpful information for developing novel composite materials, reducing the extra experimental cost.

L. Gan et al. (Eds.): ARC 2022, LNCS 13569, pp. 17–31, 2022.
https://doi.org/10.1007/978-3-031-19983-7_2

Recent enhancements of High-Performance Computing (HPC) power, especially the development of supercomputers, provide an opportunity for complex MD simulations with complex potentials. Several available HPC clusters use accelerators such as graphics processing units (GPUs) to improve the performance of MD simulations, and they can make simulations of millions of particles with sufficient FLOPs. The ever-increasing demands of MD simulations even push the development of special-purpose supercomputers like Anton supercomputers [5–7] and MDGRAPE [8,9], but they are very inaccessible and are not widely used. While Anton supercomputers are based on ASICs, some novel systems have radical architectural changes (e.g., Sunway TaihuLight Supercomputer, Fugaku, and CrayXT3), resulting in a better performance of simulations, and it makes plenty of outstanding works in simulating biological systems [10,11]. However, as the MD simulations grow more complicated, traditional general-purpose chips can no longer meet the complex demands, such as memory, bandwidth, and computing efficiency. Furthermore, the computing efficiencies, the memory wall, and the power issues are becoming more and more serious when mapping MD simulations onto leading-edge supercomputing systems. There is a significant gap between the widely-used MD simulations and the current physical systems.

Fortunately, reconfigurable computing systems, such as those based on Field Programmable Gate Array (FPGA) technology offer a brand-new computing pattern that enables researchers to use a unique data-flow computing model to achieve better performance. Implementing molecular dynamics (MD) on FPGAs has also drawn substantial attention, and serval works [12,13] are made to tap the potential capacity of FPGAs for MD simulation. However, existing studies [14,15] are focused on the simple force interaction such as $Lennard-Jones(L-J)potential$, which contains a few variables to be computed, and it is not suitable for simulating new semiconductor materials. Furthermore, most of the FPGA implementations in the literature are resided entirely on-chip for the whole computation, completely removing the dependency on off-chip devices, resulting in a limited simulation scale during MD simulations.

In this work, we extend the MD simulation with the typical multi-body potential $(Tersoff)$, and it has been widely used to analyze the three-body MD interaction between partially rigid particles such as silicon $(Si)$. As is often the case when looking for cost-effective ASIC replacement, Field Programmable Gate Arrays (FPGAs) provide a viable alternative. A customized FPGA-based solution can significantly improve energy efficiency and power consumption compared to CPU and GPU clusters. We want to explore the feasibility of making a deeply-pipelined system for MD simulations on state-of-the-art FPGAs and propose an efficient accelerator for complex $Tersoff$ multi-body potential with high power efficiency.

To our best knowledge, most of the FPGA implementations in the literature are designed for two-body MD interactions with a limited simulation scale. This work is the first attempt to develop a large-scale MD simulation for three-body interactions $(Tersoff)$ on a single-node FPGA system. Furthermore, our design for Tersoff potential is general enough, and we consider it has the potential to be used for computing some similar problems in MD without completely redesigning the hardware. We also expect that the presented work can offer some ideas for designing and implementing similar applications on FPGAs .

Our significant contributions can be summarized as follows:

- We have presented an efficient data transfer strategy for large-scale MD simulations that overlapped computation and communication, improving the utilization of on-chip memories.
- We propose a fixed-point arithmetic for $Tersoff$ potential computation, which gives a tradeoff between resource and precision.
- We have proposed a custom pipelined computation engine for $Tersoff$ potential, which brought a significant performance improvement.

The remainder of this paper will first present the basic background information on $Tersoff$ potential and prior work for MD simulaions. Then, the data transfer design between the off-chip and on-chip memory, fixed-point quantization of $Tersoff$, and a custom dataflow computing model of $Tersoff$ will be elaborated. Following this, the results are presented and evaluated comparatively with different platforms. Finally, conclusions are detailed with plans for future work.

## 2   Background

### 2.1   Classical MD with $Tersoff$ Potential

The basic workflow of MD simulations consists of four essential parts: system initialization, neighbor list generation, force interactions, and motion update. Neighbor list generation and force interactions are much more time-consuming among the four parts. In the part of neighbor list generation, a cutoff distance is introduced, and both forces and energies between particles are assumed to be zero if the distance between two particles is beyond the cutoff distance. Cell linked list algorithm is used widely in modern MD simulations to build the neighbor list. In this algorithm, the simulation domain is partitioned into several cells, the edge of cells is equal to or larger than the cutoff distance, and there are 26 neighboring cells for each particle located in the home cell.

As mentioned before, a typical three-body potential ($Tersoff$) with $N$ particles has a computational complexity of $O(N^3)$, which is far more complex than two-body algorithm. The total potential energy for the $Tersoff$ potential system can be written as $U = \frac{1}{2} \sum_i \sum_{j \neq i} U_{ij}$, where the energy $U_{ij}$ can be written as

$$U_{ij} = f_C\left(r_{ij}\right) \left[f_R\left(r_{ij}\right) - b_{ij} f_A\left(r_{ij}\right)\right] \tag{1}$$

where $f_C$ is a smooth cutoff function which contains trigonometric functions, $f_R(r) = Ae^{-\lambda r_{ij}}$ and $f_A(r) = Be^{-\mu r_{ij}}$ are the repulsive function and the attractive function, respectively.

Furthermore, the most crucial part is bond-order($\zeta$), and it takes the following forms:

$$b_{ij} = \left(1 + \beta^n \zeta_{ij}^n\right)^{-\frac{1}{2n}} \tag{2}$$

$$\zeta_{ij} = \sum_{k \neq i,j} f_C\left(r_{ik}\right) g_{ijk} \tag{3}$$

$$g_{ijk} = 1 + \frac{c^2}{d^2} - \frac{c^2}{d^2 + \left(h - \cos\theta_{ijk}\right)^2} \tag{4}$$

Here, $A$, $B$, $\beta$, $n$, $c$, $d$, $\lambda$, $\mu$ and $h$ are parameters and $\theta_{ijk}$ is the angle formed by $r_{ij}$ and $r_{ik}$.

## 2.2 Prior MD Work

In general, MD is one of the core methods in High-Performance Computing (HPC). Several well known high performance MD software packages (e.g. GRO-MACS [16], LAMMPS [17], AMBER [18], NAMD [19], CHARMM [20]) are making full use of modern HPC to achieve better performance. Furthermore, many supercomputers are used for MD simulations to get better performance. On Sunway TaihuLight supercomputer, Duan et al. [21] use the full supercomputer nodes for MD simulations, achieving a tremendous performance of over 2.43 PFlops. Meanwhile, in the year 2020, a machine learning-based simulation protocol [22] for MD can simulate over 100 million atoms more than $1ns$ per day on the Summit supercomputer, and this work can attain 91 PFLOPS (45.5% of the peak) in double precision and 162/275 PFLOPS in mixed-single/half-precision.

During the past several decades, Field Programmable Gate Arrays (FPGAs) have been explored as efficient accelerators for MD simulations. Most FPGA-based studies [23–25] only target the particle-particle (PP) computation to accelerate MD simulations, since they make up for over 92% of the runtime of simulations. However, they only accelerate non-bonded pair interactions on the FPGAs and do not use inter-FPGA communication. Although they can accelerate the interactions, the overall system is not competitive due to a limited bandwidth between the host processor and the BRAM on the FPGA card. The work proposed by Benjamin Humphries et al. [26,27] shows that the widely-used 3D FFTs in the order of $64^3$ can be successfully presented on single FPGAs, which achieve a competitive speed within a few 100 μs. Kasap et al. [28] make the first attempt to propose a production-level MD accelerator using FPGA-based parallel computers. Another work [13] presents the first full-scale FPGA-based simulation engine implemented on a single FPGA and shows that its performance is competitive with a GPU.

# 3  Efficient Data Transfer

## 3.1  Bandwidth-Friendly Particle Mapping

When it comes to large-scale particle mapping, off-chip memory (DRR4/HBM) can be used well to store particle information, especially for large-scale MD simulations. Due to the bandwidth-to-compute nature of MD simulations, it takes a large number of particles for few force interactions, and the performance is directly bound up with the available bandwidth offered by FPGAs. However, the random memory access nature of particle mapping presents an important issue: access flexibility. It is essential to offer a bandwidth-friendly particle mapping for the following computation.

---

**Algorithm 1.** A Design for Accelerating Particle Mapping

---

**Require:** $FETCH$ : get the data of particles

   $N_{cell}$: numbers of cell in in the $x, y, z$ direction

   $Cell_{size}(N_{cell})$: number of particles in each cell

   $Cell_{offsets}(N_{cell})$: new index of particles in each cell

   $Cell_{ptr}(N_{cell} + 1)$: the whole number of particles in the first $N_{cell}$ cells

**Ensure:** Resorted Particle Position: X($N$),Y($N$),Z($N$)

1: **for** $i \in atoms$ **do**                                                 ▷ Assign and count cell index
2:     $FETCH(Data(i))$
3:     $k \leftarrow cell\ index\ of\ particle\ i$
4:     $Cell_{size}(k) \leftarrow Cell_{size}(k) + +$
5:     $Cell_{offsets}(k) \leftarrow Cell_{offsets} + +$
6: $Cell_{acc} \leftarrow 0$
7: **for** $i$ in range $(0, N_{cell})$ **do**
8:     $Cell_{acc} \leftarrow Cell_{acc} + Cell_{size}(i)$
9:     $Cell_{ptr}(i) \leftarrow Cell_{acc}$
10: $Cell_{ptr}(N_{cell}) \leftarrow Cell_{acc}$
11: **for** $i \in atoms$ **do**                                                ▷ Linear reorder
12:     $k \leftarrow cell\ index\ of\ atom\ i$
13:     $j \leftarrow Cell_{offsets}(k)$
14:     $base \leftarrow Cell_{ptr}(k)$
15:     $X(base + j) \leftarrow i$
16:     $Y(base + j) \leftarrow i$
17:     $Z(base + j) \leftarrow i$

---

Since particles are randomly initialized, the particles often cannot be stored continuously in off-chip memory. The subsequent batch data transfer will bring the problem of discrete memory access and reduce bandwidth utilization. To solve this problem, we propose a bandwidth-friendly data mapping design in this work. As we adopt the cell linked list algorithm mentioned before, 27 cells (1 home cell and 26 neighboring cells ) are sent to FPGAs for each timestep computation. To increase the bandwidth utilization and decrease the data transfer latency, we should map the memory locations of potential neighboring cells and the home cell as closely as possible.

The procedure of data mapping is shown in Algorithm 1. The first loop (lines 1–5) computes the cell index of each particle $i$. Then, the second loop (lines 6–9) accumulates the number of particles sent to on-chip memory for each batch. At last, the third loop (lines 11–17) makes a linear distribution of particles. By adopting this method, particles in the same home cell or neighboring cells will be located in the off-chip memory with a sequential access pattern, and no explicit performance degradation can be seen in simulations.

### 3.2   Zigzagging Buffer Design

As the scales of MD simulations increase rapidly, the need for more FPGA on-chip resources, especially BRAMs, becomes evident. However, the main issue becomes latency with more than enough storage offered by off-chip memory, such as HBMs or GDDR. Therefore, an efficient strategy is pursued to make data transfer between on-chip memory and off-chip devices, allowing for overlapping computation and communication.

In general, the on-chip buffer strategy is always used for the prefetch design based on FPGA, which efficiently narrows the gap between data transfer and on-chip computation. Similarly, the on-chip buffer design is an essential strategy used in MD simulations. To order to utilize the architectural compute resources fully, the on-chip buffer is optimized to the minimum size and only stores the data if reused in subsequent computations. Thus, we propose a zigzagging buffer design to meet the requirement.

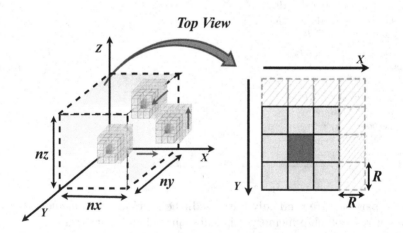

**Fig. 1.** Zigzagging buffer for MD simulaions.

As is shown in Fig. 1, $(0, 0, 0)$ is denoted for the cells with minimum coordinates, $nx$, $ny$, and $nz$ indicate the number of cells in the $X$, $Y$ and $Z$ directions, respectively. $R$ represents the following phase's atoms to be computed, which are only loaded but not computed. We assume the $X$-axis as the most frequently varying dimension, followed by the $Y$- and $Z$-directions. The on-chip buffer is employed to store multiple cells of particles for the following computation. For each batch of data ($3 \times 3 \times 3$ cells) needed to be computed, an on-chip buffer with ($4 \times 4 \times 4$ cells) is loaded into on-chip memory, prefetch a cell data in the $X$, $Y$ and $Z$ directions, respectively. The prefetched buffer will move on the $X - Y$ plane, then prefetch the data along the $Z$ axis in a zigzag motion. Computation is performed on zigzagging buffer data within the boundaries.

## 4   Fixed-Point Design

The practical algorithm using fixed-point arithmetic operation can significantly reduce the area and power consumption and obtain a cost-effective design. For brevity, we use the notation Fixed ($IWL$, $FWL$) to denote a fixed-point representation. $IWL$ and $FWL$ are integer word-length and fractional part word-length. The $IWL$ optimizations determine the dynamic data range, while $FWL$ optimizations consist of the numerical accuracy analysis.

### 4.1   Dynamic Range Analysis

Generally, overflow is quite dangerous for any practical applications in numerical simulation. Although a direct correlation between the application quality and the overflow probability is hardly determined, the dynamic range estimation usually determines the minimum and maximum values and computes the minimum number of bits for the integer part.

Most of the variables contained in $Tersoff$ potential are only influenced by the input distance ($r_{ij}$). Their range is easy to track, and the variables only change to a small degree. However, as $Tersoff$ potential contains plenty of transcendental functions computation, such as $exp$ and $pow$, the final range is hard to decide on after going through the calculation of the transcendental functions. For example, when calculating the value of Bonded-Order ($\zeta = exp(lam3 * (r_{ij} - r_{ik})^3)$), where $lam3$ is a constant parameter, $r_{ij}$ and $r_{ik}$ are the distance between different particles. If taking the method of Extreme Values Theory [29], the maximum range of bonded-order ($\zeta$) is up to 263428, resulting in the $IWL$ being 20, which is quite expensive to set such a long word length for bonded-order ($\zeta$). Hence, the first problem is whether it is necessary to cover the absolute theoretical bounds for $IWL$.

Considering that the distance $r$ is the only input value for MD simulations, it is essential to analyze the input distribution carefully. Figure 2 shows a statistic of distribution of $|r_{ij} - r_{ik}|$ and $r$ for a system containing 5k particles, over 100 K iterations. It is clear that most values of $|r_{ij} - r_{ik}|$ and $r$ concentrate in a fixed interval, respectively. The maximum value and minimum value of $|r_{ij} - r_{ik}|$ is 1.514 and 0.512, respectively. According to the formula of bonded-order ($\zeta$) discussed before, $IWL$ of $\zeta$ is limited to 10, much smaller than the absolute

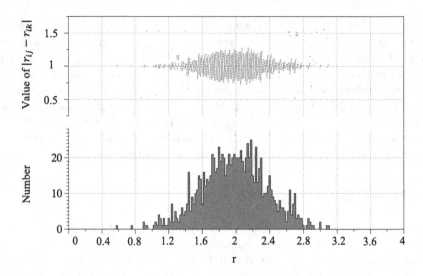

**Fig. 2.** The distribution of $r_{ij}$-$r_{ik}$ and $r$

theoretical bounds. We also apply a similar approach to determine the integer
bit width for the other fixed-point variables in the algorithm.

## 4.2   Precision Analysis

Computation in fixed-point arithmetic has limited accuracy and generates quantization error at the output. The quantization of fixed-point error is considered
a noise added to the result and evaluated by the difference between the output
with different precision. Therefore, verifying that the algorithm's fixed-point
arithmetic behavior is modified within a reasonable limit is necessary. Thus, the
second problem is whether to determine the suitable $FWL$ between the needed
accuracy and the circuit cost.

Generally, accuracies of the final results should be guaranteed before we can
apply the fixed-point strategy. However, it is difficult to model the link between
the application quality and error occurrence probability in MD simulations.
Hence, in order to determine the impact on final accuracy caused by quantization error, we propose a bit-width optimization through bit-accurate simulations
for different bit-width configurations. In this work, we find an essential indicator
(relative energy error) for the quick estimation of the accuracy from [30]. If the
relative energy error is more extensive than 0.1%, the final result will no longer
be more accurate than the baseline.

During the process of MD simulation, the force interaction $F$ is a critical
variable that needs to be quantized. We explore a set of different bit widths for
$F$ and observe the dynamic trend of the relative error and the on-chip resource
cost. According to the formulations of $F$, the maximum $IWF$ of $F$ is 8 due to
the $IWF$ of $\zeta$ is set as 10 . Hence, to analyze the impact of different $FWL$

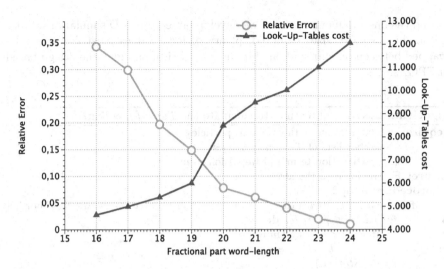

**Fig. 3.** The relative error and resource cost of LUTs according to different $FWL$ of $F$

of force $(F)$ on the whole system, we explore the $FWL$ of $F$ from 24 to 16. From Fig. 3, we observe a similar relative error of different bit-width as with the baseline, ranging from 24-bits to 16-bits, and the relative error meets the requirement of 0.1% when the bit-width is larger than 20. However, when we further reduce the bit-width of $F$, we see a surge of the relative error to a level far above the required 0.1%. The sharp accuracy reduction at the bit-width of $F$ to 20 indicates the precision threshold of the $Tersoff$. When the bit width of data decreases and cannot satisfy the precision threshold, the accuracy will break sharply. On the resource cost side, the bit-width of 20 is also a suitable choice that reduces the LUT usage from around 20000 to 10050 of the total capacity FPGA.

## 5   Custom Dataflow Design

Since the bandwidth-friendly data mapping strategy and fixed-point quantiza-tion design are proposed in Sect. 3 and Sect. 4, more attention should be paid to improving the performance of force interactions. Considering the dataflow architecture of FPGA, a custom pipelined strategy for $Tersoff$ interaction can be taken to improve the performance.

In this Algorithm 2, the overall force of particle $i$ contains two parts: repulsive force and attractive force. After generating the neighbor list, the short-range repulsive and attractive forces will be computed quickly. However, adopting the original algorithm of computing $Tersoff$ potential is quite expensive. Firstly, the original method will require an almost triple computation workload $(0(N^3))$ for $Tersoff$ interaction, and all the computation parts are employed under the serial computing pattern. Secondly, the storage capacity of local value is far beyond the on-chip memory size if we develop large-scale MD simulations. Since the on-chip memory size is limited, plenty of local values must frequently be swapped between on-chip and off-chip memory. It is a bad idea the design based on FPGAs.

---

**Algorithm 2.** Original method to calculate the $Tersoff$ potential

---
**Require:** $r$: The distance of the different particles
$\quad\quad\quad L$: Neighbor lists of different particles
$\quad\quad\quad F_A, F_R$:Attraction term and Repulsion term
**Ensure:** $F$: The force on the atom
 1: **procedure** ALGO2
 2: $\quad$ **for** each $i \in particles$ **do** $\quad\quad\quad\quad\quad\quad\quad\quad\quad$ ▷ Generate Neighbor list
 3: $\quad\quad$ **for** each $j \in particles$ **do**
 4: $\quad\quad\quad$ **if** $r_{(ij)} < cutoff$ **then**
 5: $\quad\quad\quad\quad L \leftarrow L \cup j$
 6: $\quad\quad\quad\quad Store(L)$
 7: $\quad$ **for** each $i \in particles$ **do**
 8: $\quad\quad$ **for** $j \in L_i$ **do**
 9: $\quad\quad\quad$ **if** $i \neq j$ **then**
10: $\quad\quad\quad\quad F_i \leftarrow F_i + F_R(ij)$ $\quad\quad\quad\quad\quad\quad\quad\quad$ ▷ *Repulsion term*
11: $\quad\quad\quad\quad UPDATE(F_i)$
12: $\quad\quad\quad$ **for** $k \in L_i$ **do**
13: $\quad\quad\quad\quad$ **if** $j \neq k$ **then**
14: $\quad\quad\quad\quad\quad F_i \leftarrow F_i + FORCE(\zeta_{ijk})$
15: $\quad\quad\quad\quad\quad UPDATE(F_i)$
16: $\quad\quad\quad$ **for** $k \in L_i$ **do**
17: $\quad\quad\quad\quad$ **if** $j \neq k$ **then**
18: $\quad\quad\quad\quad\quad F_A \leftarrow \zeta_{ikj}$ $\quad\quad\quad\quad\quad\quad\quad\quad\quad$ ▷ *Attraction term*
19: $\quad\quad\quad\quad\quad F_i \leftarrow F_i + F_A(j, i, k, \zeta_{ij})$
20: $\quad\quad\quad\quad\quad UPDATE(F_i)$

---

Thus, to solve this problem, a custom pipelined design is proposed for $Tersoff$ interaction. As the data prefetch strategy is adopted in this work, each batch contains 64 cells ($4 \times 4 \times 4$) for computation. As shown in Fig. 4, when the current home cell has completed the generation of the neighbor list, the process of force interactions for the current home cell and neighbor list generation for the next home cell can be operated simultaneously. Furthermore, considering the $\zeta(ijk)$ is shared in the repulsive term and attraction term at the level of $k$-loop, the local value $\zeta(ijk)$ can be pushed directly to the attraction term, which means when calculating the attraction term of the particle $i$, it is not necessary to wait for the repulsion term to be finished for all the particles. Hence, the custom computation pattern used in MD simulations can improve the performance well, allowing for overlapping different communication parts.

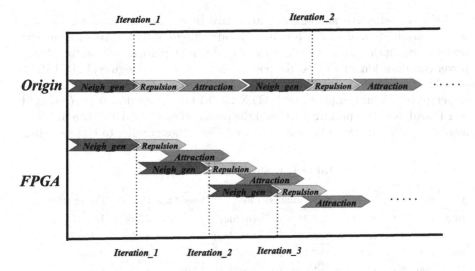

**Fig. 4.** Custom dataflow computation pattern for MD simulaions.

# 6  Evaluation

## 6.1  Environment Setup

We have implemented, tested, and verified our designs on Xilinx Alveo U200 FPGA, which has four DDR4 stacks. This high-end chip has 2586 CLBs, 6840 DSPs, 345.9 Mb block RAMs, and 2 QSFP28 (100GbE) interfaces, making it a good target for FPGA/MD. Then, our main evaluation metrics include overall performance, resource usage, power consumption, and energy evaluation.

Throughout the testing process, we select a typical crystalline structure of silicon $(Si)$, equilibrated at temperature $T = 100\,\mathrm{K}$, to characterize the performance of our implementation. The atoms are highly mobile in the simulation system while only fluctuating around their equilibrium positions in the crystalline structure. The dataset has 512 K atoms, which is too large to fit in a single FPGA's BRAM. The dataset is constrained to a bounding box of $59.5 \times 51 \times 51 \mathring{A}$, with a cutoff radius of $4.2\mathring{A}$. The simulation timestep is $2fs$.

## 6.2  Evaluation Performance

In this section, we will evaluate the performance of different platforms, including multi-core CPU, GPU, and the FPGA implementations of this work. Table 1 measures the performance of $Tersoff$ potential with 512 K atoms while using different devices. For a fair comparison, the benchmark is run on the device without any involvement of the host in the calculation. Firstly, Compared with CPU, our design implemented on FPGA has much better performance, 219.64× improvement for Intel Xeon 2690 v3 CPU with one core, and 14.69× improvement for Intel Xeon 2690 v3 CPU with eight cores.

As a cost-effective accelerator alternative in clouds and clusters, the low power consumption of FPGA is one of the advantages of HPCs. We evaluate the power consumption and power efficiency of different platforms. Due to the low power consumption for FPGA, the power efficiency of our design on U200 FPGA are 152.6× and 28.6× than that on Xeon CPU with one core and eight cores, respectively. Then, compared with GTX 2080ti GPU, our design implemented on FPGA has better performance, and the power efficiency is 4.1× than it. Much more evaluation needs to be done, but we believe these results to be promising.

**Table 1.** Evaluation performance.

| Platform | Simulation rate | Speed up | Power | Power efficiency |
|---|---|---|---|---|
| Intel 2690 v3 1-core | $1.04 \times 10^{-2}$ (ns/day) | 1 | 32 W | 1 |
| Intel 2690 v3 2-core | $3.60 \times 10^{-2}$ (ns/day) | 3.7× | 45W | 2.2× |
| Intel 2690 v3 4-core | $7.13 \times 10^{-2}$ (ns/day) | 7.1× | 64W | 3.55× |
| Intel 2690 v3 8-core | $1.34 \times 10^{-1}$ (ns/day) | 14.9× | 80W | 5.96× |
| NVIDIA GTX 2080Ti GPU | 2.17 (ns/day) | 208.65× | 184.6W | 37.68× |
| Xilinx Alevo U200 FPGA | 2.21 (ns/day) | 219.80× | 46.5W | 152.2× |

## 6.3   Resource Usage Evaluation

This section discusses the overall system resource utilization for $Tersoff$. As mentioned before, we propose an effective data transfer design to overlap computation and communication and improve the utilization of on-chip memories (BRAMs). Meanwhile, we find a rich design space for quantization of $Tersoff$ and propose a custom precision for force computation to reduce on-chip resource usage. Finally, we present a custom pipelined computation model for $Tersoff$, reducing the computational engine idling.

Table 2 lists the available resource of FPGA and several pipeline units that can fit onto a single FPGA chip. We note that our force pipeline for $Tersoff$ can include 64 pipelines. Due to the design of cell linked list, this design needs hundreds of memory modules, while the workload mapping requires each pipeline to accumulate the local variable on-chip. Because of this, a substantial on-chip memory is required. Compared with the standard floating-point implementation of $Tersoff$ based on FPGAs, our fixed-point design reduces LUT, BRAM, and DSP usage by 60.5%, 79.2%, and 74.1%, while the fixed-point design increase LUT, BRAM, and DSP use by 55.1%, 74.1%, and 48.1%, respectively.

## 6.4   Energy Evaluation

Energy evaluation adds complexity but is needed only every few iterations. We thus stream off the energy values computed by FPGA via PCIe every few iterations. A software simulator based on CPU is made to perform simulation on

**Table 2.** Overall system resource utilization

|  | Available | Force pipeline (float) | Force pipeline (fixed) |
|---|---|---|---|
| Pipelines | – | 64 | 64 |
| Kernel frequency (MHZ) | – | 300 | 300 |
| LUT | 892K | 542.88K (60.5%) | 491.18K (55.0%) |
| FF | 1.74M | 0.98M (56.4%) | 0.95M(53.2%) |
| DSP | 6.84K | 4.40K (74.1%) | 3.20K (48.1%) |
| BRAM | 35 MB | 28.04 MB (79.2%) | 26.04 MB (74.2%) |
| Latency | – | 87 | 71 |
| Power (W) | – | 49.8 | 46.5 |

the same input dataset in single precision for validation. The energy waveform is shown in Fig. 5. Our software simulator's energy waveform matches our FPGA implementation with a slight variance.

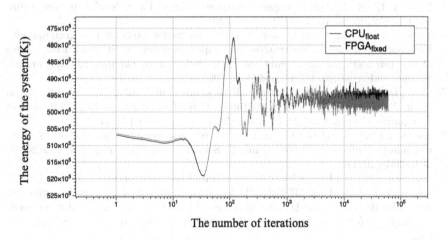

The number of iterations

**Fig. 5.** Energy Waveform

# 7   Conclusion

In this work, we focus on many-body potentials $(Tersoff)$ on a single FPGA with 512 K particles. Compared with conventional pair-wise potentials, the many-body potential $(Tersoff)$ requires much more arithmetic operations and data dependency. Due to the limited on-chip resource of FPGA, several approaches are pursued to increase simulation performance, such as input/output throughputs, pipeline design, custom precision, and parallelism.

Compared with a floating-point implementation based on NVIDIA 28080ti GPUs, our design based on Xilinx U200 FPGA is 1.2× better, and the power efficiency is 4.1× than it. In the future, we would like to find ways to improve the performance further and verify FPGAs as promising candidates for both current and next-generation supercomputing architectures.

**Acknowledgments.** This work was supported in part by the National Natural Science Foundation of China (No. 62102114, U21B2031), and the Key Research Project of Zhejiang Lab (No. 2021PB0AC01).

# References

1. Daggett, V.: Protein folding- simulation. Chem. Rev. **106**(5), 1898–1916 (2006)
2. Koyanagi, J., et al.: Evaluation of the mechanical properties of carbon fiber/polymer resin interfaces by molecular simulation. Adv. Compos. Mater. **28**(6), 639–652 (2019)
3. Jensen, F.: Introduction to computational chemistry. Wiley (2017)
4. Zhou, X.: Impact of molecular dynamics simulations on research and development of semiconductor materials. MRS Adv. **4**(61–62), 3381–3398 (2019)
5. Shaw, D.E., et al.: Anton, a special-purpose machine for molecular dynamics simulation. Commun. ACM **51**(7), 91–97 (2008)
6. Shaw, D.E., et al.: Anton 2: raising the bar for performance and programmability in a special-purpose molecular dynamics supercomputer. In: SC 2014: Proceedings of the International Conference for High Performance Computing, Networking, Storage and Analysis. IEEE, pp. 41–53 (2014)
7. Shaw, D.E., et al.: Anton 3: twenty microseconds of molecular dynamics simulation before lunch. In: Proceedings of the International Conference for High Performance Computing, Networking, Storage and Analysis, pp. 1–11 (2021)
8. Ohmura, I., et al.: MDGRAPE-4: a special-purpose computer system for molecular dynamics simulations. Philos. Trans. R. Soc. A Math. Phys. Eng. Sci. **372**(2021), 20130387 (2021)
9. Morimoto, G., et al.: Hardware acceleration of tensor-structured multilevel ewald summation method on MDGRAPE-4A, a special-purpose computer system for molecular dynamics simulations. In: Proceedings of the International Conference for High Performance Computing, Networking, Storage and Analysis, pp. 1–15 (2021)
10. Zhang, T., et al.: SW_GROMACS: accelerate GROMACS on sunway TaihuLight. In: Proceedings of the International Conference for High Performance Computing, Networking, Storage and Analysis, pp. 1–14 (2019)
11. Gao, P., et al.: Millimeter-scale and billion-atom reactive force field simulation on Sunway Taihulight. IEEE Trans. Parallel Distrib. Syst. **31**(12), 2954–2967 (2020)
12. Yang, C., et al.: Molecular dynamics range-limited force evaluation optimized for FPGAs. In: 2019 IEEE 30th International Conference on Application-specific Systems, Architectures and Processors (ASAP), vol. 2160, pp. 263–271. IEEE (2019)
13. Yang, C., et al.: Fully integrated FPGA molecular dynamics simulations. In: Proceedings of the International Conference for High Performance Computing, Networking, Storage and Analysis, pp. 1–31 (2019)
14. Chen, Y.: OpenCL for HPC with FPGAs: case study in molecular electrostatics. In: IEEE High Performance Extreme Computing Conference (HPEC). IEEE, vol. 2017, pp. 1–8 (2017)

15. Cong, J., et al.: Revisiting FPGA acceleration of molecular dynamics simulation with dynamic data flow behavior in high-level synthesis. In: arXiv preprint arXiv:1611.04474 (2016)
16. Hess, B., et al.: GROMACS 4: algorithms for highly efficient, loadbalanced, and scalable molecular simulation. J Chem. Theory Comput. 4(3), 435–447 (2008)
17. Plimpton, S.: Fast parallel algorithms for short-range molecular dynamics. J. Comput. Phys. 117(1), 1–19 (1995)
18. Salomon-Ferrer, R., Case, D.A., Walker, R.C.: An overview of the Amber biomolecular simulation package. Wiley Interdisc. Rev. Comput. Mol. Sci. 3(2), 198–210 (2013)
19. Phillips, J.C., et al.: Scalable molecular dynamics with NAMD. J. Comput. Chem. 26(16), 1781–1802 (2005)
20. Brooks, B.R., et al.: CHARMM: the biomolecular simulation program. J. Comput. Chem. 30(10), 1545–1614 (2009)
21. Duan, X., et al.: Redesigning LAMMPS for peta-scale and hundredbillion- atom simulation on Sunway TaihuLight. In: SC18: International Conference for High Performance Computing, Networking, Storage and Analysis, pp. 148–159. IEEE (2018)
22. Jia, W., et al.: Pushing the limit of molecular dynamics with ab initio accuracy to 100 million atoms with machine learning. In: arXiv preprint arXiv:2005.00223 (2020)
23. Maliţa, M., Mihăiţă, M., M ştefan, G.: Molecular dynamics on fpga based accelerated processing units. In: MATEC Web of Conferences, vol. 125, p. 04012. EDP Sciences (2017)
24. Escobar, F.A., Chang, X., Valderrama, C.: Suitability analysis of FPGAs for heterogeneous platforms in HPC. IEEE Trans. Parallel Distrib. Syst. 27(2), 600–612 (2015)
25. Khan, M.A., Chiu, M., Herbordt, M.C.: FPGA-Accelerated Molecular Dynamics. In: Vanderbauwhede, W., Benkrid, K. (eds.) High-Performance Computing Using FPGAs, pp. 105–135. Springer, New York (2013). https://doi.org/10.1007/978-1-4614-1791-0_4
26. Benjamin, H.: 3D FFTs on a Single FPGA. In: IEEE 22nd Annual International Symposium on Field-Programmable Custom Computing Machines. IEEE, vol. 2014, pp. 68–71 (2014)
27. Sheng, J., et al.: Design of 3D FFTs with FPGA clusters. In: 2014 IEEE High Performance Extreme Computing Conference (HPEC). IEEE, pp. 1–6 (2014)
28. Kasap, S., Benkrid, K.: Parallel processor design and implementation for molecular dynamics simulations on a FPGA-based supercomputer. JCP 7(6), 1312–1328 (2012)
29. Chapoutot, A., Didier, L.S., Villers, F.: Range estimation of floating-point variables in simulink models. In: Proceedings of the 2012 Conference on Design and Architectures for Signal and Image Processing. IEEE, pp. 1–8 (2012)
30. Piana, S., Klepeis, J.L., Shaw, D.E.: Assessing the accuracy of physical models used in protein-folding simulations: quantitative evidence from long molecular dynamics simulations. Curr. Opin. Struct. Biol. 24, 98–105 (2014)

# A Runtime Programmable Accelerator for Convolutional and Multilayer Perceptron Neural Networks on FPGA

Ehsan Kabir[1]([✉]), Arpan Poudel[1], Zeyad Aklah[2], Miaoqing Huang[1], and David Andrews[1]

[1] CSCE Department, University of Arkansas, Fayetteville, AR, USA
{ekabir,arpanp,mqhuang,dandrews}@uark.edu
[2] Computer Science Department, University of Thi-Qar, Nasiriyah, Iraq
zaklah@utq.edu.iq

**Abstract.** Deep neural networks (DNNs) are prevalent for many applications related to classification, prediction and regression. To perform different applications with better performance and accuracy, an optimized network architecture is required, which can be obtained through experiments and performance evaluation on different network topologies. However, a custom hardware accelerator is not scalable and it lacks the flexibility to switch from one topology to another at run time. In order to support convolutional neural networks (CNN) along with multilayer perceptron neural networks (MLPNN) of different sizes, we present in this paper an accelerator architecture for FPGAs that can be programmed during run time. This combined CNN and MLP accelerator (CNN-MLPA) can run any CNN and MLPNN applications without re-synthesis. Therefore, time spent on synthesis, placement and routing can be saved for executing different applications on the proposed architecture. Run time results show that the CNN-MLPA can be used for network topologies of different sizes without much degradation of performance. We evaluated the resource utilization and execution time on Xilinx Virtex 7 FPGA board for different benchmark datasets to demonstrate that our design is run time programmable, portable and scalable for any FPGA. The accelerator was then optimized to increase the throughput by applying pipelining and concurrency, and reduce resource consumption with fixed-point operations.

**Keywords:** FPGA · Neural network · MLP · CNN · Overlay · Flexible · Programmable · Reconfigurable · Accelerators · Custom hardware

## 1 Introduction

Deep neural networks have been applied to applications that are hard to solve using traditional rule based programming methods. A trained DNN for a

L. Gan et al. (Eds.): ARC 2022, LNCS 13569, pp. 32–46, 2022.
https://doi.org/10.1007/978-3-031-19983-7_3

particular application takes some input features and makes prediction, decision or classification. For many real time applications, a CPU based software system might not be fast enough to produce outputs as the size of the network grows for complex problems. Hence, hardware platforms like FPGA are used for DNN applications because of their massive parallel processing units to produce throughput higher than the CPU. The architecture of DNN with parallel inputs, outputs, and neurons in the hidden layers makes it possible. The reconfigurable logic blocks and interconnects, parallel memory and computing units, and low power consumption of FPGA have produced many FPGA accelerator [1,2]. Applications such as image compression, pattern recognition, signal processing, IoT device control, and biomedical applications (e.g., arrhythmia and eplileptic seizure detection etc.) are reported in [3,4]. Krisps et al. [5] showed how an artificial neural network (ANN) could be implemented within an FPGA for a real time hand detection and tracking system. Wayne et al. [6] designed a spiking neural network accelerator supporting large scale simulation on FPGA-based systems. Seul et. al. Several methods exist for compressing the size of data to reduce multiplication and addition operations for fast inference and to reduce hardware consumption. For example, [7,8] proposed binary neural network (BNN) inference engine on FPGAs for MNIST image classification with high accuracy. Convolutional neural network (CNN) [9] is used for applications such as image recognition, segmentation, speech recognition, medical diagnosis etc. Although applications with CNN is growing, MLP workloads still have a large share in open clouds operations by companies such as Facebook and Google [10,11]. However, these accelerators are customized for only one type of neural network used in a single application. Thus, the parameters for different network topologies need to be defined before synthesis for different applications. Moreover, creating custom DNN for different applications with hardware description language (HDL) or high level synthesis (HLS) code is an arduous and time consuming task. Therefore, a multi-purpose hardware accelerator is desirable to meet varied computational and memory requirements while supporting various neural networks for various applications. Some flexible and scalable accelerators for neural networks on FPGA have been reported in [12–14]. This paper presents such an accelerator for CNN and MLP applications.

The main contributions of this paper are:

- Designing a run time programmable hardware accelerator to run both CNN and MLPNN applications.
- Writing a parameterized high level synthesis code so that parameters such as number of processing elements (PEs), data representation (floating-point or fixed-point) and activation function (AF) implementation approach (BRAM lookup tables (LUTs) or synthesized logic-diffused multiplier) can be set before synthesis. This allows designers to adjust resource utilization by varying the parallel processing with PEs. It also enables changing the type of AFs and data precision.

- Making some parameters programmable (such as input size, output size, number of layers, neurons, channels and filters, size of filters and stride) so that they can be set (up to a maximum value) during run time. Thus, different topologies for different applications can be run without resynthesizing the hardware. Our experiments showed 50 h of reduction time on synthesis, placement, implementation and routing for maximum utilization on Virtex 7.
- Developing a switching technique to switch between CNN and MLP operations according to user's need. It enables the reuse of the same PEs for both MLP and CNN.
- Optimizing the accelerator to demonstrate some strategies that can be applied to make further improvement on the performance of the accelerator.
- Testing different benchmark data sets and network topologies to show programmable attributes and performance of the accelerator, and comparing them with Xilinx FINN and DPU framework for the same networks.

The rest of this paper is organized as follows. Section 2 introduces the CNN-MLPA architecture, and Sect. 3 presents the results for MLP. In Sect. 4, CNN feature of the accelerator is discussed in details along with its results. Finally, Sect. 5 concludes this paper.

## 2   CNN-MLPA Architecture

Figure 1a shows the generic structure of an CNN-MLP accelerator. It contains a 1D array of Processing Elements (PEs), a scheduler, a controller, configuration registers, local memory, and three external interface connections. Input data, weights for the filters in convolution layers (CLs), and weights in the fully connected (FC) layers are transferred through the same input channel. For a particular network, weights are fetched from DRAM according to their need and then they are stored in BRAM. The size of DRAM is the limitation for our design. The input and output interfaces are configured as FIFOs with a DMA engine (not shown) for fast transfers through the AXI-Stream interface. The AXI4-Lite interface is used to program the configuration registers and control the operation of the CNN-MLPA during run time. Users can switch between CNN and MLP during run time with a control signal. MLP is nothing but a fully connected neural network [15], whereas CNN contains convolution layers with multiple channels and filters [9,16] followed by the fully connected layers. Thus, for CNN applications, block of both convolution layers and MLPs are kept active; and for MLP applications, only the MLP block functions. The remainder of this section describes the functionality of different components of the CNN-MLPA.

### 2.1   Processing Element

Figure 1b shows the block diagram of a PE. Each PE has two input BRAMs (one for inputs and the other for weights), an output BRAM, control signals (Start,

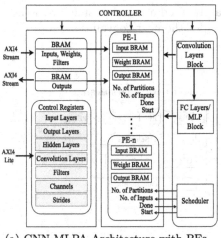 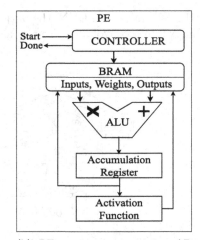

(a) CNN-MLPA Architecture with PEs.

(b) PE structure containing AR and AF unit.

**Fig. 1.** Overview of the CNN-MLP accelerator.

and Done), an adder/multiplier unit (ALU), a controller, accumulation registers (AR), and an AF unit. AR is mainly an output buffer that stores the complete or partial result of a multiplication-accumulation (MAC) operation. Then this result is sent either back to the input buffer so that it can be used for the next layer or to the output stream interface. Each PE gives output for one neuron of a layer in case of MLP operation. For CNN, each PE may be used several times depending on the number of PEs, channels and filters in a convolution layer. Two types of AFs are implemented: a step function and log sigmoid. Before synthesis, two options are provided to the system designer to implement the AFs as either computation-based functions (synthesized hardware) or using LUTs.

## 2.2 Scheduler

The responsibility of the scheduler is to partition each layer of neurons into the linear array of PEs. The scheduler divides each layer into groups of neurons equal in size of the available number of PEs. If the number of neurons in a layer is not divisible evenly by the number of PEs, the remaining neuron(s) will be assigned to the first PE(s) during the next cycle. For example as shown in Fig. 2, with 4 PEs and 10 neurons in the first hidden layer, the scheduler will sequence two groups (G1, G2) of 4 neurons and one group (G3) of 2 neurons. The second hidden layer has 7 neurons. Thus, one group (G4) of 4 neurons and one group (G5) of 3 neurons will be scheduled. All neurons in a group are processed concurrently, while different groups are processed sequentially. Based on the scheduler assignment, the controller aligns weights and inputs for each neuron in each PE's internal BRAMs. The outputs of each group within a layer are saved in the output buffer, and assigned as inputs to the next layer for

MLPNN. In case of CNN, the outputs can be used as partials sum for the next channel in a convolution layer or as inputs for the next convolution layer.

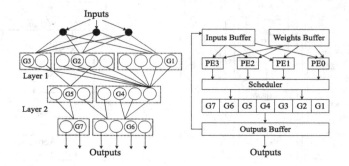

**Fig. 2.** Scheduling neurons in MLP with four PEs.

## 2.3   Controller

The controller organizes weights and inputs for the neurons. It divides the weight vector into groups, each having weights equal to the number of PEs, and allocates them into each PE's weight BRAM. It also connects the outputs of each layer with the appropriate weights, and this combination of outputs and weights is used in the next layer. The inputs are read serially from BRAM and stored in PE's input BRAM according to the number of neurons and PEs in the input layer for FCs. However, the allocation of inputs for CL depends on the input size, filter size, number of PEs, and strides. The allocation of weights and inputs for convolution operation in the convolution layer is briefly described by Fig. 3 for inputs with two channels, two filters and two PEs. Two sets of inputs in a channel can be convoluted by a filter in two PEs in parallel. Inputs (a, b, c) are arranged in PE-1's input BRAM. PE-2's input BRAM holds one stride size shifted version of inputs (b, c, d). Filter-1 has two sets of weights for Channel-1 and Channel-2, which are arranged in the temporary filter buffer. PE performs the MAC operations to produce partial sums. The same PEs are reused until convolution on Channel-1 is done. The same convolution process with Filter-1 is done on Channel-2. The outputs of both channels are accumulated in the output buffer. These operations are repeated for the same input channels with Filter-2 to produce output Channel-2. The output channels are used as input channels for the next layer.

The controller can read the AF values via the streaming input channel and store them in PE's BRAM if they are implemented as LUTs. Moreover, it calculates the number of weights being streamed to the CNN-MLPA based on the configured registers. Finally it streams the results out of the CNN-MLPA core and generates "done" signal in the output layer. It also enables users to switch between CNN and MLPNN operations.

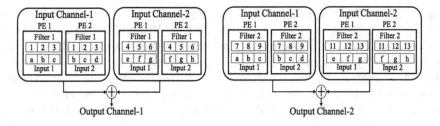

Fig. 3. Convolution layer operations.

## 2.4 Configuration Registers

The CNN-MLPA contains two sets of registers, one for the MLP block and one for the Convolution Layers (CL) block. They are used to specify the topology of the neural network during run time. The registers are described below with their corresponding parameters they store.

- Layers: number of layers in the FC block.
- Inputs: number of inputs.
- Outputs: number of outputs.
- Neurons$_{H_n}$: number of neurons in $n^{th}$ hidden layer.
- ConvLayers: number of CL in the network.
- InputSize: input size in each CL.
- OutputSize: output size in each CL.
- Filters: number of filters in each CL.
- FilterSize: filter size in each CL.
- Channels: number of channels in each CL.
- Strides: the step size of the scanning filter in each CL.

The number of registers for MLP block scales according to the maximum network configuration such as: Maximum Number of Layers (MNL), Maximum Number of Neurons (MNN), Maximum Number of Neurons in Largest Layer (MNNLL), Maximum Number of Inputs (MNI), Maximum Number of Outputs (MNO), and the registers for CL scales according to the maximum number of filters, input and output channels, size of the filters and strides in the CL. Some values for the registers such as output size from each CL can be pre-calculated and then be sent to the accelerator if the network architecture is known. For example, output size is calculated by the equation, $OutputSize = \frac{\text{Input size-Filter size+2}\times\text{Padding Layers}}{strides}$. We can stream the value to the controller directly or let the accelerator calculate it.

## 3 Evaluation and Results for MLP Operations

### 3.1 Test Platform

The CNN-MLP accelerator is implemented on Xilinx Virtex-7 (xc7vx-485tffg1761-2) FPGA board. The overall implementation contains a softcore IP named MicroBlaze running at 100 MHz frequency as the processing system (PS) and the CNN-MLPA as programmable logic (PL). The code for the accelerator was written in C++ and generated using Xilinx's Vivado-HLS 19.2 tool. After synthesis, we run C/RTL co-simulation with our testbench code in HLS to verify the functionality and output. Then, we export the RTL to vivado design suite where it is integrated with the MicroBlaze. With the help of a direct memory access (DMA) controller, communication among MicroBlaze, accelerator, and external memory (DDR3 DRAM) is established for transfer and storage of data. MicroBlaze provides programming interface to the users and enables communication with the accelerator via JTAG-UART. It transfers the input data and weights as a vector to the DRAM, and activates the DMA controller to transfer the data from DRAM to the local BRAM of the accelerator. It also assists the accelerator to be activated, read from and write to the storage. The block diagram of the overall architecture is shown in Fig. 4. AXI Timer IP is used to measure the time.

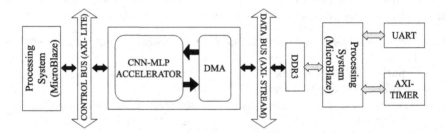

**Fig. 4.** Overview of the complete implementation.

## 3.2   CNN-MLPA Configurations

CNN-MLPA can be configured either for MLP operations or CNN operations. The MLP block will exist in both cases since CNN uses the FC layers of the MLP block. Therefore, when synthesized for CNN, it can perform MLP operations too. First, the CNN-MLPA was configured as an MLP accelerator only where the parameters are MNL, MNN, MNNLL, MNI, MNO as mentioned earlier. They are set as 6, 784, 784, 784 and 64 respectively before synthesis as a maximum bound for running the largest MLPNN we used as benchmark for MNIST dataset. Three versions of the accelerator with 4, 8 and 16 PEs and computation-based sigmoid AFs for all layers were synthesized. Then, we measured execution time and resource utilization. The results are compared with other FPGA implementations. Then we substituted sigmoid AFs with ReLU AFs, and floating-point precision with fixed-point for improving performance and resource utilization. Performance results for these tests are presented in Sects. 3.4 and 3.5.

## 3.3 Test Applications

Table 1 lists some referenced benchmarks along with the implementation platform, operating frequency and execution time. We ran these topologies on our architecture to evaluate performance of the MLP feature of the CNN-MLPA. Each application was first trained offline on a desktop PC using python. Different topologies were evaluated during the training phase. The validity of the results for each system was checked by comparing the outputs with the expected outputs produced by python, and C/RTL co-simulation result of HLS.

**Table 1.** Various FPGA implementations of MLPNN.

| Works | Dataset | Topologies (Input, Hidden layers, Output) | Implementation platform | Frequency (MHz) | Execution time/Speed up |
|-------|---------|-------------------------------------------|-------------------------|-----------------|-------------------------|
| [17] | | #1: (784, 64, 64, 10) | Zynq Zedboard | 200 | 36.1x Speed Up compared to 2.3 GHz Intel Core2 Processor |
| | | #2: (784, 128, 128, 10) | | | |
| | | #3: (784, 256, 256, 10) | | | |
| [18] | MNIST | #4: (784, 600, 600, 10) | Virtex-7 (xc7vx485tffg1761-2) | 490 | 2.514 µs |
| [19] | | #5: (784, 1024, 10) | Zynq 7000 | 300 | 4.76 µs |
| [20] | | #6: (784, 126, 126, 126, 10) | Zynq 7000 | 219 | 69 µs |
| [14] | | #7: (4, 7, 12, 3) | Kintex-7 (xc7k410t) | 330 | 430 ns |
| [18] | IRIS | #8: (4, 10, 3) | Virtex-7 (xc7vx485tffg1761-2) | 490 | 79 ns |
| [21] | HAR | #9: (14, 19, 19, 7) | Spartan-6 (xc6slx45csg324-2) | 67 | 800 ns |

## 3.4 Performance Evaluation of MLP Accelerator

The benchmarks mentioned in Table 1 are run with our accelerator at 100 MHz for three different numbers of PE. Table 2 shows the execution time for 9 different topologies for 3 different numbers of PEs for floating-point precision. The throughput here is floating-point operations per second (FLOPS), which was calculated by the ratio of floating-point multiply-accumulate (MAC) operations and execution time. All the topologies were run by changing some parameters such as the number of inputs, outputs, layers, and number of neurons in each layer during run time without the need to re-synthesize. Input data sets were pre-loaded into off-chip DRAM. The execution time obtained from AXI timer of the FPGA includes the total time taken to setup the configuration registers with parameters, transfer input and weight data from DRAM to the accelerator's local BRAMs, read that data from BRAMs, store them into PE's internal BRAMs, compute results, write final results back into the BRAMs, and send the output to the DRAM. If AFs are used as LUTs, then they must also be loaded into the BRAM. This will increase the execution time. Therefore, the time increases as the network grows.

**Table 2.** Execution time of optimized MLP accelerator for different benchmark topologies.

| Model | Topology (Inputs, Hidden layers, Outputs) | Execution time (μS) | | | Throughput for 8 PEs (MFLOP/S) |
|---|---|---|---|---|---|
| | | 4 PEs | 8 PEs | 16 PEs | |
| #1 | 784, 64, 64, 10 | 750 | 520 | 341 | 211 |
| #2 | 784, 128, 128, 10 | 1,584 | 1,095 | 708 | 215 |
| #3 | 784, 256, 256, 10 | 3,581 | 2,468 | 1,600 | 218 |
| #4 | 784, 600, 600, 10 | 11,078 | 7,700 | 4,927 | 217 |
| #5 | 784, 1024, 10 | 10,770 | 7,461 | 4,760 | 218 |
| #6 | 784, 126, 126, 126, 10 | 1,950 | 1,244 | 798 | 212 |
| #7 | 4, 7, 12, 3 | 6.1 | 6.00 | 5.88 | 49 |
| #8 | 4, 10, 3 | 4.18 | 4.19 | 4.54 | 33 |
| #9 | 14, 19, 19, 7 | 15.68 | 12.5 | 11 | 121 |

The computation time of CNN-MLPA accelerator is mainly dependent on the number of PEs and the size of the network. As the size of the two hidden layers increased from Model 1 to Model 4 of Table 2, we can see that the execution time increases. This trend will be different if convolution layers are used. Many hyper parameters of CNN affect its inference time. Most of the time inside PEs is spent on MAC operations. Moreover, computation-based sigmoid activation function contains exponential and division operations. These operations take many clock cycles. Now, if the network size grows for limited PEs, the number of groups of PEs will be high according to the partitioning technique described earlier in Sect. 2.2. The maximum number of PEs depends on the available resources of the FPGA platform. One PE can do several MAC operations at the same time. Applying loop unrolling pragma in Vivado HLS would process multiple loops in parallel, affecting the performance and resource utilization. This is one method for optimization in HLS based design. Here, the PEs are partially optimized with pipeline and unroll directives. All the loops are pipelined with initiation intervals that do not violate the timing constraints. Moreover, log-sigmoid activation function is replaced by ReLU activation function [22], which is very simple to implement on hardware and takes less clock cycles to execute. The execution time was brought down to half by this approach. If the number of PE is increased, more operations are executed in parallel, thus decreasing the time. However, for smaller network like the Models 7 and 8 of Table 2, the impact of large number of PEs is not significant because they will remain unused. The execution time can also be decreased by designing the accelerator to use LUTs for AFs and represent the data with fixed-point precision before synthesis. But it may reduce accuracy. We chose the bit width in such a way that the accuracy was preserved.

The results in Table 3 are derived for 16 PEs for 8 bit (4 bit integer part & 4 bit fractional part) inputs and weights at the input layer. Intermediate layers required at most 12 bits (8 bit integer part & 4 bit fractional part)

**Table 3.** Result comparison of floating-point and fixed-point precision for 16-PE design.

| Model | Topology | Execution time (μS) | | Accuracy at 8 Bit | Frame per second | Throughput (OP/S) |
|-------|----------|--------------|-------------|-------------------|------------------|-------------------|
| | | 32 Bit float | 8 Bit fixed | precision | at 8 Bit precision | at 8 Bit precision |
| #4 | 784, 600, 600, 10 | 7,700 | 2,637 | 100% | 380 | 634 MOPS |
| #3 | 784, 256, 256, 10 | 2,468 | 854 | 100% | 1170 | 628 MOPS |
| #1 | 784, 64, 64, 10 | 520 | 180 | 99% | 5556 | 610 MOPS |

to maintain good accuracy. The precision was determined by analyzing the maximum and minimum values of inputs and trained weights with python script so that all the values within this range can be represented by fixed-point precision with minimum error. The precision for intermediate layers was determined by experiments because different network size may require different precision. Same accuracy as 32 bit floating-point precision was achieved in this method. Both the area and execution time were also reduced. Table 3 reports throughput in terms of both OP/S and frame per second (FPS).

## 3.5 Resource Utilization and Performance Comparison with Other Works

This section shows the resource utilization and performance of the programmable CNN-MLPA with MLP feature only. It also reports comparison on resource utilization and throughput with other MLP related works. The term normalized throughput (ratio of OP/S & total LUT or DSP utilized) was introduced for better comparison because different works adopt different parallelism strategies and use different FPGA platforms. Moreover, our design was not fully optimized for maximum resource consumption. We report the versions synthesized for running the largest network for MNIST dataset in Models 4 and 6 of Table 2. Model 4 represents the maximum number (600) of neurons in a layer and Model 6 represents the total number of layers (5), which are set before synthesis so that both can be run on the CNN-MLPA. The maximum number of 32-bit weights was chosen to be 850,000 because Model 4 requires around 835,000 weights. It almost exceeds the available BRAM resources. The input BRAMs of PEs also put pressure on on-chip memory. By directing Vivado HLS to allocate distributed RAM [23], also known as LUT-based RAM for PEs, the consumption of 36K

**Table 4.** Result comparison with other works.

| MLP Designs | FPGA | LUT | DSP | BRAM | FF | Throughput (OP/S) | Normalized throughput [OP/($S \times LUT \times 1000$)] |
|-------------|------|-----|-----|------|-----|-------------------|-------------------------|
| CNN-MLPA (Our Work) | XC7VX485T | 18,218 | 6 | 222 | 11670 | 610 M | 33.5 |
| NAFOSTED'17 [20] | XC5VLX-110T | 218,528 | – | – | 139,391 | 3.8 G | 17.4 |
| FPL'21 [3] | XC7Z020 | 11,845 | 184 | 61 | 16,461 | 3 M | 0.250 |
| DLAU'17 [17] | XC7Z020 | 53,200 | 220 | 280 | 106,400 | 192 M | 3.594 |
| IJEECS'19 [2] | Altera 5CSEMA5F31C6 | 7,137 | 70 | – | 11,053 | 12.7 M | 1.7 |
| Xilinx FINN'17 [8] | ZC706 | 91,131 | – | 4.5 | – | 1.9 T | 20849 |

BRAMs was brought down to 81.07%. Our design can also fetch additional weights from DRAM when required to avoid over utilization of BRAMs.

The CNN-MLPA shows better normalized throughput compared with all other works except Xilinx FINN in Table 4. Xilinx FINN outperforms us by a large number because it relies mainly on binary neural network training before inference. Thus, different networks need to go through the training cycle first. Furthermore, it can only be used with PYNQ boards [24] for interfacing with python, and it is not run time programmable. Our design is synthesized only once for all networks. Therefore, the latency increases with larger networks because the same resources are being utilized sequentially. Larger network will require more resources for equivalent performance. If the loops for the PEs in HLS can be unrolled efficiently, the resource utilization will be increased for better throughput.

## 4    Accelerator with CNN Feature

When CNN is run on the CNN-MLPA, both convolution layer (CL) block and MLP block shown in Fig. 1a are functional. Thus, the maximum limit for the configuration parameters of the convolution layers as described in Sect. 2.4 are also set based on the largest CNN being run. The largest CNN we ran was VGG-16 based on which the maximum values for input size, output size, number of filters and channels, filter size were chosen. Model specific parameters are sent during run time to execute different CNN topologies within the limit. We tested the programmable feature of the accelerator with three custom CNNs. Their network topologies and performance are reported in Table 5. These three CNNs perform MNIST digit classification. Some other benchmarks such as VGG-16, LeNet and SqueezeNet were also executed.

We used ReLU AF after each convolution layer. For the custom CNNs in Table 5, the whole convolution block is followed by two FC layers in the MLP block before outputs are generated. Thus, a CNN with one convolution layer was represented as 'Input→ Conv1→ ReLU→ FC→ ReLU→ FC→ ReLU→ Output'. The convolution layers have input and output channels. The number of output channels from a CL, which works as input for the next CL, depends on the number of filters used to scan the data of the input channels. The filters scan with a step size known as stride. Their weights are multiplied with the inputs and then the partial sums are accumulated. This operation is done in one PE. Thus, the same PE will operate several times. The number of times the same PE is used depends on the total number of PEs and input channels, and the size of filters and stride. An adder is used outside PE to sum up all the output of the same location of the channels (as shown in Fig. 3).

### 4.1    Results for Full CNN-MLP Acceleration

This section shows the performance and resource utilization when both convolution layer block and MLP block are operational. Table 5 includes result of the execution time, frame per second, throughput and accuracy at fixed-point precision for three custom CNNs. 10 bit (6 bit integer part & 4 bit fractional part) precision for inputs and weights and 16 bit (6 bit integer part & 8 bit fractional part) precision for outputs and intermediate values were found to preserve the same accuracy as floating-point after some experiments on the 3 CNNs. The precision might be different for other very deep CNNs. It also shows the combinations of various parameters (filter, channel, stride, padding) used in the convolution layers. The number of MAC operations in the convolution layers is higher than the FC layers of CNN. The time also grows with the increase in convolution layers. The time can be reduced by using more PEs in CLs because they have more parallel operations than FC layers.

**Table 5.** Performance of CNN-MLPA for 3 CNN architectures.

| Model | CNN architecture | Filter size (No.× Width × Height) | Input channels | Stride, padding | Test accuracy (%) | Execution time (mS) | Frame per second | Throughput (OP/S) |
|---|---|---|---|---|---|---|---|---|
| 1 | Input → Conv1 → ReLU → FC → ReLU → FC→ ReLU→ Output | Layer-1: (1 × 8 × 8) | Layer-1: 1 | Layer-1: (1,0) | 97 | 0.209 | 4784 | 0.65 G |
| 2 | Input → Conv1 → ReLU → Conv2 →ReLU → →FC →ReLU → FC→ReLU→ Output | Layer-1: (1 × 8 × 8) Layer-2: (3 × 3 × 3) | Layer-1: 1 Layer-2: 1 | Layer-1: (1,0) Layer-2: (2,0) | 98 | 0.219 | 4566 | 0.92 G |
| 3 | Input → Conv1 → ReLU → Conv2 →ReLU → → Conv3 →ReLU → →FC →ReLU → FC→ReLU→ Output | Layer-1: (3 × 3 × 3) Layer-2: (8 × 6 × 6) Layer-3: (3 × 3 × 3) | Layer-1: 1 Layer-2: 3 Layer-3: 8 | Layer-1: (1,0) Layer-2: (2,0) Layer-3: (1,0) | 99 | 0.237 | 4219 | 1.3 G |

The comparison of resource utilization, throughput in terms of both OP/S and FPS and normalized throughput (ratio of OP/S & total LUT or DSP utilized) between our work and others for different benchmarks is shown in Table 6. It also contains some custom CNN implementation done by us and others using Xilinx DPU [25] on Zynq UltraScale+ MPSoC ZCU104 Evaluation board. It shows how CNN-MLPA can support various CNN networks using the same resources. The CNN-MLPA was not fully optimized for any particular network, but was optimized for all networks. Therefore, the normalized throughput is not the best but close to other custom designs, which supports only one network. The DSP utilization of CNN-MLPA is also lower than other designs. When compared with the Xilinx DPU, we got higher throughput of the models in Table 5 with CNN-MLPA when DPU was configured with single core. Our design is also portable to any FPGA while DPU is only supported by a few platforms.

**Table 6.** Result comparison with other works for different benchmarks.

| Models | Designs | FPGA | LUT | DSP | BRAM 36k | FF | Throughput (OP/S) | Normalized Throughput [**OP**/($S \times LUT \times 1000$)] |
|---|---|---|---|---|---|---|---|---|
| LeNet-5 | CNN-MLPA (This Work) | XC7VX485T | 70878 | 96 | 361 | 58422 | 120 M | 1.7 |
| | Electronics'21 [26] | XCZU9EG | 61,713 | 123 | 102 | 27,863 | 141 M | 2.28 |
| | ICEIC'20 [27] | XCZU9EG | 32,598 | 143 | 95 | 33,585 | 201 M | 6.14 |
| VGG-16 | CNN-MLPA (This Work) | XC7VX485T | 70878 | 96 | 361 | 58422 | 418 | |
| | YUAN et al.'21 [28] | VCU118 | 781,000 | 4096 | 1779 | 243,802 | 2558 G | 3275 |
| | FCCM'21 [29] | XCVU9P | 469,288 | 2100 | 27 | 663,488 | 49.92 G | 106 |
| SqueezeNet/ZynqNet | CNN-MLPA (This Work) | XC7VX485T | 70878 | 96 | 361 | 58422 | 19 | |
| | Micro-processors and Microsystems'20 [30] | XC7Z020 | 38,038 | 172 | 97.5 | 25,036 | 5.5 G | 145 |
| | ARC'18 [31] | ZC702 | 13,418 | 149 | 124 | 18,114 | 1.1 G | 87 |
| Custom CNNs | Xilinx DPU (Single Core)-In Our Lab | ZCU104 | 49,383 | 710 | 255 | 98735 | 118 M | 2.38 |
| | Xilinx DPU (Dual Core) - Electronics'22 [25] | ZCU104 | 103,700 | 1,380 | 290 | 198,900 | 7 G | 66 |
| | Xilinx DPU - SEEDA-CECNSM'21 [32] | XC7Z020 | 31,812 | 194 | 117.5 | 58,169 | 4.1 M | 0.128 |

# 5   Conclusion

In this paper, we presented a run time programmable accelerator on FPGAs to run both Convolutional Neural Network (CNN) and Multilayer Perceptron Neural Network (MLPNN) of any topology without re-synthesizing the accelerator every time for different networks. It partitions the operations of a network into groups of available processing elements (PEs). The advantages of this design are reusability and scalability over custom accelerators that can execute only specific DNN applications. The execution time and resource utilization are reported for some benchmark datasets to show how they vary with the number of PEs, precisions and activation functions (AF). It can be synthesized either for MLPNN or CNN. If synthesized for CNN, it can run both MLP and CNN applications. The synthesis is done only once after configuring parameters such as data precision, number of PEs, and implementation method for the AFs for a particular FPGA. Then it becomes efficient for handling a wide range of CNN and MLPNN topologies with varying accuracies and performance. Performance in terms of execution time may degrade for some networks, which can be considered as a trade-off for the flexibility, scalability and portability of the CNN-MLPA architecture.

# References

1. Zhao, M., Hu, C., Wei, F., Wang, K., Wang, C., Jiang, Y.: Real-time underwater image recognition with FPGA embedded system for convolutional neural network. Sensors **19**(2), 350 (2019)
2. Ann, L.Y., Ehkan, P., Mashor, M.Y., Sharun, S.M.: FPGA-based architecture of hybrid multilayered perceptron neural network. Indonesian J. Electr. Eng. Comput. Sci. **14**(2), 949–956 (2019)
3. Ngo, D.M., Temko, A., Murphy, C.C., Popovici, E. FPGA hardware acceleration framework for anomaly-based intrusion detection system in IoT. In 2021 31st International Conference on Field-Programmable Logic and Applications (FPL), pp. 69–75 (2021)
4. Jiang, W., et al.: Wearable on-device deep learning system for hand gesture recognition based on FPGA accelerator. Math. Biosc. Eng. **18**(1), 132–153 (2021)

5. Krips, M., Lammert, T., Kummert, A.: FPGA implementation of a neural network for a real-time hand tracking system. In: 2002 Proceedings of the First IEEE International Workshop on Electronic Design, Test and Applications, pp. 313–317 (2002)
6. Cheung, K., Schultz, S.R., Luk, W.: A large-scale spiking neural network accelerator for FPGA systems. In: Villa, A.E.P., Duch, W., Érdi, P., Masulli, F., Palm, G. (eds.) ICANN 2012. LNCS, vol. 7552, pp. 113–120. Springer, Heidelberg (2012). https://doi.org/10.1007/978-3-642-33269-2_15
7. Liang, S., Yin, S., Liu, L., Luk, W., Wei, S.: FP-BNN: binarized neural network on FPGA. Neurocomputing **275**, 1072–1086 (2018)
8. Umuroglu, Y., et al.: FINN: a framework for fast, scalable binarized neural network inference. In Proceedings of the 2017 ACM/SIGDA International Symposium on Field-Programmable Gate Arrays, pp. 65–74 (2017)
9. LeCun, Y., Bengio, Y., Hinton, G.: Deep learning. Nature **521**(7553), 436–444 (2015)
10. Wu, C.J., et al.: Machine learning at Facebook: understanding inference at the edge. In 2019 IEEE International Symposium on High Performance Computer Architecture (HPCA), pp. 331–344. IEEE (2019)
11. Jouppi, N., Young, C., Patil, N., Patterson, D.: Motivation for and evaluation of the first tensor processing unit. IEEE Micro **38**(3), 10–19 (2018)
12. Aklah, Z., Andrews, D.: A flexible multilayer perceptron co-processor for FPGAs. In: Sano, K., Soudris, D., Hübner, M., Diniz, P.C. (eds.) ARC 2015. LNCS, vol. 9040, pp. 427–434. Springer, Cham (2015). https://doi.org/10.1007/978-3-319-16214-0_39
13. Majumder, K., Bondhugula, U.: A flexible FPGA accelerator for convolutional neural networks. arXiv preprint arXiv:1912.07284 (2019)
14. Sanaullah, A., Yang, C., Alexeev, Y., Yoshii, K., Herbordt, M.C.: Application aware tuning of reconfigurable multi-layer perceptron architectures. In: 2018 IEEE High Performance extreme Computing Conference (HPEC), pp. 1–9. IEEE (2018)
15. Fine, T.L.: Feedforward Neural Network Methodology. Springer, Cham (2006). https://doi.org/10.1007/b97705
16. Stanford University. cs231n convolutional neural network for visual recognition
17. Wang, C., Gong, L., Qi, Yu., Li, X., Xie, Y., Zhou, X.: DLAU: a scalable deep learning accelerator unit on FPGA. IEEE Trans. Comput. Aided Des. Integr. Circ. Syst. **36**(3), 513–517 (2016)
18. Medus, L.D., Iakymchuk, T., Frances-Villora, J.V., Bataller-Mompeán, M., Rosado-Muñoz, A.: A novel systolic parallel hardware architecture for the FPGA acceleration of feedforward neural networks. IEEE Access **7**, 76084–76103 (2019)
19. Abdelsalam, A.M., Boulet, F., Demers, G., Langlois, J.P., Cheriet, F.: An efficient FPGA-based overlay inference architecture for fully connected DNNs. In: 2018 International Conference on ReConFigurable Computing and FPGAs (ReConFig), pp. 1–6. IEEE (2018)
20. Huynh, T.V.: Deep neural network accelerator based on FPGA. In: 2017 4th NAFOSTED Conference on Information and Computer Science, pp. 254–257 (2017)
21. Basterretxea, K., Echanobe, J., del Campo, I.: A wearable human activity recognition system on a chip. In: Proceedings of the 2014 Conference on Design and Architectures for Signal and Image Processing, pp. 1–8. IEEE (2014)
22. Si, J., Harris, S.L., Yfantis, E.: A dynamic ReLU on neural network. In: 2018 IEEE 13th Dallas Circuits and Systems Conference (DCAS), pp. 1–6. IEEE (2018)

23. Fazakas, A., Neag, M., Festila, L.: Block RAM versus distributed RAM implementation of SVM classifier on FPGA. In: 2006 International Conference on Applied Electronics, pp. 43–46 (2006)
24. Python productivity for zynq. http://www.pynq.io/board.html
25. Hussein, A.S., Anwar, A., Fahmy, Y., Mostafa, H., Salama, K.N., Kafafy, M.: Implementation of a DPU-based intelligent thermal imaging hardware accelerator on FPGA. Electronics 11(1), 105 (2022)
26. Cho, M., Kim, Y.: FPGA-based convolutional neural network accelerator with resource-optimized approximate multiply-accumulate unit. Electronics 10(22), 2859 (2021)
27. Cho, M., Kim, Y.: Implementation of data-optimized FPGA-based accelerator for convolutional neural network. In: 2020 International Conference on Electronics, Information, and Communication (ICEIC), pp. 1–2 (2020)
28. Yuan, T., Liu, W., Han, J., Lombardi, F.: High performance CNN accelerators based on hardware and algorithm co-optimization. IEEE Trans. Circ. Syst. I: Regul. Pap. 68(1), 250–263 (2021)
29. Bhowmik, P., Pantho, J.H., Mbongue, J.M., Bobda, C.: ESCA: event-based split-CNN architecture with data-level parallelism on ultrascale+ FPGA. In: 2021 IEEE 29th Annual International Symposium on Field-Programmable Custom Computing Machines (FCCM), pp. 176–180 (2021)
30. Mousouliotis, P.G., Petrou, L.P.: CNN-grinder: from algorithmic to high-level synthesis descriptions of CNNS for low-end-low-cost FPGA socs. Microprocess. Microsyst. 73, 102990 (2020)
31. Mousouliotis, P.G., Petrou, L.P.: SqueezeJet: high-level synthesis accelerator design for deep convolutional neural networks. In: Voros, N., Huebner, M., Keramidas, G., Goehringer, D., Antonopoulos, C., Diniz, P.C. (eds.) ARC 2018. LNCS, vol. 10824, pp. 55–66. Springer, Cham (2018). https://doi.org/10.1007/978-3-319-78890-6_5
32. Flamis, G., Kalapothas, S., Kitsos, P.: Workflow on CNN utilization and inference in FPGA for embedded applications: 6th south-east Europe design automation, computer engineering, computer networks and social media conference (seeda-cecnsm 2021). In: 2021 6th South-East Europe Design Automation, Computer Engineering, Computer Networks and Social Media Conference (SEEDA-CECNSM), pp. 1–6 (2021)

# A Multi-FPGA Scalable Framework for Deep Reinforcement Learning Through Neuroevolution

Javier Laserna, Andrés Otero$^{(\boxtimes)}$ ⓘ, and Eduardo de la Torre ⓘ

Universidad Politécnica de Madrid, Madrid, Spain
{joseandres.otero,eduardo.delatorre}@upm.es, j.laserna@alumnos.upm.es

**Abstract.** The application of Deep Neural Networks (DNN) for reinforcement learning has proven effective in solving complex problems,
such as playing video games or training robots to perform human tasks.
Training based on reinforcement implies the continuous interaction of the
agent powered by the DNN and the environment, vanishing the typical
separation between the training and inference stages in deep learning.
However, the high memory and accuracy requirements of gradient-based
training algorithms prevent using FPGAs for these applications. As an
alternative, this work demonstrates the feasibility of using Evolutionary
Algorithms (EA) for training DNNs and their usage in reinforcement
learning scenarios. Unlike backpropagation, EA-based training of neural
networks, referred to as neuroevolution, can be effectively implemented
on FPGAs. Moreover, this paper shows how the inherent parallelism of
EAs can be effectively exploited in multi-FPGA scenarios to accelerate the learning process. The proposed FPGA-based neuroevolutionary
framework has been validated by building a system capable of learning
autonomously to play the Pong Atari game in less than 25 generations.

**Keywords:** Reinforcement learning · Neuroevolution · Convolutional
Neural Networks · Multi-FPGA

## 1 Introduction

Nowadays, the predominant technique for training Deep Neural Network (DNN)
models is backpropagation. Backpropagation is based on the computation of
the gradient of the error function with respect to the network weights for each
input-output pair. This gradient is calculated for one layer at a time, iterating
backward from the last layer to the input. Then, network weights are updated
so that the expected error is minimized. Backpropagation has reported excellent
accuracy results when training huge DNNs with over a million neurons.

The high numerical accuracy and the amount of memory required to compute the weight's gradient across the network layers make Graphics Processing

This project has been funded by the Spanish Ministry for Science and Innovation under
the project TALENT (ref. PID2020-116417RB-C42).

Units (GPUs) the best choice for gradient-based training [10]. On the contrary, FPGAs beat GPUs in DNN inference, i.e., when the capabilities learned during training are put to work, since they offer higher power efficiency and throughput than GPUs [13]. However, separating the training/inference processes prevents the implementation of systems requiring the continuous adaptation of the network models after deployment, a feature referred to as lifelong learning [15]. Of particular interest are scenarios where autonomous agents learn from their own experience by actively interacting with the environment, a strategy known as Reinforcement Learning (RL). Unlike supervised learning, where agents learn by passively observing example input/output pairs, in RL, agents learn from the rewards received from the environment in response to their previous actions. These rewards reflect how well the agent is doing [17]. In RL, there may be no distinction between training and test phases, requiring the continuous adaptation of the control policy to changes in the environment or the system itself. Deep Reinforcement Learning (DRL) is a particular case of RL, in which a DNN makes the decisions on how to respond to the incoming stimuli from the environment. DRL is an effective technique that has achieved very significant results in the context of robotics, video games, and smart grids, among many others [9].

This paper proposes a novel framework for continuously training DNN-based deep reinforcement learning models on FPGAs having these application scenarios in mind. Unlike the state-of-the-art, the proposal in this work is to use an Evolutionary Algorithm (EA), a bio-inspired optimization and solution searching tool, to train the system. The use of EAs for training neural networks is known as neuroevolution. This work demonstrates that neuroevolution is an alternative to backpropagation that can be efficiently implemented in FPGAs.

Learning based on EAs involves maintaining a population of potential candidate solutions that are randomly mutated and combined to obtain agents increasingly suitable for solving a given problem. The quality of each possible solution has to be evaluated by measuring its performance when interacting with the environment. As shown in this work, this process can benefit from the inherent parallelism offered by multi-FPGA systems by allowing the evaluation of multiple DNN models simultaneously for each new generation. The evolutionary process is repeated during a given number of generations, up to having a good enough solution (i.e., a fitted agent, using RL terminology) for the problem.

Neuroevolution has already shown its benefits for reinforcement learning in software-based solutions. However, the original contribution of this work is to show the adaptation of neuroevolution-based DRL to FPGAs. The proposed framework relies on the Versatile Tensor Accelerator (VTA) included in the Apache TVM framework [3] for evaluating the performance of each potential candidate DNN. Candidate networks are evaluated in parallel using multiple FPGA System-on-Chips (SoCs) connected through a local area network. The capabilities of the proposed framework are demonstrated by developing an agent capable of playing the Pong Atari video game against a computer.

The rest of this paper is structured as follows. Section 2 reviews the related work on neuroevolution for DRL. The background technologies used in this work are described in Sect. 3, while the neuroevolutionary framework is described in Sect. 4. The detailed SW/HW architecture of the neuroevolutionary agents is described in Sect. 5. Experimental results are described in Sect. 6, while conclusions and future work are shown in Sect. 7.

## 2 Related Work

Neuroevolution has proven surprising results in complex human tasks like beating video games such as the Atari games [11,16]. Previous work also shows that neuroevolution can deal directly with visual input, which makes network training highly complex due to the high dimensionality of the space of possible solutions [8]. Using only visual information is also the approach proposed in this work.

All these works constitute purely software solutions that do not include hardware acceleration. Although there are some works dealing with evolution of neural networks in FPGAs (such as our previous work in [5]), these are limited to shallow neural models with limited computing capabilities. As far as we know, the only experience of the implementation of deep neuroevolution in FPGAS is the work presented by IBM research in [1]. Authors report training a DNN to beat the Atari 2600 games using deep neuroevolution implemented in a custom-designed system, the IBM Neural Computer. This system comprises 432 Xilinx FPGAs interconnected in a 3D mesh network topology, with a total power consumption about 4 kW. Each of the nodes relies on a PCIe 2.0 connection to communicate with the external computer that acts as the host. The DNN integrated in each node is the DNNBuilder. Results provided in this paper demonstrate that gradient-free optimization methods are competitive for training DNNs over FPGAs. However, different from the architecture proposed in our work, the system proposed by IBM research is implemented on a custom ultra-high performance board designed specifically to be installed in a cloud infrastructure, not appropriate for the embedded domain. Differently, in this work a distributed scheme intended to be deployed in a fog/edge scheme is proposed. In this scheme, the different accelerator boards can be physically distributed along an Internet of Things infrastructure, working collaboratively through standard Internet services to retrain the controller when needed. Moreover, using a custom board also limits the accessibility of the end-users to neuroevolution and reduces flexibility. The proposal in this work uses commercial devices and relies uniquely on open-source accelerator IPs, which is envisaged as a critical factor for the adption of the framework by the community.

## 3 Background Technologies

The main components integrating the FPGA-based neuroevolutionary framework proposed in this paper are explained next.

## 3.1 OpenAI Gym

OpenAI Gym is a toolkit for developing and benchmarking reinforcement learning algorithms [2]. The OpenAI Gym library has a comprehensive collection of different environments that can be used to compare the performance and accuracy of machine models. For this work, interest is focused on the Atari subset of environments (Fig. 1). This environment targets the simulation of the games present in the Atari 2600, a game console that was very popular in the 80s and had many arcade-style games available.

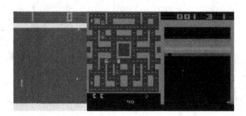

**Fig. 1.** Example of OpenAI Gym Atari games. From left to right: Pong, MsPacman, Breakout

The OpenAI environment simulates the game's behavior running in a software simulator of a real Atari machine. It is implemented in Python and can be integrated into the embedded processors of the FPGA SoC selected to implement the framework. Among the possible games included in Atari, the Pong has been selected as use case.

## 3.2 Versatile Tensor Accelerator

The evaluation of each DRL agent during the neuroevolution process requires the execution of multiple neural network inferences. This is one of the more time-consuming tasks that can benefit more from the parallelization capabilities of FPGAs. This work relies on the Versatile Tensor Accelerator (VTA) [12] for accelerating these inferences. This solution is embedded in the Apache TVM framework [3] and delivers an end-to-end workload solution that provides a complete software stack that can map high-level models down to the programming interface exposed by the VTA. The DNN model can be programmed in different software frameworks (TensorFlow, PyTorch, Keras, among others). Then a relay graph optimizer is responsible for translating the DNN model to a graph representation. Finally, the TVM operator optimizer and the TVM just-in-time runtime compiler execute the DNN model graph representation over the hardware architecture. This hardware architecture is parameterized by the size of the shared input/output SRAM memory, the size of the General Matrix Multiply (GEMM) core integrated within the VTA, and the data widths.

### 3.3   Pyro Library

Pyro [6] is a Python library that allows building applications where objects can communicate over the network with minimal programming effort, using standard Python method calls. It supports almost every possible parameter and return value types. It provides powerful features that enable building distributed applications quickly and effortlessly.

## 4   Neuroevolutionary Framework Overview

The proposed neuroevolutionary framework is composed of a set of FPGA SoCs (Xilinx Zynq-7000) connected over a local area network to a Personal Computer (PC) that acts as the master node, as shown in the scheme in Fig. 2. The PC executes the evolutionary algorithm that proposes candidate configurations for the neuroevolutionary agents interacting with the environment (i.e., the Pong Atari game). These agents are internally implemented as DNNs, as described in section V. The EA directly proposes new weights and biases for these DNNs to create new candidate agents. Every generation, the possible DNN solutions (i.e., the set of weights proposed by the EA) are distributed throughout the FPGA SoCs connected over the network to be evaluated when interacting with the Atari. The model candidates are distributed using Pyro. In each of these FPGA SoCs, the evolved neural network model will try to infer the best action for every output given by the OpenAI gym environment. This closed-loop workflow between the environment and the agent will run in each node until the game is finished (i.e., when any player reaches 21 points). A fitness result describing the quality of the agent is sent back to the primary node when this happens. When all the models finish, the controller node classifies the models by their fitness and applies the mutation operator to generate a new generation of neural network models. Crossover, the other typical bioinspired operator, has not been included in the algorithm since it did not provide any benefit according to preliminary results. Repeating this process over a significant number of generations produces an optimal model trained to play the Pong game successfully, as it will be shown in the experimental results section. It must be noticed that the evolved agent plays against a fixed algorithm already implemented in the OpenAI environment. The system is fully scalable, supporting a variable number of FPGAs running in parallel. In this work, experimental results have been carried out with 1, 2, 4, and 8 FPGA SoCs.

Next, further details are provided regarding the evolutionary algorithm and the distribution of fitness evaluation processes throughout the FPGA SoCs.

### 4.1   Evolutionary Algorithm Overview

The training of the neuroevolutionary agents is guided by the evolutionary algorithm described in Algorithm 1. It is an iterative algorithm in which bio-inspired transformations are applied to a population of potential solutions repetitively

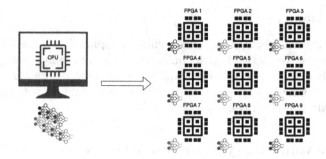

**Fig. 2.** Structure of the distributed neuroevolutionary framework.

during $G$ generations (lines 1 to 19). Each solution in the population is a set of weights and biases for the DNN featuring the neuroevolutionary agents. The initial population is generated via the $\lambda$ function, which randomly produces the parameters for each specific model from a uniform distribution (line 4). Afterward, for every generation, a population of $N$ individuals is generated by applying a mutation operator over the population of the previous generation (lines 6 and 7). In this case, the mutation is implemented taking inspiration from Evolutionary Strategies, hence, by adding Gaussian noise with a standard deviation $\sigma$. Once the new generation is created, the fitness function $F$ evaluates the models according to their performance in solving the given problem, in this case, playing Pong against the machine (line 9). Notice that this step is executed in parallel on the FPGA SoCs. The fitness metric for each individual is used to sort them according to their performance (line 11) and the set of best candidates $C$ (elite population) is created according to this order (lines 13 and 15). The elite population is the set of individuals that persist between generations. A reevaluation of all the individuals in the elite population is performed and the individual with the best performance is set as the *Elite* (line 17). This *Elite* model will not be affected by mutation during the next generation (line 18).

For the experimental results provided in the paper, the values of the hyper-parameters of the algorithm have been fixed empirically to the values described in Table 1.

**Table 1.** Hyper-parameters table

| Hyper-parameter | Value |
|---|---|
| Generations number ($G$) | 250 |
| Population size ($N$) | 1000 |
| Selected individuals ($T$) | 200 |
| Mutation power ($\sigma$) | 0.005 |
| Number of elites ($E$) | 1 |

**Algorithm 1.** Genetic algorithm

**Require:** number of generations $G$, population size $N$, selected individuals $T$, initialization function $\lambda$, mutation power $\sigma$, fitness function $F$, elite population $C$, number of re-evaluations $n$.

**Ensure:** $N >= T$; $0 < \sigma < 1$; $E = 0$

1: **for** $g = 1, 2..., G$ generations **do**
2:     **for** $i = 1, ..., N - 1$ **do**
3:         **if** $g = 1$ **then**
4:             $\theta_i^{g=1} = \lambda()$ {initialize random DNN}
5:         **else**
6:             $k = $ uniformRandom$(1,T)$ {select parent}
7:             $\theta_i^g = \theta_k^{g-1} + \sigma \cdot snrv()$ {mutate}
8:         **end if**
9:         Evaluate $F_i = F(\theta_i^g)$ {play Pong and get the score}
10:     **end for**
11:     Sort $\theta_i^g$ with descending order by $F_i$
12:     **if** $g = 1$ **then**
13:         Set Elite Candidates $C \leftarrow \theta_{1...T}^{g=1}$
14:     **else**
15:         Set Elite Candidates $C \leftarrow \theta_{1...T}^g \cup$ {Elite}
16:     **end if**
17:     Set Elite $\leftarrow arg\ max_{\theta \in C}\ \frac{1}{n} \sum_{j=1}^n F(\theta)$
18:     $\theta^g \leftarrow$ [Elite,$\theta^g$ - {Elite}] {only include elite once}
19: **end for return** Elite

## 4.2 Distribution of Evolutionary Processes

The distribution of the models to be evaluated from the master node (the PC) to the FPGA SoCs is done using the Pyro library, which only requires the PC to know the IP address and ports associated with each FPGA SoC. Once the training starts, the master node instantiates as many processes as secondary nodes registered in a pool of resources. Associated to each resource, there is a flag responsible for registering whether the node is busy or whether it has been released and is ready to take on a new load. Semaphores are used to synchronize all the processes.

Next, the internal structure of each neuroevolutionary agent integrated into each FPGA SoC is provided.

## 5 Detailed SW/HW Architecture of the Neuroevolutionary Agents

We describe now the framework component that runs in each FPGA SoC. The ZYNQ-Z1 device has been selected for this implementation [4]. This platform has as the processing system (PS) and as the programmable logic (PL). The Atari Pong environment and the preprocessing step are implemented in the PS. A Debian Linux operating system has been implemented in the processors to make the development easier. The evolved DNNs running over the VTA architecture included in the Apache TVM framework has been implemented in the PL. Both partitions, shown in Fig. 3, are described in the following subsections.

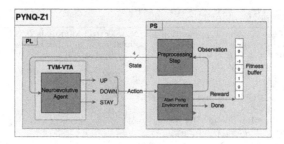

**Fig. 3.** FPGA SoC architecture for deep neuroevolution.

## 5.1 Software Subsystem

**Atari Game Model.** The particular architecture of the Atari Pong environment used in this work is represented in Fig. 4. This scenario has one input and four outputs. The input to the environment is called *action*, and it mimics the interaction that would produce a human player in the case of a real Atari game machine. In this environment, only the right side pad (green) can be controlled, and for this input, the user is allowed to go up, go down or do nothing. These three different types of action will be the output of the machine learning agent. After setting the input for a step in the simulation, this OpenAI gym environment computes the action and evolves the system to the next state. The output of the environment comprises the next game frame (observation), if a player has scored or not (reward), if the game has finished or not (done), and some relevant information about the environment (info). This model is integrated as a software process in the embedded processor of each SoC.

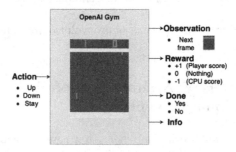

**Fig. 4.** Atari Pong environment architecture (Color figure online)

**Video Frame Preprocessing.** The preprocessing routine performs the necessary actions to adjust the visual output of the Atari Pong environment to make it compatible with the input of the DNN accelerator. These actions include deleting the scoreboard, down-sampling the resolution to 84 × 84 pixels, and changing the background colors and pads to grayscale. Then, the preprocessing module batches four consecutive frames and inserts them into the neural network (Fig. 5). Notice that the system needs more than one frame to infer the ball's and pad's trajectory, not only the instantaneous position. The system is prepared to work with visual information without requiring extra sensors, an approach known as visual servoing in robotics.

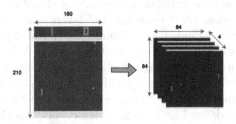

**Fig. 5.** Preprocessing step

## 5.2  Hardware Subsystem

The evolved DNN is the entity responsible for deciding the optimal sequence of actions to be executed to try and beat the other player (in this case, the program embedded in the OpenAI model). Each action corresponds to a movement of the joystick: up, down, and stay (see Fig. 6). To take the decision, the DNN receives the state of the environment as the input.

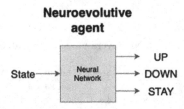

**Fig. 6.** Modular representation of the DNN in the neuroevolutionary agent.

The DNN interacts with the Atari Pong environment moving the player pad. This movement generates a new game frame that is provided to the preprocessing stage, feeding back the latest state of the game to the DNN. Therefore, the neural network closes the loop between the environment output and the received actions, as shown in Fig. 3. These steps are repeated until the game ends. At this point, the reward buffer is returned to the master node as the fitness of the neural network loaded in the agent.

The associated fitness value represents the goodness of each candidate model after playing a complete game. A point will be added to this fitness if the evolved solution scores. Conversely, a point will be subtracted if the Atari model scores. The game finishes when any of the two players achieve +21.

Among all the possible DNN topologies in the literature, we have selected a Convolutional Neural Network (CNN) appropriate for dealing with visual input data [18]. The internal structure of the CNN model is represented in Fig. 7. This network contains a feature extraction part and a classifier part. The feature extraction part comprises three convolutional layers and a pooling layer. The pooling layer has been included as a dummy layer exclusively to be able to package the CNN model in the format required by the VTA accelerator. This is why it does not produce a change in the output dimensions. On the other hand, the binary classifier part is composed of a flattened layer that serves as a nexus for the two dense layers that connect the CNN output. The parameters of all these layers are defined in Table 2. This network has three outputs, each associated with an action of the joystick. The action for which the DNN provides the highest value will be the one introduced to the environment.

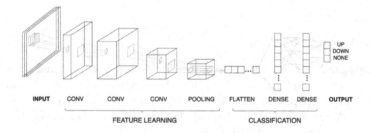

**Fig. 7.** Diagram of a convolutional neural network (CNN)

**Table 2.** CNN layers parameters table

| Operation | Filter size | Stride | Output | Activation |
|---|---|---|---|---|
| Input image | – | – | $84 \times 84 \times 4$ | – |
| Convolution | $8 \times 8$ | $4 \times 4$ | $20 \times 20 \times 32$ | ReLU |
| Convolution | $4 \times 4$ | $2 \times 2$ | $9 \times 9 \times 64$ | ReLU |
| Convolution | $3 \times 3$ | $1 \times 1$ | $7 \times 7 \times 64$ | ReLU |
| MaxPooling2D | – | – | $7 \times 7 \times 64$ | – |
| Flatten | – | – | 3136 | – |
| Dense | – | – | 512 | – |
| Dense | – | – | 3 | – |

The CNN is executed over the VTA accelerator included in the Apache TVM framework. To do so, the model weights proposed by the EA are encoded using the TVM tools into a graph format that can be understood by the tensor processor VTA.

# 6    Experimental Results

The experimental results carried out to validate the proposed multi-FPGA based platform for deep RL are described in this section. The evaluation of the solution will be carried out in terms of the achieved fitness and the training performance.

## 6.1    Fitness Evaluation

The proposed fitness function consists of the sum of all the rewards obtained from the simulation environment during training, as shown in Eq. 1. These individual rewards $Fi_i$ consist of the following values: 0 if no agent has scored a goal, the value 1 if the player scores a goal, and the value $-1$ if the machine scores a goal.

$$fitness = \sum_{i=0}^{N} F_i \qquad (1)$$

The fitness evolution during training is shown in Fig. 8, where it can be observed that the proposed framework manages to beat the machine, i.e., it obtains a positive fitness in less than 25 generations. Moreover, it can be seen that, after 172 generations, almost perfect score (20 vs. 21) is achieved by the developed agent. It must be noticed that the fitness value represented in the figure corresponds to the best individual in the population since this will be the individual to be selected for the final deployment.

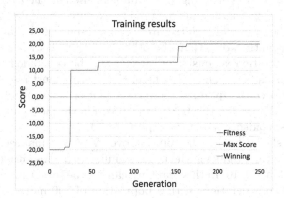

**Fig. 8.** Evolution of the fitness of the best individual of the population during training

## 6.2    Architecture Evaluation

In this section, we will evaluate the framework's performance in terms of training time for a variable number of FPGA accelerators. These results are summarized in Table 3. Apart from showing the total time, the final value is broken down by each of the parts involved in evaluating the DNN model: execution time of the neural network (DNN), execution time of a game episode on the OpenAI gym simulation environment (Env), time required for sending the model to the FPGA node (Send), total execution time of a game (Iter), and total training time for a generation (Total). These time results shown in the table are the average execution time for all the FPGAs in the cluster. The slight differences in the DNN evaluation and the environment time depending on the number of FPGA is due to the changing traffic in the Ethernet network.

**Table 3.** Execution times.

|          | DNN (ms) | Env (ms) | Send (s) | Iter (s) | Total (h) |
|----------|----------|----------|----------|----------|-----------|
| 1 FPGAs  | 504,9*   | 140,6    | 6,957    | 63,001   | 4,1       |
| 2 FPGAs  | 504,3*   | 141,0    | 6,805    | 63,002   | 2,04      |
| 4 FPGAs  | 503,7    | 140,8    | 8,574    | 62,811   | 1,075     |
| 8 FPGAs  | 504,7    | 141,1    | 6,811    | 63,281   | 0,546     |

From the results in the Table 3, we can state that the FPGA-based solution is fully distributed and scalable, enabling the successful resolution of the deep RL problem in a feasible time.

The same neuroevolutionary system has been deployed on a PC processor (Intel Core i5 - 10400 with 6 cores running at 4,30 GHz), a gaming GPU (AMD Ryzen RX 570), as well as on a single VTA implemented on the Zynq-7020 device. The graph in Fig. 9 shows the time required to execute a complete iteration (one set) for each of the proposed architectures. These results show that a single VTA solution is significantly worse than the other two solutions when only the time required for an iteration is considered. It can also be concluded that the GPU solution is the fastest solution of the three. However, it must also be noted that the nominal power consumption of these three platforms is entirely different (65 w for the CPU, 450 w for the GPU, and 5 W for the SoC, according to the manufacturer's spreadsheets and the report in [7]).

However, as shown below, the solution over VTA is enhanced when we use distributed computing, reducing the times significantly. This situation is graphically represented in Fig. 10. In this graph we can see the total time elapsed during the training of two generations with a population of 100 models each one (240 iterations in total with the parent's reevaluation). For these results, one can see the effect of a distributed computation of the VTA solution on the total training time. As the number of FPGA nodes in the network doubles, the training time is reduced by about half. The scalability limit will be imposed by the size of the population of candidate DNNs evaluated by the evolutionary algorithm in every generation.

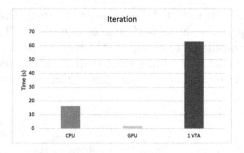

**Fig. 9.** Iterations times for a single CPU, a high-end GPU and 1 VTA instance

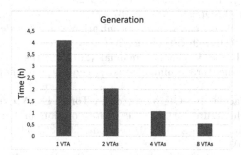

**Fig. 10.** Generations times with a variable number of hardware accelerators.

## 7 Conclusions and Future Work

This paper demonstrates the feasibility of using solutions based on evolutionary algorithms to accelerate the training of DNNs on commercial FPGAs as an alternative to gradient-based algorithms, which are not that suitable for FPGA implementations. This feature is demonstrated in the context of reinforcement learning applications, in which an agent running on an FPGA accelerator is continuously interacting with an environmental model to learn how to control it, using the accumulated experience. An Atari game included in OpenAI has been selected as the use case to demonstrate the possibilities of the provided solution. Experimental results show that the system can train the network and almost linear scalability when using a multi-FPGA scenario is achieved. This will be only bounded by the size of the population.

Future work will address the extension of the proposed framework to all the rest of the games included in the OpenAI Atari environments and other DNN training problems to show the generalizability of the solution. The adaptation to new environments is straightforward since these environments share a standard interface. Only the fitness function should be adapted to the particularities of each game. A physical setup is also being prepared to demonstrate that the framework can effectively control mechanical systems. Other DNN training scenarios, such as supervised classification, will be demonstrated in addition to applying it to reinforcement learning problems. Moreover, other automated libraries to execute DNNs in FPGAs, such as FINN [19] or Brevitas [14], will be evaluated and compared with the performance offered by VTA. Another possibility that is being considered to accelerate the training process is implementing the environmental model in hardware since their python-based implementation in the embedded device takes an amount of time that is not negligible.

# References

1. Asseman, A., Antoine, N., Ozcan, A.S.: Accelerating deep neuroevolution on distributed fpgas for reinforcement learning problems. J. Emerg. Technol. Comput. Syst. **17**(2) (2021). https://doi.org/10.1145/3425500
2. Brockman, G., et al.: Openai gym (2016)
3. Chen, T., et al.: Tvm: end-to-end optimization stack for deep learning. arXiv preprint arXiv:1802.04799, vol. 11, no. 20 (2018)
4. Digilent: Pynq-z1 board reference manual (2017). https://reference.digilentinc.com/_media/reference/programmable-logic/pynq-z1/pynq-rm.pdf. Accessed 8 July 2021
5. García, A., Zamacola, R., Otero, A., de la Torre, E.: A dynamically reconfigurable bbnn architecture for scalable neuroevolution in hardware. Electronics **9**(5) (2020). https://doi.org/10.3390/electronics9050803, https://www.mdpi.com/2079-9292/9/5/803
6. Irmen: Pyro4 framework (2021). https://github.com/irmen/Pyro4. Accessed 8 July 2021
7. Kachris, C., Falsafi, B., Soudris, D.: Hardware Accelerators in Data Centers. Springer, Heidelberg (2019)
8. Koutník, J., Schmidhuber, J., Gomez, F.: Evolving deep unsupervised convolutional networks for vision-based reinforcement learning. In: Proceedings of the 2014 Annual Conference on Genetic and Evolutionary Computation, pp. 541–548. GECCO'14, Association for Computing Machinery, New York, NY, USA (2014). https://doi.org/10.1145/2576768.2598358
9. Liu, X., Xu, H., Liao, W., Yu, W.: Reinforcement learning for cyber-physical systems. In: 2019 IEEE International Conference on Industrial Internet (ICII), pp. 318–327. IEEE (2019)
10. Luo, C., Sit, M.K., Fan, H., Liu, S., Luk, W., Guo, C.: Towards efficient deep neural network training by fpga-based batch-level parallelism. J. Semicond. **41**(2), 022403 (2020)
11. Mnih, V., et al.: Playing atari with deep reinforcement learning (2013)
12. Moreau, T., et al.: A hardware-software blueprint for flexible deep learning specialization. IEEE Micro **39**(5), 8–16 (2019)
13. Nurvitadhi, E., et al.: Can fpgas beat gpus in accelerating next-generation deep neural networks? In: Proceedings of the 2017 ACM/SIGDA International Symposium on Field-programmable Gate Arrays, pp. 5–14 (2017)
14. Pappalardo, A.: Xilinx/brevitas (2021). https://doi.org/10.5281/zenodo.3333552
15. Parisi, G.I., Kemker, R., Part, J.L., Kanan, C., Wermter, S.: Continual lifelong learning with neural networks: A review. Neural Netw. **113**, 54–71 (2019)
16. Petroski Such, F., Madhavan, V., Conti, E., Lehman, J., Stanley, K.O., Clune, J.: Deep neuroevolution: genetic algorithms are a competitive alternative for training deep neural networks for reinforcement learning. arXiv e-prints. arXiv:1712.06567 (Dec 2017)

17. Russell, S., Norvig, P.: Artificial intelligence: a modern approach (2002)
18. Sze, V., Chen, Y.H., Yang, T.J., Emer, J.S.: Efficient processing of deep neural networks: a tutorial and survey. Proc. IEEE **105**(12), 2295–2329 (2017)
19. Umuroglu, Y., et al.: Finn: a framework for fast, scalable binarized neural network inference. In: Proceedings of the 2017 ACM/SIGDA international symposium on field-programmable gate arrays. pp. 65–74 (2017)

# Development Progress of SWLBM a Framework Based on Lattice Boltzmann Method for Fluid Dynamics Simulation

Chu Xuesen[1,2,3](✉) [iD], He Xiang[4], Li Fang[5], Liu Zhao[6], and Yang Guangwen[1,6]

[1] Department of Computer Science and Technology, Tsinghua University, Beijing 100084, China
chuxs@cssrc.com.cn
[2] China Ship Scientific Research Center, Wuxi 214082, China
[3] Taihu Laboratory of DeepSea Technological Science, Wuxi 214082, China
[4] Jiangnan Institute of Computing Technology, Wuxi 214083, China
[5] National Research Center of Parallel Computer Engineering and Technology, Beijing 100084, China
[6] National Supercomputing Center in Wuxi, Wuxi 214072, China

**Abstract.** SWLBM is a software framework based on Lattice Boltzmann Method (LBM) for Computational Fluid Dynamic (CFD) running on Sunway many-core processors. In this paper, we review the achievements of code developing in early stage and introduce the development progress recently of this software, including the development of parallel optimization for Sunway new-generation supercomputing system, functional extensions of the software like pre-process function for mesh generation from a geometry file with STL file and BMP file, Immersed boundary condition for moving subject simulation. Some applications with SWLBM will be introduced to show the advantage of this software over other CFD code in large-scale simulations. SWLBM is still under development, with the continuous improvement of functions, it will play a greater role in the field of fluid simulation.

**Keywords:** Lattice Boltzmann Method · High performance computing · Sunway many-core processor · Computational Fluid Dynamic

## 1 Introduction

Computational Fluid Dynamic is one of classical application styles on High Performance Computing (HPC) systems. Sunway supercomputing systems are designed by National Research Center of Parallel Computer Engineering and Technology based on Sunway many-core processors. One of them is the Sunway TaihuLight which is set in National Supercomputing Center in Wuxi, ranked No.1 on HPC worldly Top500 list during the years 2016–2017. Lattice Boltzmann Method is a class of CFD methods developed since 1990 s, which traces back to Lattice Cellular Automata (LCA) [1, 2]. This methods solve Boltzmann equation usually LBGK equation instead of the Navier-Stokes equation which is usually solved by other CFD methods, but it was certificated similar between LBGK to Navier-Stokes equation by Chapman-Enskog expansion [3, 4]. The scheme of this method is normally described as collide and stream phases, the information communication needed for flow field evolution is locally. As scheme friendly for parallel computation LBM was widely researched on HPC area, and showed its capability in solving problems which need ultra-scale simulation in many areas [5–9].

SWLBM (also named SunwayLB - Sunway Lattice Boltzmann Method code) is jointly developed by a team composed of members from China Ship Scientific Research Center, National Supercomputing Center in Wuxi and Jiangnan Institute of Computing Technology. The code is specially designed for Supercomputers which use Sunway many-core processors based on Lattice Boltzmann Method since 2017. The main motivation of this code developing is to produce an efficient tool to solve problems within days in industrial area which acquire extreme super-size computing with Sunway Supercomputers. In this paper we will briefly review the works we have done in early stage when the code was established and will introduce the development progress recently in the latter part.

## 2 Typical Works in Early Stage

The early stage for this code development is during the year 2017–2018. The works were focused on optimization the efficiency of parallel algorithms on Sunway Taihu-Light supercomputer with many-core processors SW26010. The code involved with LBGK equation with the Lattice scheme called D3Q19 model [2] which is widely used. Smagorinsky model [10] was embedded in the code for Large Eddy Simulation (LES) when flow simulated at high Reynolds number, and do Direct Numerical Simulation (DNS) without any turbulence models for low Reynolds number situation. The details of those works could be found in reference [11–14].

### 2.1 Optimization Schemes for SW26010

The SW26010 processor has 260 heterogeneous cores divided by four core groups (CGs) which providing a peak performance of 3.06TFlops. As in Fig. 1 shows, each CG is composed of one management processing element (MPE) and 64 computing processing elements (CPEs).

The SWLBM code was optimized with multi-levels parallelization including MPI A thread and SIMD. The orchestrated strategy includes carefully designed domain decomposition consider with MPI load balance, data blocking in CG level with efficient data exchange scheme, thread-level data reuse, maximize the utilization of DMA (Direct Memory Access) bandwidth and 64k LDM, manual loop unroll and instructions reordering to exploit computational potential of the pipelines and 256-bit vectorization instructions of CPEs.

As the final result, SWLBM achieve high level parallel efficiency performance. The performance experiments were done up to the largest size with 5.6 trillion lattice cells running on 160,000 CGs and 10,400,000 cores, achieved a sustained performance 4.7 PFlops. Amdahl's law [15] for strong scaling and Gustafson's law [16] for weak scaling was shown in Fig. 2.

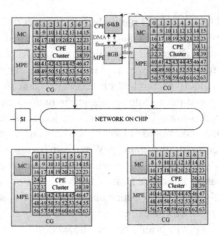

**Fig. 1.** Architecture of SW26010 [13]

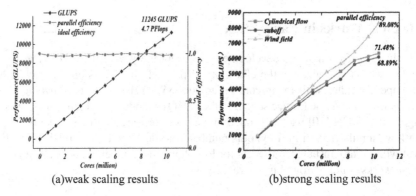

(a)weak scaling results                    (b)strong scaling results

**Fig. 2.** Performance and parallel efficiency of weak scaling and strong scaling tests [12]

## 2.2 Typical Applications

Direct numerical simulations of turbulence flow were typical application in this stage. The benchmark cases like flow past a circular cylinder at Re = 3900, channel flow at $Re_t = 180$ were simulated.

**Flow Past a Circular Cylinder at Re = 3900.** The flow past circular cylinder has been one of the highly researched topics especially at Re = 3900 [17–19]. This case was set as experimental example for weakly scaling testing. And a process completely DNS of this case was done with lattice size of 4000 * 1000 * 4000 to verify the capability to solve specific problems by SWLBM. The resolution was 200 referenced to the diameter of cylinder. It costs 0.3s per step with parallel size of 2000CGs and more than one million steps evolution of the flow field was simulated to obtain the regular flow structure for analyzing. The simulation result of Q Criterion was shown in Fig. 3. It could be found the distinguishable complex vortex structures could be captured by SWLBM.

**Fig. 3.** Q-Criterion of flow past circular cylinder at Re = 3900

**Channel Flow at $Re_t = 180$.** Channel flow is another topic which is widely researched for turbulence studies [20, 21]. The channel flow at $Re_t = 180$ was directly simulated with lattice size of 1024 * 256 * 256 and cost 0.041 s per step with 64 CGs. The results agrees quantitatively with the DNS results take by Moser et al. [19] (see Fig. 4.)

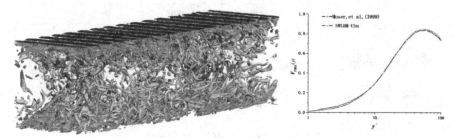

**Fig. 4.** Vortex structure and statistical quantitative comparison with other DNS [19]

## 3  Recently Development Progress

Afterward the focus of work on SWLBM development was shifted to function extending since 2019. Various pre-processing functions were developed to enhance the ability of SWLBM dealing with practical problems. Lattice schemes like D3Q27 and MRT, sub-grid scale models like WALE model and Vreman model for Large Eddy Simulation were included in SWLBM gradually. Immersed boundary conduction was also introduced for solving moving subject problems. Parallel optimization would be done after each new functions involved. Another development progress on parallel optimization issue is the work taken in transplant SWLBM code to new generation Sunway many-core processors SW26010Pro.

## 3.1  Optimization Works for SW26010Pro

The new generation Sunway many-core processor is SW26010Pro [22], one hetero-geneous CPU consists of 6 CGs (see in Fig. 5). There are some significant updates of SW26010Pro related to SWLBM's performance comparing to SW26010. First SW26010Pro has 512-bit SIMD enables 8 FP64/FP32 data to be processed in a sin-gle instruction. Second LDM was updated to 260 k. The corresponding optimization of SWLBM was developed. The precision of the main date types in SWLBM was updated from FP32 to FP64. The DMA and SIMD operation were optimized too. Another ver-sion of SWLBM was also developed with A thread replaced by SWACC for hybrid parallelization. Simulation of flow past SUBOFF was set as a case for optimization per-formance testing with lattice size of 3000 * 600 * 600. The performance could be found in Table1 testing with 64CGs. Either A thread or SWACC version could get about 120x speedup according to MPI version which just running with MPE.

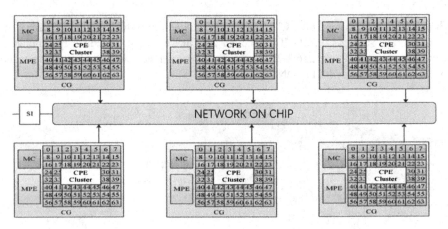

**Fig. 5.**  Architecture of SW26010Pro

## 3.2  Pre-processing Functions Within SWLBM

In order to solve industrial problems, a CFD software should have a robust pre-processing module to handle arbitrarily geometries involved for simulation. The pre-processing job in SWLBM in to define the lattice inside the computational domain into different styles like FLUID, SOLID, BOUNDARY. Different functions were designed corresponding to different input sources for pre-process in SWLBM. Here pre-processing with inputs from STL geometry files and BMP files will be introduced.

**Pre-process with STL Files.**  STL is one of the popular formats of file to describe the structure of the geometry. It represents a surface geometry using facets. The facets define the surface of a 3D object and is uniquely identified by a unit normal, and by three vertices. An efficient algorithm for pre-processing of Lattice Boltzmann method based on STL file was developed for SWLBM, the details could be found in reference

**Table 1.** Optimization performance of SWLBM with SW26010Pro.

| Functions | MPE(MPI) | MPE(MPI) + CPE(A thread) | SpeedUp | MPE(MPI) + CPE(SWACC) | SpeedUp |
|---|---|---|---|---|---|
| Halo_send() | 0.102174 s | 0.002502 s | 40.84 | 0.004456 s | 22.93 |
| Communicate() | 0.285495 s | 0 | N/A | 0.011618 s | 24.57 |
| Halo_receive() | 0.105054 s | 0.003720 s | 28.24 | 0.005093 s | 20.63 |
| Boundary() | 1.011485 s | 0.007940 s | 127.39 | 0.009438 s | 107.17 |
| Stream() | 24.271920 s | 0.402023 s | 60.37 | 0.384242 s | 63.17 |
| Collide() | 44.281064 s | 0.159458 s | 277.70 | 0.180118 s | 245.84 |
| Total | 70.058357 s | 0.578840 s | 121.03 | 0.596119 s | 117.52 |

[23]. The process from STL file to final result simulated with SWLBM with CHN-T1 airplane model is shown in Fig. 6.

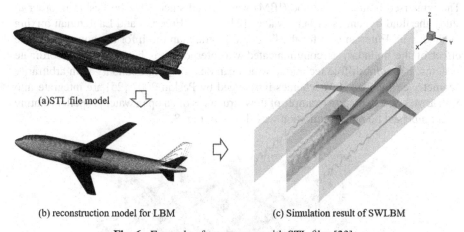

(a)STL file model

(b) reconstruction model for LBM        (c) Simulation result of SWLBM

**Fig. 6.** Example of pre-process with STL files [23]

**Pre-process with BMP Files.** Another pre-processing function was to reconstruct a 2D image with BMP file into 3D geometry. The other format images could transform into BMP format firstly and then saved as a monochrome bitmap with 1-bit color depth. The pre-processing function could load the file and judge the lattice's style according to the color value, and generate the third dimension with slice copy. The typical usage of such function is to simulate the flow fields past certain LOGs. Normally those flows were simulated with lattice size of 1000 * 500 * 500, finishing within one hour with 2000CGs of SW26010 for 100,000 steps. An example of flow past Tsinghua University's LOG was shown in Fig. 7.

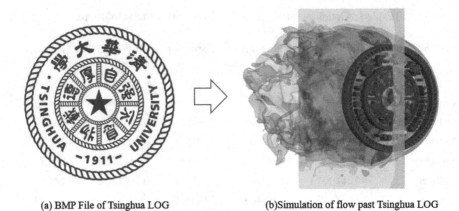

(a) BMP File of Tsinghua LOG          (b)Simulation of flow past Tsinghua LOG

**Fig. 7.** Example of pre-process with BMP file

### 3.3  Immersed Boundary Conditions

The immersed boundary method (IBM) was created since 1972 by Peskin in order to study the fluid dynamics of heart valves [24]. It is a Eulerian and Lagrangian mixing method, with Eulerian grid for the fluid and Lagrangian mesh for the boundaries. The effect of the boundary is communicated via interpolations between both coordinate systems. It is a mesh-free technique which can deal moving boundary with arbitrarily geometry easily. The IBM schemes introduced by Peskin 2002 [25] are integrate into SWLBM. The calculation example of flow structures of an open water propeller rotating with immersed boundary condition was shown in Fig. 8.

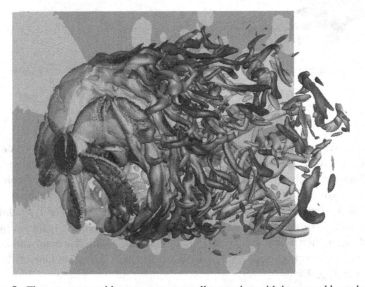

**Fig. 8.** Flow structure with open water propeller rotating with immersed boundary

### 3.4 Other Expert Applications with SWLBM

SWLBM was originally designed to handle ultra-large scale simulation problems. So, the professional application scenarios with SWLBM are those industry cases which sensitive to the high resolution of the computational domain, like wind field, turbulence flow, muti-scale problem and so on. Some expert applications will be introduced following.

**Wind Field Simulation.** Wind field simulation is a popular subject from research of wind farm in wind power industry to forecasting dispersion of air pollution, simulation of urban ventilation corridor in environmental engineering study. With the efficient heterogeneous parallelization SWLBM could simulate wind field much faster than other CFD code such as OpenFOAM. The simulation of wind field of the Beijing Olympic Park was shown in Fig. 9. The area of 4 km$^2$ was calculated in this case with lattice setting 4000 * 4000 * 1000 of 1 m resolution. It is finish within 24 h with 2000CGs for 200,000 steps evolution simulating.

**Fig. 9.** Wind field of the Beijing Olympic Park

**Large Scale Wake Simulation.** Wake flow study of underwater vehicle is a popular topic in ship engineering area. Most former simulations are limited in an area of few times the length of the vehicle due to huge amount of calculation required in such problem. Because not only the region near vehicle needs high resolution in order to capture the flow structure formed, but also needs high resolution wake region to maintain the flow field evolution spread with low dissipation. Due to huge scale simulation capability and low diffusion characters of LBM scheme, SWLBM can handle such problem much easier than other software. A 20 km region of wake flow of a suboff with length of 87 m was simulated with the resolution of 0.1 m. The lattice size is 200000 * 1000 * 1500 (300billion), the calculation was taken with 18,000CGs of SW26010Pro with time cost 0.68 s per step. The wake structure simulated is shown in Fig. 10.

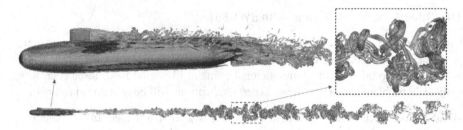

**Fig. 10.** Large scale wake simulation of suboff

## 4 Conclusions

In this paper, we report our development progress of SWLBM the CFD software for Sunway supercomputers based on Lattice Boltzmann Method. Heterogeneous parallel optimizations were designed for SW26010 at early stage and updated for SW26010Pro recently, with efficient hybrid parallel strategy SWLBM lead to more than 100x speedup. Variety pre-process functions enable SWLBM to realize flow field simulation with arbitrarily geometry. Various applications with SWLBM including turbulence flow simulation, wind field simulation, large scale wake simulation showed the powerful capability of SWLBM to deal ultra-large-scale simulation with Sunway supercomputers.

SWLBM is still under developing. Much more function will be planned to develop in the future such as free surface models, thermal models and so on. The post-process functions will also to be expand for result data analyzing. We are sure SWLBM could be a powerful tool on Sunway supercomputers for industry application.

## References

1. McNamara, G.R., Zanetti, G.: Use of the Boltzmann equation to simulate lattice-gas automata. Phys. Rev. Lett. **61**(20), 2332 (1988)
2. Qian Y., d'Humières D., Lallemand P.: Lattice BGK models for Navier–Stokes equation. EPL (Europhys. Lett.) 17(6), 479 (1992)
3. Lallemand, P., Luo, L.: Theory of the lattice Boltzmann method: dispersion, dissipation, isotropy, galilean invariance, and stability. Phys. Rev. E **61**(6), 6546–6562 (2000)
4. Luo, L.: Unified theory of lattice Boltzmann models for nonidealgases. Phys. Rev. Lett. **81**(8), 1618–1621 (1998)
5. Pohl, T., et al.: Performance evaluation of parallel large-scale lattice boltzmann applications on three supercomputing architectures. In: SC'04. Washington, DC, USA. IEEE Computer Society, p. 21 (2004)
6. Williams, S., Carter, J., Oliker, L., Shalf, J., Yelick, K.: Lattice Boltzmann simulation optimization on leading multicore platforms. In: Parallel and Distributed Processing, IPDPS 2008, pp. 1–14
7. Godenschwager, et al.: November. a framework for hybrid parallel flow simulations with a trillion cells in complex geometries. In Proceedings of the International Conference on High Performance Computing, Networking, Storage and Analysis, p. 35. ACM (2013)
8. Bauer, et al.: Massively parallel phase-field simulations for ternary eutectic directional solidification. In Proceedings of the International Conference on High Performance Computing, Networking, Storage and Analysis. ACM (2015)

9. Rettinger, C., Godenschwager, C., Eibl, S., Preclik, T., Schruff, T., Frings, R., Rüde, U.: Fully resolved simulations of dune formation in riverbeds. In: Kunkel, J.M., Yokota, R., Balaji, P., Keyes, D. (eds.) ISC High Performance 2017. LNCS, vol. 10266, pp. 3–21. Springer, Cham (2017). https://doi.org/10.1007/978-3-319-58667-0_1

10. Smagorinsky, J.: General circulation experiments with the primitive equations. Mon. Wea. Rev. **91**, 99–164 (1963)

11. Chu, X., Liu, Z., Shi, S., Meng, H., Lv, X., Han, J.: Development progress on SWLBM CFD software on sunway architecture. In: The 10th National Conference on Fluid Mechanics, HangZhou China (2018)

12. Liu, Z.: SunwayLB: enabling extreme-scale lattice boltzmann method based computing fluid dynamics simulations on sunway taihulight. In: IEEE International Parallel and Distributed Processing Symposium (IPDPS) (2019)

13. Lv, X., Liu, Z., Chu, X., Shi, S., Meng, H., Huang, Z.: Extreme-scale simulation based LBM computing fluid dynamics simulations. Comput. Sci. **47**(4), 13–17 (2020)

14. Li, F., Li, Z., Xu, J., Fan, H., Chu, X., Li, X.: Research on adaptation of CFD software based on many-core architecture of 100P domestic supercomputing system. Comput. Sci. **47**(1), 24–30 (2020)

15. Amdahl, G.M.: AFIPS Conference Proceedings, vol. 30, pp. 483–485 (1967). https://doi.org/10.1145/1465482.1465560

16. Gustafson, J.L.: Communications of the ACM 31(5), 532–533 (1988). https://doi.org/10.1145/42411.42415

17. Kravchenko, A.G., Moin, P.: Numerical studies of flow over a circular cylinder at ReD = 3900. Phys. Fluids **12**(2), 403–417 (2000)

18. Franke, J., Frank, W.: Large eddy simulation of the flow past a circular cylinder at ReD = 3900. J. Wind Eng. Ind. Aerodyn. **90**(10), 1191–1206 (2002)

19. Parnaudeau, P., Carlier, J., Heitz, D., et al.: Experimental and numerical studies of the flow over a circular cylinder at Reynolds number 3900. Phys. Fluids **20**(8), 12–287 (2008)

20. Cao, P., Chu, X., Wang, J., et al.: Simulation of channel flow with lattice boltzmann method by DNS and LES. Aerodyn. Res. Exp. **33**(02), 98–104 (2021)

21. Moser, R.D., Kim, J., Mansour, N.N.: Direct numerical simulation of turbulent channel flow up to Re = 590. Phys. Fluids **11**(4), 943–945 (1999)

22. Ma, Z., He, J., et al.: BAGUALU: targeting brain scale pretrained models with over 37 million cores. In Proceedings of the 27th ACM SIGPLAN Annual Symposium on Principles and Practice of Parallel Programming (PPoPP'22)

23. Xiaoxiao, Z., Zhang, W., Xuesen, C., et al.: An efficient algorithm for pre-processing of lattice Boltzmann method based on STL files. ACTA Aerodynamica Sinica **39**(03), 44–50 (2021)

24. Peskin, C.S.: Numerical analysis of blood flow in the heart. J. Comp. Phys. **25**, 220–252 (1977)

25. Peskin, C.S.: The immersed boundary method. Acta. Numer. **11**, 479–517 (2002)

# Entropy-Based Early-Exit in a FPGA-Based Low-Precision Neural Network

Minxuan Kong[1(✉)] and Jose Luis Nunez-Yanez[2]

[1] University of Bristol, Bristol, UK
mk16085@bristol.ac.uk
[2] Linköping University, Linköping, Sweden
jose.nunez-yanez@liu.se

**Abstract.** In this paper, we investigate the application of early-exit strategies to fully quantized neural networks, mapped to low-complexity FPGA SoC devices. The challenge of accuracy drop with low bitwidth quantized first convolutional layer and fully connected layers has been resolved. We apply an early-exit strategy to a network model that combines weights and activation with extremely low bitwidth and binary arithmetic precision based on the ImageNet dataset. We use entropy calculations to decide which branch of the early-exit network to take. The experiments show an improvement in inferred speed of 1.52× using an early-exit system, compared with using a single primary neural network, with a slight accuracy decrease of 1.64%.

**Keywords:** Early-exit · Neural network · Low-cost FPGAs · Hardware acceleration

## 1 Introduction

The deployment of deep neural networks (DNNs) on edge devices is increasingly popular and this brings new energy and performance challenges. For example, the inference speed of neural networks (NNs) on CPUs is generally limited by the lower level of parallelism present in the hardware with just a few arithmetic units available. On the other hand, GPU devices offer significantly better performance with a large number of parallel streaming processors but these are designed to work with data types wider than the few bits used in quantized neural network (QNN) models, which limits their performance. The deployment of heavily quantized NNs on field-programmable gate arrays (FPGAs) has resulted in very high performance and low energy consumption [1]. However, despite the efficiency of quantized models, significant performance and complexity trade-offs

This research was partially funded by the Royal Society Industry fellowship, INF\R2\192044 Machine Intelligence at the Network Edge (MINET), EPSRC HOPWARE EP\RV040863\1 and Leverhulme trust international fellowship High-performance video analytics with parallel heterogeneous neural networks IF-2021-003.

L. Gan et al. (Eds.): ARC 2022, LNCS 13569, pp. 72–86, 2022.
https://doi.org/10.1007/978-3-031-19983-7_6

are required to map DNNs with millions of parameters in low-cost FPGAs with limited resources.

In this research, we build an early-exit image classification system based on the FINN framework [2]. Our demonstrator is based on a low-cost Xilinx Zynq-7020 SoC PYNQ-Z2 (FPGA) board and a Logitech C160 webcam. FINN [3] is a framework that specifically targets QNNs, with emphasis on generating dataflow-style architectures customized for each network. The resulting FPGA accelerators are highly efficient and can yield high throughput and low latency. Our target system design is shown in Fig. 1. Both webcams capturing and direct image inputs are applicable to this recognition system with a heterogeneous NN deployed to achieve optimal performance. The proposed early-exit system contains a primary network, which has more network layers and can achieve better accuracy but is slower; and a small-scale network, which has fewer network layers with high efficiency but it is relatively low accuracy. The computing layers, including the first convolutional layer and fully connected (FC) layer of the NN, are executed on the programmable logic (PL). However, the entropy evaluation module will be executed in the processing system (PS). The deployment strategy will be explained in detail in Sects. 3 and 4. The uncertainty evaluation module based on entropy estimations is used to decide which network should be applied during inference. These two NNs cooperate with each other to form a high-performance adaptive system with optimized processing time.

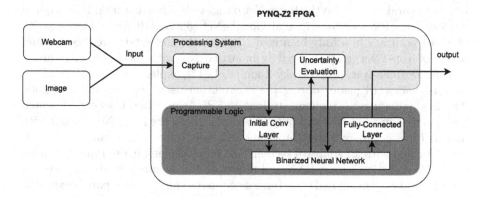

**Fig. 1.** Overview of the system

The main contributions of this research can be summarized as follows:

- We propose the application of an early-exit strategy that targets a hardware-based neural network with sub-byte precision for weights and activations.
- We optimize accuracy and execution time mixing different sub-byte precisions for weight and activations in different layers.
- We evaluate the accuracy and execution time by changing the entropy of the uncertainty evaluation module with different image perspectives captured by the camera.

## 2    Background and Related Work

The deployment of DNNs on FPGAs has become popular due to their design flexibility, good performance, and low energy consumption. However, the limited resources available in embedded FPGAs requires significant trade-offs between performance and complexity. The current progress in DNNs dictates that the number of required parameters has reached the order of millions or even billions. For example, CoAtNet-7 [4], the most advanced NN as of writing this publication, achieves 90.88% of top-1 accuracy when applied to the ImageNet dataset and contains 2.44 billion parameters. Other widely-used NNs such as VGG [5], GoogLeNet [6], and Res-Net [7] have also reached the level of millions of parameters. The increase in parameters significantly improves the accuracy of DNNs, but it makes the deployment on low-cost edge devices challenging.

In recent years, the need for floating-point multiply-add operations has been reduced by using weight and activation quantization, with extreme cases such as Binarized Neural Networks (BNNs) eliminating the need for multiplications altogether. Kim and Smaragdis [8] believe that in a fully binarized NN, some inactive neurons can be pre-served as zero weight, while others are served as one weight during the calculation. They achieved 98.7% of accuracy on the MNIST dataset using the proposed BNN system. In a BNN only XNOR and bit counting operations are used instead of multiplication/addition. XNOR-Net [9] is proposed by the research group of Rastegari, which applied the binary convolutional neural network to the ImageNet dataset classification task. It is inspired by Alex-Net [10], Res-Net [7], and GoogLeNet [6]. XNOR-Net achieves 51.2% of Top-1 accuracy in a fully binarized NN with the ResNet-18 architecture and 65.5% of Top-1 accuracy in a partly binarized NN with the GoogLeNet architecture. DoReFa-Net, proposed by Zhou et al. [11], explored the accuracy of the forward/backward passes during the convolution using low bit-width weights. This made effective NN implementations on FPGAs possible. They experimented with partly binarized NNs and fully binarized NNs on the ImageNet dataset with 53% of Top-1 accuracy with 8-bit weight and 8-bit activation. Kwan et al. [12,13] experimented with an adaptive system that varies the number of frames used for image classification with a BNN and improved the accuracy to 70.4% based on the FINN library using real data frames as input. The inference part is executed on the PL, while a filter that adapts the system is executed on the PS.

The early-exit strategy has been proposed as a way to adapt the classification effort to the complexity of the task. The objective is to improve performance and reduce energy requirements with a minimum accuracy drop. BranchyNet [14] was proposed with the core idea of early exiting by introducing an early-exit system in the DNN. Branchy-LeNet (B-LeNet) on the MNIST dataset and Branchy-ResNet (B-ResNet) on the CIFAR10 dataset are both modifications from the original Le-Net and Res-Net NNs. B-LeNet and B-ResNet achieve 99.25% and 79.17% respectively, which have a negligible accuracy drop or even slightly increased accuracy compared with the 99.20% and 80.70% accuracy of the original network. At the same time, B-LeNet and B-ResNet also achieved 4.7× and 1.9× speed improvement compared with the original networks on an NVIDIA GeForce

GTX TITAN X (Maxwell) 12GB GPU. In our research, we will create an early-exit NN using similar techniques to BranchyNet. Teerapittayanon et al. [15] also applied BranchyNet to the portable-edge-cloud heterogeneous computing system with the NN model divided into three parts. Wang et al. [16] proposed a dual dynamic inference framework for DNN training containing Input-Adaptive Dynamic Inference (IADI) and Resources-Adaptive Dynamic Inference (RADI). The IADI can dynamically choose the sub-network that is the most time-effective with minimal degradation of accuracy, while RADI decides the confidence of early exit. This framework is applied on Res-Net trained with CIFAR-10 resulting in up to 4× computational saving with the same or higher accuracy compared with the SkipNet [17]. Lo et al. [18] proposed authentic operation (AO) and dynamic network sizing under the early-exit concept. AO is used after an initial inference is performed locally to decide whether the input should be transferred to the edge server for further inference or to present the output directly. The dynamic network determines the number of NN layers being used. Neshatpour et al. [19] decomposed the convolutional neural network (CNN) into a continuous number of smaller networks that are capable of image classification, and an early-exit strategy is introduced afterwards. Li et al. [20] and Phuong et al. [21] introduced multiple early-exit branches to the DNN model with the ImageNet dataset. More recent research shows that multiple early-exit branches can improve the efficiency of inference as demonstrated in SDN [22] and SPINN [23]. However, adding multiple exit branches into the NN system will increase the complexity of the network and in this research, we focus on a single exit branch due to the limited resources available in the selected Zynq-7020 FPGA board.

The training method of the early-exit networks shown above is known as joint training. In joint training, all the layers in a model are trained simultaneously. In our research, the early-exit branch network will be trained separately from the primary network. The primary network will be trained in the initial phase. Then, the early-exit branch will be introduced and trained while the pretrained primary model is made immutable. Since the branch network is trained separately, it is not required to train the whole network from scratch but only re-train the corresponding branches if there are modifications or additions to the branch network.

There is also a similar concept of the primary network and subordinate network written as Multi-Precision CNNs in the research work done by Amiri et al. [24]. In that work, NNs were trained independently, and they did not share the same data structure. In this research, we will still retain the multi-CNN concept but the early-exit branch network will share a part of the structure with the primary network. This will reduce the NN size and the NN training process.

In contrast to the previous work that considers DNNs mapped to CPUs and GPUs, we deploy the early-exit strategy on an FPGA-based BNN with the FINN framework [2]. Umuroglu et al. have implemented a BNN with FINN into a ZC706 embedded FPGA platform. It has been demonstrated that up to 12.3 million image classifications per second with 0.31 μs latency on the MNIST with 95.8% accuracy, while reached up 21096 image classifications per second with

283 µs latency on the CIFAR-10 and SVHN dataset with respectively 80.1% and 94.9% accuracy. This previous FINN research has targeted less challenging datasets with fewer image categories so the whole network can fit in the device memory. Zhang et al. [25] proposed FracBNN, a BNN which is deployed on a Zynq Ultrascale+ MPSoC device and achieved 71.8% Top-1 accuracy. Although the accuracy of FracBNN is better than our model, the FracBNN model is too large to be deployed on our low-cost FPGA device. Furthermore, we need to build an early-exit branch network based on the primary network increasing complexity, which will make FracBNN implementation even more problematic.

## 3    Early-Exit Topology and Training

In this section, we present the early-exit topology and demonstrate the training method of the NN. Python version 3.6.9 and PyTorch 1.10.2 with GPU support and dependencies were installed on an 8-core vCPU, Tesla P100 GPU, and 53GB of machine RAM. There are other frameworks for training available such as PyTorch, TensorFlow, and Caffe. However, to maintain compatibility with the FINN tools, our method uses PyTorch to train the NN model and uses the Brevitas [26] tool to quantize the model. The model is then converted from .npz to .onnx format which is ready for deployment on the FPGA. The model is trained with the ILSVRC12 dataset which is derived from the ImageNet dataset.

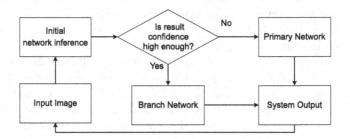

**Fig. 2.** The flow chart of the primary and early-exit configuration of NN system

The early-exit system contains a primary NN and an early-exit branch and both are mapped to a Xilinx Zynq-7020 SoC PYNQ-Z2 FPGA board. As shown in Fig. 2 and Fig. 3, every sample will go through some layers of the NN for initial inference until it reaches a junction. An evaluation will be performed to compare the current entropy of the sample with the entropy set by the user. The entropy is defined as: $entropy(y) = \sum_{l \in L} y_l log_2 y_l$, where $y$ is a vector that contains probabilities of all possible classification labels and $l$ contains all possible classification labels. If the current entropy is smaller than the threshold entropy set on the primary network, the sample will go through the early-exit network for further inference and present the result with maximum probability. If not, the sample will go through the primary network and the label with maximum probability will be returned. The inferring system will repeat the same procedure and continue in a loop after the classification result of the latest input image has been produced. The uncertainty evaluation algorithm is demonstrated as follows:

$$r = f_{exit}\,(x)$$
$$y = softmax\,(r)$$
$$e = entropy(y)$$
$$\text{if } e < e_T \text{ then}$$
$$\text{return } argmax(y),$$

where $f_{exit}$ is the output of the network and $e_T$ is the entropy of training. The early-exit network system follows the same procedure for every image inference.

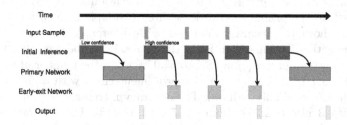

**Fig. 3.** The processing timeline for the system

Figure 4 shows the structure of the primary and early-exit NNs. The primary network structure is based on Dorefa-Net and the early-exit network is a pruned version of the primary network with fewer convolutional layers and FC layers. Both primary and early-exit networks share the same data structure at the initial inference part of the NN. The first stage of our approach trained the NN layers with 1-bit weight and 2-bit activation but remains the first convolutional layer and FC layers unquantized with floating-point precision to guarantee the prediction accuracy of the NN. This is because the first layer is connected to the image input which contains 8-bit pixels. Hence, there will be a significant

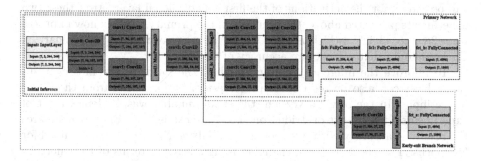

**Fig. 4.** The primary and early-exit model topology

accuracy drop if it is binarized. However, the unquantized layers are not able to be deployed on the PL side of FPGA and make the entire system less efficient. The previous version of the NN system achieves 52.29% of Top-1 accuracy and 63.62% of Top-5 accuracy for the primary network, and 48.17% of Top-1 accuracy and 59.38% Top-5 accuracy for the early-exit branch network. In order to improve the efficiency of the network after being deployed on the PYNQ-Z2 board, we kept the quantized NN layers as their original and set up a series of experiments to find an optimization method that can satisfy both accuracy requirements and fully quantized layers. The FC layers are quantized to 1-bit weight and 2-bit activation directly as they do not impact the NN accuracy as significantly as the first convolutional layer does. The FC layers will produce a one-hot vector output. However, for the first convolutional layer, a variety of bits of quantization targeting the weight and activation are tested from 1 bit to 4 bits based on the primary network, with each sample trained for 35 epochs. Figure 5 (a) shows the accuracy difference with different weight precision while keeping the activation binarized. From the figure, it can be seen that the accuracy significantly improves from 28% to 35.07% when the number of weight bits increases from 1 to 2. The accuracy improvement effect with a higher number of weight bits is gradually reduced. The accuracy increase when replacing 2-bit weights with 3 bits is 2.35% from 35.07% to 37.42%. The accuracy improvements comparing 3-bit and 4-bit weight is only 1.24% from 37.42% to 38.66%. If the accuracy is the only factor that is taken into the consideration, it is obvious that a higher weight bit count will result in higher NN inference accuracy. However, this increases in weight bits will result in additional computation and resource consumption. Hence, to balance NN inference efficiency and accuracy, the weight of the first convolutional layer will be quantized to 2 bits. Figure 5 (b) demonstrates the effects on accuracy with different counts of activation bits. The weights of the first convolutional layer are quantized to 2 bits in this scenario. The accuracy behaviour in this experiment is similar to the weight experiment. The accuracy increases sharply with the gain of 8.25% from 35.07% to 43.32% when the activation bit number is changed from 1 to 2. However, the accuracy only improves approximately 1% when the activations are quantized to 3 bits or 4 bits, with 44.86% and 45.89% respectively. Similarly, in order to achieve the best combination of accuracy and NN execution efficiency, a 2-bit quantization will be chosen for the activations of the first convolutional layer. After these two experiments presented above, the accuracy of the primary network now improves from 28% to 43.32%, which is close to the accuracy of the NN with binarized FC layers only that achieves an accuracy of 49.76%.

To improve the inference accuracy further, the stride of the first convolutional layer can also be reduced to preserve more information from the direct image input. In the original version, the stride number was 4. Hence, a set of experiments with a range of stride from 4 to 1 are carried out. Figure 6 compares the results of accuracy with different strides. All the NN samples are trained for 35 epochs. The effect of stride changing is significant in terms of the inference accuracy as an increment of approximately 5.5% is achieved for each step of the

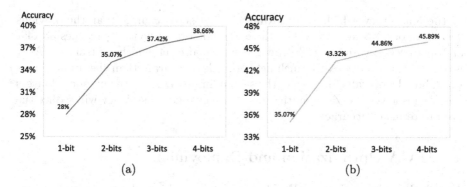

**Fig. 5.** Accuracy with different levels of weight quantization (a) Accuracy with different levels of activation quantization (b)

stride change from 4 to 2 reaching 53.64% of Top-1 accuracy with the stride equals to 2. When the stride is set to 1, the accuracy increases to 55.51% with a step increment of 1.87%, which is less significant than the previous change. Thus, the stride number of the first convolutional layer is set to 2 as an optimal solution with the best balance between efficiency and accuracy.

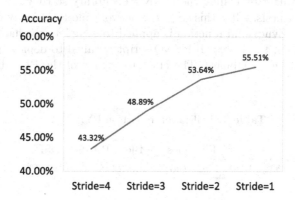

**Fig. 6.** The comparison of accuracy with different stride

The fully-quantized primary network was trained for 60 epochs to achieve the optimal inference accuracy, while the early-exit network was trained afterwards using the pre-trained model from the primary network using transfer learning techniques. Thus, instead of training the entire early-exit network, the initial layers of NN can be directly used from the pre-trained primary network. Only the layers that are different from the primary network need to be trained from scratch. This design makes the early-exit system achieve better integration, flexibility, and ease of modification if any further enhancements and development are carried out. The primary network reaches 59.38% of Top-1 accuracy and 72.81%

of Top-5 accuracy, which is approximately 7% more accurate than the previous version of our NN system. While the early-exit branch network reaches 53.14% of Top-1 accuracy and 65.64% Top-5 accuracy after 60 epochs of training. As it is expected, the early-exit branch network is less accurate than the primary network, but the overall efficiency of the system improves since the number of layers executed is lower. In addition, the confidence evaluation strategy will reduce the drop in terms of accuracy.

## 4    FPGA Optimization and Deployment

After training the NNs, the FINN framework is used in order to deploy the NNs on the PYNQ-Z2 platform using a multi-layer offload architecture. The process of deployment is shown in Fig. 7. Brevitas is applied to achieve NN quantization. Brevitas is a PyTorch library for quantization-aware training (QAT). Although PyTorch has already quantized the NN, the quantization in PyTorch only targets CPU backends and Brevitas has been designed to target FPGA and Data Processing Unit (DPU) backends. Thus, the trained model needs to be imported to Brevitas to convert the quantization format to target the FPGAs backend. Then, the NN model is imported to FINN using the ModelWrapper. The next step is to convert the network layers that will be deployed on the FPGA into their HLS equivalent by calling the FINN HLS library so they are available for Vivado HLS synthesis. After this step, the network model is ready for hardware generation. The ZynqBuild function is applied to complete the hardware generation step. Finally, the DeployToPYNQ script is called to deploy the hardware to the PYNQ-Z2 FPGA board. The clock frequency of the PL will be fixed at 50 MHz.

**Table 1.** Utilization report on PYNQ-Z2

| LUTs | FlipFlops | Block RAMs | DSPs |
|------|-----------|------------|------|
| 51632 (97%) | 42538 (40%) | 139 (99%) | 69 (32%) |

Table 1 shows the utilization of PL resources which is close to the maximum. Therefore, the hardware proposed accelerator is maximizing the utilization of the FPGA device.

## 5    Evaluation

### 5.1    Entropy Threshold Evaluation

In this section, we evaluated the efficiency and accuracy obtained when changing the entropy value for the uncertainty evaluation module. Figure 8 shows how changes in entropy affect the percentage of samples that take the early-exit

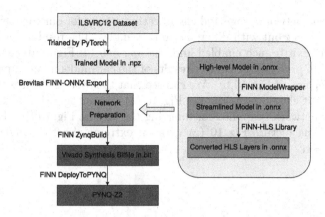

**Fig. 7.** The deployment procedure of NN on the PYNQ-Z2 FPGA

branch, as well as how it affects the frequency that the system chooses to select the early-exit branch. It shows that there is an inflection point of entropy value which indicates a rapid decrease in terms of accuracy. Hence, it can be deduced that the value of the inflection point of the entropy value will be a trade-off that satisfies the required inference speed while maintaining accuracy. In the rest of the paper, we set the threshold value to 0.14 for the further evaluation that corresponds to the inflection point.

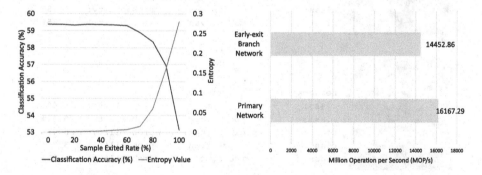

**Fig. 8.** The overall accuracy of the heterogeneous NN with varying entropy threshold

**Fig. 9.** The MOPS comparison for primary network and branch network

## 5.2   Camera Input Evaluation

In this section, we verify that the system is able to adaptively select the optimal branch of the NN according to the different camera angles while classifying the same object. Our demonstrator is based on a Logitech C160 webcam. The size of every input sample is fixed at $224 \times 224 \times 3$ pixels. Figure 10 demonstrates examples of the network usage and classification results for our early-exit system on the same object but with different camera angles. The results were obtained with the early-exit branch enabled and *entropy* = 0.14. Figure 10 clearly shows that the system presents the correct results of the car model in all camera angles, with the exception of Fig. 10 (e). We can see that the system chooses the branch network while it classifies the picture Fig. 10 (a) and outputs the correct results. The primary network is applied for inferring the picture Fig. 10 (b). The system fails to infer the picture Fig. 10 (c) with an extreme shooting angle with the primary network.

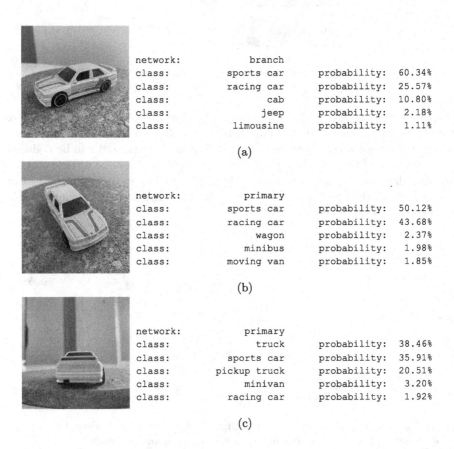

```
network:              branch
class:            sports car      probability:   60.34%
class:            racing car      probability:   25.57%
class:                   cab      probability:   10.80%
class:                  jeep      probability:    2.18%
class:             limousine      probability:    1.11%
```

(a)

```
network:             primary
class:            sports car      probability:   50.12%
class:            racing car      probability:   43.68%
class:                wagon      probability:    2.37%
class:              minibus      probability:    1.98%
class:           moving van      probability:    1.85%
```

(b)

```
network:             primary
class:                truck      probability:   38.46%
class:           sports car      probability:   35.91%
class:          pickup truck      probability:   20.51%
class:              minivan      probability:    3.20%
class:           racing car      probability:    1.92%
```

(c)

**Fig. 10.** Examples of network usage and inference results

### 5.3  Performance and Accuracy Evaluation

To test the performance, we prepared 100 images randomly captured from the Logitech C160 webcam. Figure 11 shows the execution time evaluation for the early-exit NN system. As shown in Fig. 11 (a), The majority of the execution time in this NN model is spent in the FC layers. Thanks to the pruned network layers in the branch network, the execution time of the convolutional layers in the branch network is 1.43× faster than the primary network and is 2.44× faster than the primary network in terms of the FC layers. The overall time cost of the early-exit branch network is 2.08× lower than the primary network, which achieves 146.27ms and 304.75ms respectively as it can be seen in Fig. 11 (b). Although the FC layer contains most of the parameters in the NN, it requires lower computation than the convolutional layer. It can also be observed that the execution time of the convolutional layer and FC layers on the PS are not proportional to the number of parameters in the corresponding layers.

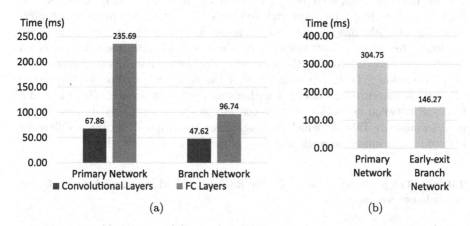

**Fig. 11.** The time costs comparison for each part of networks (a) and The total time cost comparison of networks (b)

Figure 9 compares the MOPS of the primary network and the branch network. Binarized network layers executed on the PL achieve a performance of 16167.29 MOPS for the primary network. The performance of the PL when the early-exit branch network is executed is 14452.86 MOPS.

To validate the hardware acceleration, we execute the entire NN system on the PS only. Also, an initial comparison is set up for our NN on an Intel i5-9300H 8-core CPU machine at 45W TDP (Thermal Design Power) and an NVIDIA RTX2060 GPU machine at 160W TDP by executing the original PyTorch validation code. Table 2 compares the time cost of the network executed on the various devices described above. It can be calculated that the acceleration rate for this NN is about 350× if the whole NN is executed on the PS. When the NN is tested on the Intel CPU, the time consumption is more than twice compared with PL. The execution time on the GPU is very close to the PL. This is because the layers that are implemented onto the PL are quantized as BNN layers. This allows all the network layers parameters to be stored in the initial memory of the PL without accessing the external memory. Moreover, BNNs eliminate the multiplication operations and replace them with XORing and zero-counting logic, which is also an efficient optimization targeting FPGA backends.

**Table 2.** Heterogeneous NN performance comparison on selected devices

| Device | PS on PYNQ-Z2 | i5-9300H CPU | RTX2060 GPU | PL on PYNQ-Z2 |
|---|---|---|---|---|
| Time (ms) | 78,710.55 | 548.86 | 218.33 | 224.52 |
| Time-cost Ratio | 350.57× | 2.44× | 0.87× | – |

To verify the system accuracy, we used the validation dataset of ILSVRC12. The accuracy is compared between executing just the primary network and deploying both the primary network and the early-exit branch network for inference. Table 3 highlights the threshold value, exit rate, and gain in terms of acceleration of the early-exit network system. The threshold value is set at 0.14, which is approximately the same as the entropy loss of the primary network during the training session. The results indicate that the early-exit system is 1.52× more efficient compared to the network without an early-exit branch. There is also a trade-off between network accuracy and efficiency. An accuracy drop of 1.64% is observable in Table 3, which is lower than the original accuracy difference between the primary network and the early-exit branch network.

**Table 3.** The performance result for the primary network, the branch network, and the early-exit system

| Networks | Accuracy | Time (ms) | Gain | Threshold | Exit rate |
|---|---|---|---|---|---|
| Primary Network Only | 58.74% | 304.75 | – | – | – |
| Branch Network Only | 52.76% | 146.27 | – | – | – |
| Early-exit System | 57.10% | 200.66 | 1.52x | 0.14 | 65.68% |

## 6    Conclusions and Future Work

In this paper, we present an early-exit system with a primary network and an early-exit branch network applied to a binarized neural network to improve overall system performance. The PyTorch framework is used for NN training and Brevitas is applied for NN model conversion. The quantized (partly binarized) NN model is based on the FINN framework for dataflow optimization targetting the PYNQ-Z2 FPGA backend.

The deployed NNs on the PL achieve an excellent hardware acceleration result compared with other devices with similar accuracy to the original primary network and very low energy consumption. The topology of the early-exit branch network further improves the processing rate by 2.08× compared to the primary network. The overall system is 1.52× more efficient compared to just using the primary network with a minor accuracy drop of 1.64% using the validation dataset of ILSVRC12.

In future work, we intend to evaluate other FPGA devices with more resources such as the Zynq Ultrascale+ development platform to create more complex systems with multiple exits or better accuracy NN models. A method to automatically evaluate the optimal location of early exits and their total number is also an interesting research path. Moreover, the implementation of NN to decent CPU and GPU can also be optimized. We also aim to extend our work to other application areas, such as object detection and abnormal event monitoring.

# References

1. Lentaris, G., et al.: High-performance embedded computing in space: evaluation of platforms for vision-based navigation. J. Aerosp. Inf. Syst. **15**(4), 178–192 (2018)
2. Xilinx Reasearch Labs, "Fast, scalable quantized neural network inference on FPGAs," Xilinx. https://github.com/Xilinx/finn
3. Umuroglu, Y.: FINN: a framework for fast, scalable binarized neural network inference. In: 25th International Symposium on Field-Programmable Gate Arrays (2017)
4. Dai, Z., Liu, H., Le, Q. V., Tan, M.: CoAtNet: marrying convolution and attention. In: arXiv:2106.04803 (2021)
5. Simonyan, K., Zisserman, A.: Very deep convolutional networks for large-scale image recognition. In: arXiv:1409.1556 (2014)
6. Christian, S.: Going deeper with convolutions. In: Proceedings of the IEEE Conference on Computer Vision and Pattern Recognition, Boston, USA, (2015)
7. He, K., Zhang, X., Ren, S., Sun, J.: Deep residual learning for image recognition. In: Proceedings of the IEEE Conference on Computer Vision and Pattern Recognition, Las Vegas, USA (2016)
8. Kim, M., Smaragdis, P.: Bitwise neural networks. arXiv:1601.06071 [cs.LG]
9. Rastegari, M., Ordonez, V., Redmon, J., Farhadi, A.: XNOR-Net: imagenet classification using binary convolutional neural networks. arXiv:1603.05279v4 [cs.CV] 2 Aug 2016
10. Krizhevsky, A., Sutskever, I., Hinton, G.E.: ImageNet classification with deep convolutional neural networks. Commun. ACM **60**(6), 84–90 (2012)
11. Zhou, S., Wu, Y., Ni, Z., Zhou, X., Wen, H., Zou, Y.: DoReFa-Net: training low bitwidth convolutional neural networks with low bitwidth gradients. arXiv:1606.06160
12. Kwan, E.Y.L., Nunez-Yanez, J.L.: Entropy-driven adaptive filtering for high-accuracy and resource-efficient FPGA-based neural network systems. Electronics **9**(11), 1765 (2020)
13. Kwan, E.: Real Time Object Recognition with Binary. University of Bristol, Bristol (2020)
14. Teerapittayanon, S., McDanel, B., Kung, H.: BranchyNet: fast inference via early exiting from deep neural networks. In: 2016 23rd International Conference on Pattern Recognition (ICPR) (2017)
15. Teerapittayanon, S., McDanel, B., Kung, H.T.: Distributed deep neural networks over the cloud, the edge and end devices. In: 2017 IEEE 37th International Conference on Distributed Computing Systems (ICDCS) 2017
16. Wang, Y., et al.: Dual dynamic inference: enabling more efficient, adaptive, and controllable deep inference. IEEE J. Sel. Top. Sign. Process. **14**, 623–633 (2020)

17. Wang, X., Yu, F., Dou, Z.-Y., Darrell, T., Gonzalez, J.E.: SkipNet: learning dynamic routing in convolutional networks. In: Ferrari, V., Hebert, M., Sminchisescu, C., Weiss, Y. (eds.) ECCV 2018. LNCS, vol. 11217, pp. 420–436. Springer, Cham (2018). https://doi.org/10.1007/978-3-030-01261-8_25

18. Lo, C., Su, Y.Y., Lee, C.Y., Chang, S. C.: A dynamic deep neural network design for efficient workload allocation in edge computing. In: 2017 IEEE International Conference on Computer Design (ICCD) (2017)

19. Neshatpour, K., Behnia, F., Homayoun, H., Sasan, A.: Exploiting energy-accuracy trade-off through contextual awareness in multi-stage convolutional neural networks. In 20th International Symposium on Quality Electronic Design (ISQED) (2019)

20. Li, H., Zhang, H., Qi, X., Yang, R., Huang, G.: Improved techniques for training adaptive deep networks. In: 2019 IEEE/CVF International Conference on Computer Vision (ICCV) (2019)

21. Phuong,M., Lampert, C.H.: Distillation-based training for multi-exit architectures. In: IEEE/CVF International Conference on Computer Vision (ICCV) (2019)

22. Kaya, Y., Hong, S., Dumitras, T.: Shallow-deep networks: understanding and mitigating network overthinking. In: International Conference on Machine Learning (ICML) (2019)

23. Laskaridis, S., Venieris, S.I., Almeida, M., Leontiadis, I., Lane, N.D.: SPINN: synergistic progressive inference of neural networks over device and cloud. In: Proceedings of the 26th Annual International Conference on Mobile Computing and Networking (MobiCom) (2020)

24. Amiri, S., Hosseinabady, M., McIntosh-Smith, S., Nunez-Yanez, J.L.: Multiprecision convolutional neural networks on heterogeneous hardware. In: Design, Automation & Test in Europe Conference & Exhibition (DATE), pp. 419–424 (2018)

25. Zhang, Y., Pan, J., Liu, X., Chen, H., Chen, D., Zhang, Z.: FracBNN: accurate and FPGA-efficient binary neural networks with fractional activations. In: 29th ACM/SIGDA International Symposium on Field-Programmable Gate Arrays, FPGA (2021)

26. Pappalardo, A.: Xilinx/brevitas, Zenodo 2021. https://doi.org/10.5281/zenodo.3333552

# FPGA-Extended General Purpose Computer Architecture

Philippos Papaphilippou[1]($^{\boxtimes}$)(iD) and Myrtle Shah[2](iD)

[1] Department of Computing, Imperial College London, London, UK
`p.papaphilippou17@alumni.imperial.ac.uk`
[2] ChipFlow Ltd, Cambridge, UK

**Abstract.** This paper introduces a computer architecture, where part of the instruction set architecture (ISA) is implemented on small highly-integrated field-programmable gate arrays (FPGAs). Small FPGAs inside a general-purpose processor (CPU) can be used effectively to implement custom or standardised instructions. Our proposed architecture directly address related challenges for high-end CPUs, where such highly-integrated FPGAs would have the highest impact, such as on main memory bandwidth. This also enables software-transparent context-switching. The simulation-based evaluation of a dynamically reconfigurable core shows promising results approaching the performance of an equivalent core with all enabled instructions. Finally, the feasibility of adopting the proposed architecture in today's CPUs is studied through the prototyping of fast-reconfigurable FPGAs and profiling the miss behaviour of opcodes.

**Keywords:** Computer architecture · Memory hierarchy · Reconfigurable extensions

## 1 Introduction

There has been considerable maturity around traditional software on today's CPUs. This has led to easier development through high-quality libraries and debug tools, as well as relatively mature programming models and verification routines. Additionally, a variety of software and hardware abstractions have enabled portability of code, such as with virtual memory and cache hierarchies, and enabled more effortless increase in performance, such as through instruction-level parallelism.

However, general purpose processors leave a lot to be desired in terms of performance, hence the increase in the use of computation offloading to specialised processors. These include graphics processing units (GPUs), FPGAs and even purpose-built silicon in the form of application-specific integrated circuits (ASICs).

---

The first author is now with Huawei Technologies R&D (UK) Limited.

L. Gan et al. (Eds.): ARC 2022, LNCS 13569, pp. 87–102, 2022.
https://doi.org/10.1007/978-3-031-19983-7_7

One consideration in today's hardware specialisation technologies is the fact that they are mostly based on the non-uniform memory-access model (NUMA). Large off-chip memories are found in the majority of today's high-end FPGA offerings, resulting in power-hungry and expensive setups, as well as in limitations in programming models and complications in deployment and data movement.

While promising techniques like wide single-instruction multiple-data (SIMD) instructions [17] in CPUs attempt to close the gap between specialised and general purpose computing [10], this gap is wider than it has ever been. This is because of the increased need for highly customised architectures in trending workloads [26], whose functionality cannot be efficiently expressed with a fixed general purpose ISA and architecture.

In this paper, we extend the most common computer architecture in today's systems (modified Harvard architecture [15]) to introduce FPGA-based instruction implementations in general purpose systems. In contrast to current research, this goes beyond embedded and heterogeneous processors, and introduces multiprocessing for operating systems and fine-grain reconfiguration, as with standardised instruction extensions. A feasibility study shows promising performance for supporting reconfigurable extensions on-demand, especially when supporting fast FPGA reconfiguration. The list of contributions is as follows:

1. The "FPGA-extended modified Harvard Architecture", a novel computer architecture to introduce FPGAs working as custom instructions, enabling context-switching and other advanced concepts for higher-end applications.
2. A comprehensive evaluation with fine-grain reconfiguration (at the instruction-level), providing insights on the impact of the reconfiguration time and the operating system's scheduler properties for multi-processing.
3. Feasibility studies elaborating on the readiness of current SoC technology to adopt the proposed approach.

## 2  Challenges

The research on FPGAs implementing instructions can be considered an attempt to overcome a series of challenges in current systems. This work addresses challenges found in existing research on custom instructions.

*Current CPUs and Discrete FPGAs.* One challenging design choice that relates to both hardware and software is the selection of instructions that would be more beneficial to include as part of the instruction set architecture (ISA). With a fixed ISA, vendors can select a subset of instructions, such as with the modularity of RISC-V [3], or design custom instructions. For general purpose computing it is difficult to predict what the most appropriate instructions will be. For instance, some applications may be ephemeral, as with some deep learning models, for which specialised hardware becomes obsolete faster.

Another challenge is hardware complexity. Supporting a high-number of instructions is expensive, but sometimes this has been unavoidable for widening the applicability of general purpose processors. For example, Intel's AVX2 and AVX-512 include thousands of instructions [17], and RISC-V's unratified vector extension hundreds [1]. The related implementation complexity, such as with AVX-512, is associated with a decrease in operating frequency and power efficiency, and area increase [11,14]. Additionally, AVX-512 is suboptimal for certain workloads, where a serial code could surpass them in terms of performance and scalability [11]. Expanding the ISA can also harm the SoC scalability to many-cores, which heavily relies on core miniaturisation and power efficiency.

When using FPGAs as accelerators, one of the most limiting bottlenecks to performance is the bandwidth to main memory [21]. For example, even with Intel's Xeon+FPGA, although the FPGA is directly connected to the memory controller it only achieves 20 GB/s [7]. The memory hierarchy tends to always favour CPU performance, hence the presence of expensive off-chip memories in high-end FPGA boards. This heterogeneity is considered to impact FPGA development and increases the cost and deployment of FPGAs in the datacenter [22].

*FPGAs Implementing Instructions.* The basic limitation of the related work on FPGA-based instructions is the focus on embedded and/or heterogeneous systems, with no notion for multi-processing, context-switching and other advanced micro-architectural features. The use of embedded FPGAs (eFPGAs) has many practical applications in embedded systems [5,18], but there is currently no computer architecture to "hide" reconfiguration from traditional software.

One challenge in existing methods of introducing FPGAs as custom instructions is the need for manual intervention for reconfiguration. Although the recommended procedures to handle bitstreams can be well documented, deviating from conventional software development could be detrimental for adoption [5].

By initially focusing on highly-customised instructions and more complex accelerators, there has been less opportunity for modern processors to gradually adopt small reconfigurable regions as part of their core. It is more complex to derive conclusions from specific custom instructions and accelerators, as their exploration usually shifts the focus to specialisation and optimisation.

## 3   Solution

The proposed solution is the "FPGA-extended modified Harvard Architecture", which unifies the address space for instructions, data, as well as for FPGA bitstreams. When compared to the traditional modified Harvard architecture, the proposed solution also adds a separate bitstream cache at level 1, to provide bitstreams for FPGA-instructions after an instruction opcode is ready. The idea is for a computing core that features reconfigurable slots for instructions, to be able to efficiently fetch instruction bitstreams transparently from the software. Fig. 1 (left) introduces the proposed computer architecture.

This architecture assumes that the computing core features fast-programmable FPGAs that can be used to implement instructions. This can

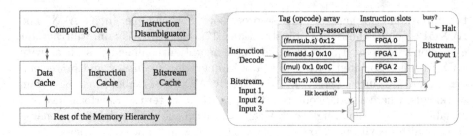

**Fig. 1.** Proposed computer architecture (left) and instruction disambiguator (right)

be achieved with the help of a small cache-like structure, the *instruction disam-biguator*, shown in Fig. 1 (right). On every instruction decode there is a request to this unit to see if there is an instruction implementation for the requested instruction. It operates as a fully-associative cache and uses opcodes (plus any additional fields for defining functions) as tags to determine the bitstream loca-tions. On an opcode miss, it requests the instruction bitstream from the bit-stream cache, while on a hit it multiplexes the operands to the appropriate slot.

The *bitstream cache* is a separate cache specifically designed for FPGA bit-streams, and can increase the performance of the reconfigurable core. Similarly to today's modified Harvard architecture, the L1 instruction and data caches are still separated and connected to a unified cache, allowing easier simultane-ous memory accesses for pipelining the instructions. Since the instruction dis-ambiguator unit waits for an instruction opcode to be ready, a bitstream fetch phase can be placed subsequently to the instruction decode pipeline stage in heavily-pipelined processors. This cache is separated to also allow different fea-tures than the rest of the caches, such as with wider blocks to facilitate the increased width to carry bitstreams, as opposed to instructions (see Sect. 5.2).

This approach enables the applications to be agnostic of the reconfiguration aspect. An operating system can provide ISA extensions (or part of them) in the form of bitstream libraries, while the hardware fetches the corresponding bitstreams on demand. Sharing the same address space for the bitstreams also enables keeping bitstreams in software binaries, so that they can provide custom instruction extensions alongside their data segment for acceleration potential.

## 4 Evaluation

This evaluation works as a proof of concept, thus any platform limitations are not handed-down over the proposed computer architecture. As our proposal concerns a fundamentally different computer architecture and targets high-end hardened processors, future research on a detailed evaluation would involve fabrication.

The framework for evaluating the performance of the proposed architecture[1] is based on Simodense [22], an open-source FPGA-optimised RISC-V softcore,

---

[1] Source code available: https://github.com/pphilippos/fpga-ext-arch.

which was heavily modified to facilitate our study on the system effects of our proposal. This study extends it with the "F" extension for single-precision floating-point support. This resulted in the RV32IMF, where "I" is the base 32-bit integer and "M" is the integer multiplication/division extension [3]. Most of the "I" instructions introduce one cycle of latency, while the "M" instructions occupy 4 non-blocking cycles of latency. The "F" extension is pipelined with a latency of 6 cycles, excluding the fused multiply-add instructions that yield a 12-cycle latency. RISC-V's "Zicsr" and a set of control status registers (*mstatus, mie, mcause, mepc* and *mtvec*) were also added to support the experiment of Sect. 4.3.

The main addition is the instruction disambiguator. Its functionality here is to process opcodes (and related fields) and add artificial latency when there is an instruction slot miss (or hit). All required instructions actually pre-exist on the softcore, emulating the performance overhead of the proposal as observed by the software. The instruction opcodes are first being resolved through the instruction cache, and the instruction slot disambiguator here works as an L0 instruction cache that uses opcodes as cache tags and adds latency on opcode accesses.

With respect to the size and complexity of the reconfigurable instructions, we explore a compartmentalisation scenario, where instructions are grouped into single reconfigurable regions according to their logic similarity. There are 3 groups for the "M" extension ({*mul, mulh, mulhsu, mulhu*}, {*div, divu*}, {*rem, remu*}), and 7 groups for the "F" extension {*fadd.s, fsub.s*}, {*fmul.s*}, {*fdiv.s*}, {*fsgnj.s, fsgnjn.s, fsgnjx.s, fmin.s, fmax.s, fle.s, flt.s, feq.s*}, {*fsqrt.s*}, {*fcvt.w.s, fcvt.wu.s, fcvt.s.w, fcvt.s.wu*}, {*fmadd.s, fmsub.s, fnmsub.s, fnmadd.s*}), totalling 10 groups. The number of free slots is parameterisable.

This emulates an environment where the CPU has no space for all extensions, and the workload exhibits competitiveness for a limited number of instruction slots. This instruction selection and granularity is indicative, thus a more complete ISA research would be appropriate to decide what fraction of instructions remains hardened in final products. Such an exploration would relate to the features and performance of the embedded FPGAs, while still allowing custom extensions.

The resulting codebase is synthesisable and also passed benchmark-based test cases on a Xilinx Zynq UltraScale+ FPGA. However, as the resulting framework ran relatively fast using Verilator 4.224, we opted to use simulations instead.

### 4.1   Benchmark Classification

The utilised benchmark suite is Embench [23], providing a selection of benchmarks with different attributes of interest. It was ported for use in our infrastructure, and each benchmark was made to run as a thread instead of a process. This required some additional modification, such adding thread safety for shared local libraries. Some benchmarks with double-precision floating point arithmetic were modified to use single-precision to make use of the "F" extension.

In order to quantify the impact of the studied extensions on the benchmark performance, they are first seen individually. There are four binaries/runs per benchmark, one for each of the following fixed specification combinations: RV32I, RV32IF, RV32IM and RV32IMF. When a useful instruction is absent from the specification of the compiler, it is replaced by a sub-optimal pre-defined routine, as specified by the application binary interface (ABI). The underlying softcore supports their superset RV32IMF and can run all 4 binaries per benchmark.

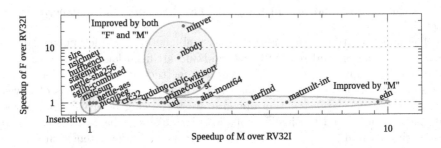

**Fig. 2.** Task classification based on the speedups of RV32IM and RV32IF over RV32I

The benchmark classification is illustrated in Fig. 2. The axes represent the speedup of using one of "M" or "F" over only the base instruction set RV32I. As expected, the five benchmarks that used floating point all seem benefit from "F" (*minver, wikisort, st, nbody* and *cubic*), while "M" seems a relatively more popular set amongst the benchmark selection (*crc32, qrduino, primecount, ud, aha-mont64, tarfind, matmult-int* and *edn*). The remaining 9 benchmarks are classified as "insensitive", which exhibit different properties such as being control-heavy. Interestingly, there is no class where an Embench benchmark is only benefited from "F" and not from "M" here.

### 4.2  Single-Program

For the evaluation of the proposed architecture under single benchmarks, we select the "improved by both F and M" class from the classification of the previous section. This is done to focus on workloads where there is demand for both instruction extensions, before introducing multi-processing.

In this experiment with simulated reconfigurability, there are six data series for different miss and hit latency combinations for the instruction slot disambiguator. There are 10-cycle, 50-cycle and 250-cycle miss latencies representing both reconfiguration technologies that approach a latency closer to that of CPU instructions, and slower which could be achievable with more traditional partial reconfiguration techniques. For each of the three, there are versions with and without a hit latency, which is useful to represent potential discrepancies between the CPU core and the fabric (e.g. frequency drops).

Figure 3 presents these results for 4 available instruction (group) slots. The y axis shows the slowdowns over when running with a fixed specification with both "M" and "F" (RV32IMF). Note that all series regard slowdowns, but the term speedup is also kept for consistency. There are also the RV32I and *max(IM, IF)* series. The latter represents the maximum performance between the fixed specifications RV32IM and RV32IF per individual run.

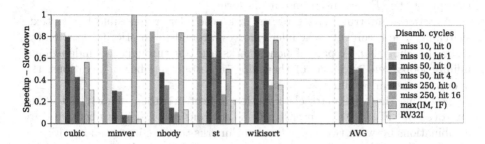

**Fig. 3.** Approaching RV32IMF with reconfigurability for single benchmarks

When selecting the (50, 0)-cycle latency configuration, it can still approach selecting the best extension per benchmark (*max(IM, IF)* series) with an average performance at around 71% of RV32IMF. It also exceeds the *max(IM, IF)* performance in benchmarks like *st* and *wikisort*, where the use of "F" instructions is used more sporadically. Over a fixed baseline, when considering both the benchmarks classes "improved by both F and M" and "improved by M" (latter not in Fig. 3), a (50, 0)-cycle latency configuration is 2.46x, 1.4x and 3.62x faster than RV32IF, RV32IM and RV32I respectively.

When comparing the versions for with and without a hit latency (darker shades in Fig. 3), there is a considerable performance degradation at the higher latency values. For instance, for 250-cycle misses and 16-cycle hits, the approach performs similarly to featuring no instructions from "M" and "F", at 20% of the RV32IMF performance. However, targeting a 0-to-few-cycle observable hit latency in future implementations, such as with fast FPGAs or more pipelining, seems to provide promising performance. This includes the (50, 4)-cycle combination, which updates the above comparison of (50, 0) to a speedup of 1.75x, 1.05x and 2.7x over RV32IF, RV32IM and RV32I respectively.

A general conclusion with regards to the latencies is that there is a sensible point where the approach is still helpful. For each workload there could be detailed curves with smaller latency intervals than the indicative values here. A similar argument can be made for the number of slots and other attributes. Though, analyzing specific points would be less significant, as this would relate more directly to the specification of the FPGAs and the core.

### 4.3   Multi-program

The effects of multi-processing are studied with the help of an operating system. FreeRTOS [8], a real-time operating system, was selected to provide a minimal framework allowing experimentation with a task scheduler. A single binary is obtained, containing both the FreeRTOS task scheduler and the benchmarks as threads. This is run as a bare-metal application by the adopted softcore to study the effects of context switching under our proposal for multi-programming. The main modification to FreeRTOS was the porting of the context-switching routine to support the "F" extension in our platform.

A periodic interrupt is set by its task scheduler, responsible for context-switching. The FreeRTOS scheduler enforces a round-robin priority between the tasks (benchmarks). A pair of benchmarks are run through two independent infinite loops, and once one of them does a certain number of iterations, the operating system terminates.

Following the benchmark classification of Sect. 4.1, the category that is not improved by "F" or "M" ("insensitive") is not considered. The studied pairs are combinations between two of the five benchmarks that are improved by "F" and "M" (totalling 10) and combinations between one from the latter category with one from the eight benchmarks that are only improved by "M" (totalling 40).

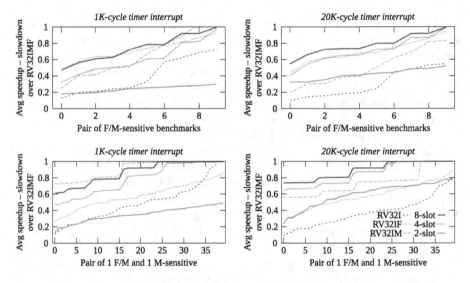

**Fig. 4.** Multi-programming using the reconfigurable approach with 2, 4 or 8 slots versus subsets of RV32IMF, under different scheduler timings. All series are sorted individually.

Figure 4 presents the results of this experiment with a 50-cycle miss latency (no hit latency) from the single-program experiments, as well as with variations of it for a different number of slots (2 and 8). The latter variations are added to elaborate on the slot interaction with this multi-program case, as the competitiveness between the slots is increased. The y-axes are the average speedups for each of the paired benchmarks over their corresponding runtimes with RV32IMF.

The left plots in Fig. 4 use binaries compiled for a 1000-cycle (1K) timer interrupt for context-switching, while the right plots present the results for a

20-fold increase in the timer interrupt delay. With the shorter 1K-cycle delay, all runtimes increase due to the additional instructions coming from the interrupt handler of the operating system. However, due to the different instruction distributions amongst the benchmarks, this also increases the instruction slot misses, hence the 20K-cycle versions improve the speedups of the reconfigurable approach. For instance, the average speedup of 4-slot series improves from 0.62 to 0.71 (i.e. from 38% to 29% slowdown) for the top selection of pairs, and from 0.82 to 0.9 for the benchmark pairs of the bottom plots in the figure.

One observation when combining the benchmarks of the same class (Fig. 4 top) is that the reconfigurable approach remains at the similar levels of performance degradation as with the last section (single-program). For instance, the average speedup for the 4-slot with 50-cycle reconfiguration and a 20K-cycle timer is 0.71, while the last section's corresponding average was also around 0.71.

From Fig. 4 (bottom right) we can see that the potential of reconfiguration is relatively higher when combining benchmarks with different extension preferences. The average speedup over RV32IMF for the 2-slot, 4-slot and 8-slot approaches is 0.62, 0.9 and 0.94 respectively, under 20K-cycle interrupts.

The proposed reconfigurable approach is shown to be more well-rounded than fixed extensions. For example, RV32IF performs significantly better than RV32IM in the pairs of the upper half of Fig. 4, but this is reversed for the pairs of the lower part. When considering all 50 of the aforementioned benchmark combinations for 20K cycle interrupts, the 4-slot version is 3.39x, 1.48x and 2.04x faster on average when compared to RV32I, RV32IM and RV32IF respectively, at an average of 0.82x the performance of RV32IMF. Finally, fine-tuning the operating system's scheduler parameters could be a cheap but necessary step to fully take advantage of the proposed computer architecture.

## 5   Feasibility

It is also important to comment on the readiness of current technologies to support such fast reconfiguration in future SoCs. The main evaluation refrained from elaborating on this aspect to enable a discussion through system effects.

### 5.1   Reconfiguration Latency Representativeness

In order to demonstrate that future CPUs which feature FPGAs as functional units can be reprogrammed under a latency of the order of magnitude studied in Sects. 4.2 and 4.3, we present an example fast-reconfigurable FPGA architecture and prototype it in simulation.

The modelled FPGA is based on a traditional FPGA fabric layout but directly exposes a wide configuration bus which can be loaded from a wide bitstream cache. In contrast, typical FPGA architectures such as UltraScale+ constrain the reconfiguration port width to 32 bits [29]. The test designs for the FPGA were based on the RISC-V bit manipulation extension [2], including *clmul* (carry-less multiply) and *bextdep* (bit extract and deposition).

The FPGA is modelled inside nextpnr [24] using the viaduct plugin framework for architectures, with a Verilog simulation model to confirm that bitstreams can be loaded in the target latency and function correctly. There are two connections between the FPGA fabric and the CPU. A wide configuration bus based on the Pico Co-Processor Interface (PCPI) from PicoRV32 [28] is loaded through an L1 cache. Once the FPGA is configured, the fabric itself can also receive instruction operands and source register values; and returns a destination value after some cycles. This approach also enables partial instruction decoding; so one bitstream could implement multiple related instructions.

A series of optimisations are applied to the architecture to minimise the configuration array size (and hence cache size and configuration port width) and reconfiguration latency. The first relates to the removal of features less likely to be useful for this application, such as block RAM (BRAM) for storing large states. The inclusion of DSPs is not explored, though this could further reduce the configuration state by avoiding the use of fabric resources e.g. for multipliers.

An optimisation relates to the type of the look-up tables (LUTs), which are basic building blocks in FPGAs. 4-LUTs (i.e. with 4 inputs totalling 16 entries) are used rather than 6-LUTs. In this way the size of the configuration information is reduced; full instead of one-hot muxes is used for the routing; and the number of routing resources is generally minimised whilst keeping target designs routable. LUT permutation and route-throughs in place and route were used to partially compensate for the latter. The benefit of 4-LUTs in this context is shown with the experiment of Fig. 5, that determines the minimum configuration FPGA array size necessary to implement the *bextdep* benchmark. Future work includes further optimising the internal architecture, such as with fracturable LUTs.

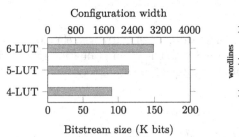

**Fig. 5.** LUT type versus bitstream size

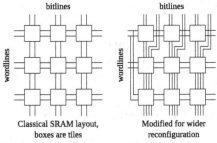

**Fig. 6.** Modification of SRAM FPGAs

When configured for 1680 LUTs, the bitstreams are a total of 91 kbits, requiring a 1824-bit wide configuration port for a 50-cycle reconfiguration latency. This is within the reasonable range of wide datapaths (see Sect. 5.2), and it could be reduced at the expense of latency. Similarly, a 250-cycle latency (that still benefited some applications) would only require a 365-bit-wide port.

A necessary architectural change was to keep the entire configuration data path equal to the number of bitlines, rather than narrowing to an 8-bit or 32-bit external port or memory mapped configuration interface. This can then be loaded at full rate, in the target number of cycles, directly from the bitstream cache.

FPGAs generally use static RAM (SRAM) cells to store the configuration bits; and a word/bit line architecture to configure them. Architectures typically have a similar number of word and bitlines to ease routing. However, this would generally lead to unacceptably high configuration latencies for this application. Reducing the configuration latency requires more bitlines and fewer wordlines – the number of wordlines being equal to the latency, all things being equal. A diagrammatic example of the implication of increasing wordlines to reduce latency is shown in Fig. 6, simplified to few tiles and word/bitlines (showing only four configuration bits per tile, rather than a typical value of about a thousand).

This prototype uses a chain of shift registers to store the configuration bits. A configuration word is being shifted through the chain each configuration cycle (the chain is 50 deep, 1824 wide). This is for brevity, but has not challenged the routability of the test case. The operating frequency aspect is left as future work, but does not seem prohibitive at the moment, given the margins for a hit latency (Sect. 4.2) and reports for instruction-like tasks operating in the GHz range [4].

## 5.2 Bitstream Cache Dimensions

To better understand the bitstream cache requirements for high-end processors, a separate study is conducted on a commercial x86 platform with a higher instruction variety (such as with vector instructions). By using dynamic binary instrumentation (DBI), this section explores the spatial needs and temporal localities with respect to the bitstream usage by comparing it to the traditional instruction and memory usage.

The study of cache size requirements would normally involve measuring the *working set* by simulating caches of different sizes and levels and pinpointing the size where the miss rate declines sharply. However, this could use assumptions relating to data and instructions, such as about the longevity of the working set (benefiting from multiple cache levels) and the access pattern (the notion of working set implies certain access distributions in space and time).

Through a custom Intel Pin [19] tool, on every dynamic instruction call, a routine updates a series of data structures for statistics on the opcodes, instruction pointers (IPs) and memory locations (where applicable). Each opcode is perceived as a separate bitstream. This represents the worst case to avoid specialisation in the observations, since it also includes control flow and data movement instructions, which are expected to be the most frequent [6,12], as well as for similar instructions that could be grouped together. A mask is applied to ignore the last 6 bits for a 64-byte-granularity in data and instruction blocks, which is commonly found in today's x86 systems.

The data structures inside the Pin tool are mainly hashsets that provide the number of unique opcodes, instruction and data blocks. On every $n \in \mathbb{N}$ number of instructions, the 3 corresponding sets are cleared and their cardinality is saved in lists (implemented as maps of <cardinality, occurrence> pairs to conserve memory). This provides the distribution of compulsory miss cardinalities occurring in the specified periods of time (measured in instructions) for each of the opcode, instruction and memory cache blocks. For the instructions and data, the algorithm's input would represent the stream observed right before the L1 instruction and L1 data caches. Though, the spatiotemporal locality scope of this experiment extends beyond the L1 caches. For the opcodes, this stream is considered to be observed from the bitstream disambiguator.

The benchmark suite selection for the single-program experiment is the single-core part of Geekbench 5. This is a series of 21 compute-intensive benchmarks ranging from encryption to machine learning, and are run one by one. The same instance of the Intel Pin tool is used for the entirety of all Geekbench benchmarks.

These results are illustrated in Fig. 7. The $x$-axis summarises the time period the hashsets are collecting information for, and is used to observe temporal locality. The $y$-axis shows the observed median cardinalities for each hashset, and represents the compulsory misses for each type of cache block (bitstream for opcode, instruction for IPs and data for data addresses). The shaded regions underneath show the lower and upper quartiles of the cardinalities in each corresponding list of hashsets. As shown, the opcode count starts from below 16 for the shorter time slices, while peaking at below 64 for the longer time slices.

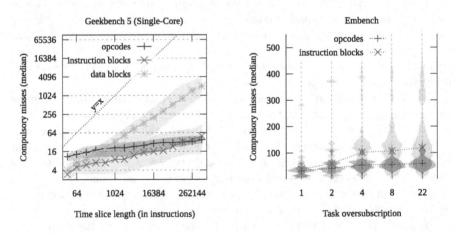

Fig. 7. Reuse behaviour in single-program    Fig. 8. Reuse behaviour in multi-program

Another observation is that the opcode series is "flatter" than the other curves, meaning that there is higher reuse of opcodes than instruction and memory blocks. It is also longer lasting. This could have been conjectured, but the relationship between the 3 types of reuse is a result of multiple factors. For instance, each instruction and data block already covers multiple locations (64-byte granularity), whose reuse also depends on the memory access pattern. From the opcode's perspective, CISC ISAs like x86-64 include a rather high number, as with Intel Pin's catalogue of over 8000 entries. The fact that the instruction and data series have a steeper upwards slope can also justify the need for multi-level cache hierarchies, as their requirements grow more rapidly with time.

For the multi-program study, the same Pin tool (but with added thread safety mechanisms) is used on the adapted Embench suite of Sect. 4.3. This time each benchmark is run as a thread using *pthreads* in Linux/x86-64 and is pinned down to the same core for oversubscription. The benchmark suite is compiled as a single binary, and with the *-march = native* flag to promote vectorisation. The idea of oversubscription here is to attempt increasing opcode demand, similar to the operating system's frequent migration of hundreds of tasks.

The results of the multi-program experiment are shown in Fig. 8, where the median compulsory misses are measured for different amounts of task oversubscription to a single core. The time window size is fixed to 32768 instructions. Superimposed to the medians are violin plots, which are used to visually provide more detailed distribution information than percentiles. The data behaviour was fairly similar to the instruction blocks in this instance, hence its omission for readability. As predicted, there is higher reuse of opcodes than instructions among the different tasks when oversubscribed. For example, when all 22 tasks are run concurrently, the median and maximum opcode misses reach 59 and 152 respectively, while the respective numbers for instructions are 119 and 672.

These numbers show that the bitstream cache is feasible with today's technology on SoCs. Specifically, a 64-block bitstream cache is shown to be enough for relatively long periods of time in both the single-program and multi-program experiments. This totals 768 KB of SRAM when using 12 KB bitstreams, being inline with the example FPGA architecture of Sect. 5.1. By observing recent processor trends that feature, for example, up to 256 MB L3 caches [25], the sub-MB size requirement is in the L2 territory. Additionally, a sub 2048-bit datapath that is demonstrated in Sect. 5.1 is only needed between this cache and the instruction disambiguator, as the expected latency profile of the bitstream cache makes progressively-loaded bitstream blocks meaningful, even with 128/256-bit datapaths to L2. Given the oversubscription experiment results and the read-only nature of the bitstreams from the FPGA's view, future multicores would also benefit from sharing of the bitstream cache(s).

These conclusions are drawn with the worst case approach in mind, such as by associating compulsory misses with the desirable cache size, and by not classifying opcodes into groups. A fraction of the reported desirable bitstream cache could still benefit future high-end CPUs with FPGAs working as instructions.

# 6    Related Work

Earlier research focused on using FPGAs as a functional unit. Garp [16] targets embedded processors without multi-processing support, but it introduces the idea of combining a bitstream alongside the process binary. It does not make FPGAs transparent, as it requires configuration instructions. DISC [27] is an earlier work that elaborates on reconfiguration in a similar context. Its instruction decoder is similar to the proposed instruction disambiguator by using caching. It is not a general-purpose computer architecture, as the processor has a separate ISA from the host processor. Chimaera [30] provides a reconfigurable array to dynamically load FPGA-based instruction implementations. This is somewhat reminiscent of the proposed bitstream cache, but only supports specially-compiled software. Architectures like CCA [13] and RISPP [9] aimed to improve the adaptability of embedded systems by providing a set of specialised functional units that can be dynamically selected at run-time. The latter does not involve FPGAs.

FABulous [18] is an open-source framework for integrating FPGAs into an ASIC. One of its applications is for the implementation of eFPGAs, also for the purposes of extending hardened cores. A RISC-V SoC with eFPGAs is presented as a use case. Related research studied the integration of SIMD units [20], but the insights were platform-related, such as with regards to Xilinx' partial reconfiguration. The custom instruction usage is limited to specialised kernels, and concepts like context-switching are not studied.

## 7   Conclusions

The FPGA-extended modified Harvard architecture can be used to transparently fetch standardised ISA extensions or custom instructions through the computer's memory hierarchy. The disambiguator unit works as an L0 cache for the FPGA slots and requests and multiplexes the bitstreams and instructions to reconfigurable regions. The evaluation showed promising results, generally surpassing the performance of a core with a constrained extension subset. The operating system in such computers is shown to benefit from longer times between context-switches to compensate for the reconfiguration time. Finally, a low reconfiguration latency is deemed necessary for the efficiency of the proposal, and our feasibility study finds this possible by mainly using existing FPGA building blocks and a cache with appropriate dimensions for providing the bitstreams.

**Acknowledgement.** We would like to thank Anuj Vaishnav for his feedback on an earlier version. The second author mainly contributed with the Sect. 5.1.

## References

1. RISC-V "V" Vector Extension, Version 0.9 (2020)
2. RISC-V "B" Bitmanip Extension, Version 0.94-draft (2021)
3. Waterman, A., Asanovic, K.: The RISC-V instruction set manual, volume I: Unprivileged ISA, version 20191214-draft. RISC-V Foundation, Technical report (2020)
4. Achronix Semiconductor Corp.: Speedcore architecture. https://www.achronix.com/speedcore-architecture. Accessed 10 Apr 2022

5. Ahmed, S.Z.: eFPGAs: Architectural explorations, system integration & a vision-ary industrial survey of programmable technologies. Ph.D. dissertation, Université Montpellier II-Sciences et Techniques du Languedoc (2011)
6. Akshintala, A., Jain, B., Tsai, C.-C., Ferdman, M., Porter, D.E.: X86-64 instruction usage among C/C++ applications. In: Proceedings of the 12th ACM International Conference on Systems and Storage, pp. 68–79 (2019)
7. Alonso, G., Istvan, Z., Kara, K., Owaida, M., Sidler, D.: doppioDB 1.0: machine learning inside a relational engine. IEEE Data Eng. Bull. **42**(2), 19–31 (2019)
8. Barry, R.: FreeRTOS reference manual: API functions and configuration options. Real Time Engineers Limited (2009)
9. Bauer, L., Shafique, M., Henkel, J.: RISPP: a run-time adaptive reconfigurable embedded processor. In: 2009 International Conference on Field Programmable Logic and Applications, pp. 725–726. IEEE (2009)
10. Bordawekar, R., Bondhugula, U., Rao, R.: Can cpus match GPUs on performance with productivity?: experiences with optimizing a flop-intensive application on CPUs and GPU. IBM Research Report, RC25033, Technical report (2010)
11. Cebrian, J.M., Natvig, L., Jahre, M.: Scalability analysis of AVX-512 extensions. J. Supercomput. **76**(3), 2082–2097 (2020)
12. Chang, Y.-J.: Exploiting frequent opcode locality for power efficient instruction cache. In: Proceedings of the 18th ACM Great Lakes Symposium on VLSI, pp. 399–402 (2008)
13. Clark, N., Blome, J., Chu, M., Mahlke, S., Biles, S., Flautner, K.: An architecture framework for transparent instruction set customization in embedded processors. In: 32nd International Symposium on Computer Architecture (ISCA 2005), pp. 272–283. IEEE (2005)
14. Gottschlag, M., Schmidt, T., Bellosa, F.: AVX overhead profiling: How much does your fast code slow you down? In: Proceedings of the 11th ACM SIGOPS Asia-Pacific Workshop on Systems, Series APSys 2020, pp. 59–66. ACM (2020)
15. Grosbach, J.H., Conner, J.M., Catherwood, M.: Modified harvard architecture processor having program memory space mapped to data memory space. US Patent 6,728,856, 27 April 2004
16. Hauser, J.R., Wawrzynek, J.: Garp: a MIPS processor with a reconfigurable coprocessor. In: Proceedings of the 5th Annual IEEE Symposium on Field-Programmable Custom Computing Machines Cat. No. 97TB100186), pp. 12–21. IEEE (1997)
17. Intel (R), Intel (R): Intel intrinsics guide. https://software.intel.com/sites/landingpage/IntrinsicsGuide/
18. Koch, D., Dao, N., Healy, B., Yu, J., Attwood, A.: FABulous: an embedded FPGA framework. In: The 2021 ACM/SIGDA International Symposium on Field-Programmable Gate Arrays, pp. 45–56 (2021)
19. Luk, C.-K., et al.: Pin: building customized program analysis tools with dynamic instrumentation. ACM Sigplan Not. **40**(6), 190–200 (2005)
20. Ordaz, J.R.G., Koch, D.: A soft dual-processor system with a partially run-time reconfigurable shared 128-bit SIMD engine. In: 29th International Conference on Application-specific Systems, Architectures and Processors (ASAP), pp. 1–8. IEEE (2018)
21. Papaphilippou, P., Luk, W.: Accelerating database systems using FPGAs: a survey. In: 2018 28th International Conference on Field Programmable Logic and Applications (FPL), pp. 125–130. IEEE (2018)

22. Papaphilippou, P., Kelly Paul, H.J., Luk, W.: Simodense: a RISC-V softcore optimised for exploring custom SIMD instructions. In: 2021 31st International Conference on Field-Programmable Logic and Applications (FPL), pp. 391–397 (2021)
23. Patterson, D., Bennett, J., Dabbelt, P., Garlati, C., Madhusudan, G., Mudge, T.: Embench: a modern embedded benchmark suite (2020)
24. Shah, D., Hung, E., Wolf, C., Bazanski, S., Gisselquist, D., Milanovic, M.: Yosys+nextpnr: an open source framework from verilog to bitstream for commercial FPGAs. In: IEEE 27th Annual International Symposium on Field-Programmable Custom Computing Machines (FCCM) (2019)
25. Suggs, D., Subramony, M., Bouvier, D.: The AMD "Zen 2" processor. IEEE Micro **40**(2), 45–52 (2020)
26. Wang, Y.E., Wei, G.-Y., Brooks, D.: Benchmarking TPU, GPU, and CPU platforms for deep learning. arXiv preprint arXiv:1907.10701 (2019)
27. Wirthlin, M.J., Hutchings, B.L.: DISC: the dynamic instruction set computer. In: Field Programmable Gate Arrays (FPGAs) for Fast Board Development and Reconfigurable Computing, vol. 2607, pp. 92–103. SPIE (1995)
28. Wolf, C.: PicoRV32-a size-optimized RISC-V CPU (2019)
29. Xilinx Inc.: Vivado Design Suite User Guide, Partial Reconfiguration - UG909 (v2018.1) (2018)
30. Ye, Z.A., Moshovos, A., Hauck, S., Banerjee, P.: CHIMAERA: a high-performance architecture with a tightly-coupled reconfigurable functional unit. ACM SIGARCH Comput. Archit. News **28**(2), 225–235 (2000)

# Multi-spectral In-Vivo FPGA-Based Surgical Imaging

Majed Alsharari[1,5(✉)] ⓘ, Lorenzo Niemitz[2], Simon Sorensen[2], Roger Woods[1] ⓘ,
Ray Burke[2], Stefan Andersson Engels[2,3], Carlos Reaño[4], and Son T. Mai[1]

[1] Queen's University Belfast, Belfast BT9 5AF, Northern Ireland, UK
{malsharari01,r.woods,thaison.mai}@qub.ac.uk
[2] Tyndall Institute, Lee Maltings Complex Dyke Parade, Cork T12 R5C, Ireland
{lorenzo.niemitz,simon.sorensen,ray.burke,
stefan.andersson-engels}@tyndall.ie
[3] Department of Physics, Kane Science Building, University College Cork,
Cork, Ireland
[4] Universitat de València, 46100 Valencia, Spain
carlos.reano@uv.es
[5] Jouf University, Sakaka 72341, Saudi Arabia
malsharari@ju.edu.sa
https://www.qub.ac.uk/schools/eeecs/, https://www.ipic.ie/,
http://research.ucc.ie/profiles/D006/stefan.andersson-engels@tyndall.ie,
http://www.uv.es/caregon2, https://www.ju.edu.sa

**Abstract.** Intelligent and adaptive in-vivo, catheter-based imaging systems with enhanced processing and analytical capability have the potential to enhance surgical operations and improve patient care. The paper describes an intelligent surgical imaging system based on a 'chip on tip', which reduces the need for conventional imaging. The associated embedded system provides real-time, in-vivo imaging analysis and data display for surgeons, enhancing their ability to detect clinically significant tissue. The paper presents initial work on an field programmable gate array implementation of a contrast limited adaptive histogram equalization algorithm, Hessian matrix construction and region of interest function on the AMD-Xilinx's Kria KV260 board. It outlines optimizations undertaken to reduce the BRAMs by 38%, DSP48 blocks by 80%, flip-flops by 33% and LUTs by 36%, thus creating a design operating at 121 FPS.

**Keywords:** Surgical imaging · Field programmable gate array

## 1 Introduction

In current surgical practice, surgeons still rely heavily on external, 'gold standard' imaging systems such as X-ray, CT and MRI. In-vivo imaging systems such as endoscopes, intravascular ultrasound are standard but can be further

---

Partially supported by Jouf University.

L. Gan et al. (Eds.): ARC 2022, LNCS 13569, pp. 103–117, 2022.
https://doi.org/10.1007/978-3-031-19983-7_8

enhanced and using smart and integrated micro cameras. This offers the potential to enhance surgical procedures and outcomes by providing high quality, diagnostic images from deep within the body using micro-scale image sensors on a micro catheter platform.

As an example, the unprocessed in-vivo images in the femoral artery, distal to proximal, of a porcine model with different illumination RGB and Near Infra-Red (NIR) are shown in Fig. 1. Fig 1(a) shows a clear field of the marker band of a balloon catheter, a commonly used medical device for cardiac procedures, and Fig 1(b) gives the same location illuminated using 940nm NIR. Commercial micro-camera integrated circuits are available, but they are not specifically designed for biophotonics applications such as surgical guidance, based on diffuse reflectance imaging, fluorescence and reflectance for specific biomarkers. Commercially available micro-cameras [8] are limited by resolution, image quality, sensitivity, field of view, etc., thus limiting their use in-vivo.

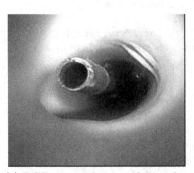

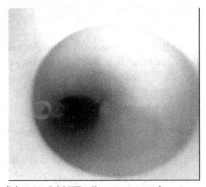

(a) RGB image showing the marker band of a balloon catheter

(b) 940nM NIR illumination showing a diffuse image with some ability to image through the blood field.

**Fig. 1.** Multispectral images from inside the femoral artery of a porcine model (Courtesy of Tyndall National Institute).

Using integrated image sensors in-vivo to successfully allow, for example, specular reflection and effective viewing of a beating heart, poses image processing and data analytics challenges. This can be resolved by employing smart, adaptive algorithms on an embedded system to enhance the image effectively, but requires adoption of a suitable low power technology and careful design. The Tyndall National Institute (TNI) in collaboration with clinicians and the medical device industry, are creating an intelligent surgical system (ISS) based on a custom CMOS image sensor and embedded processing unit which provides both image sensor power management and image processing capability to convert the detected signals at the edge or interface into clinical significant medical images, in real time. This paper describes the collaboration with Queen's University to implement the image processing functionality on an field programmable gate array (FPGA) on the AMD-Xilinx's Kria KV260 AI board.

The work uses multispectral image processing to recover the best possible RGB images, including enhancement with at least two NIR wavelengths. A contrast limited adaptive histogram equalization (CLAHE) algorithm [5] is employed to help outline specific features such as tumours, by suppressing the contrast of each pixel based on its neighbouring values. A Region of Interest (ROI) algorithm highlights intra-operative ROIs to the clinician, by applying convolution procedures using the derivatives of Gaussian kernel to construct the Hessian matrix of each pixel with the eigenvalues used by an edginess or ROI function. In this paper, we undertake a number of optimisations for the implementation of this functionality using the AMD-Xilinx Vitis High-Level Synthesis (HLS) tools.

The paper is structured as follow: Sect. 2 briefly describes the ISS, followed by an explanation in Sect. 3 of the processes and algorithms used for the detection of blood vessels. The system architecture is then described in Sect. 4 and followed by the results in Sect. 5. Conclusions are given in Sect. 6.

## 2 Intelligent Surgical System

The proposed ISS consists of a front-end comprises a micro camera and light source, and a small embedded processor with intelligent image processing functionality, connected via a fiber optic cable to a transceiver (see Fig. 2). The front-end module needs to have a small footprint within a microcatether (3–6 Fr.) in order to allow surgeons to navigate to the narrow regions inside body organs. The challenge is to undertake the design of this functionality in a lower power, FPGA technology that provides the adaptive processing to support evolving requirements. The back-end comprises a high performance computing resource which, in the future, will incorporate additional intelligence (AI) capability, gleaned by surgeons from operations as they are performed.

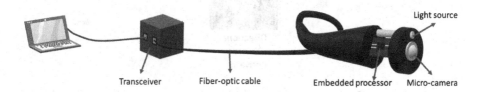

**Fig. 2.** Visualisation of the overall system design.

Images are captured by the micro-camera, and an automated multispectral light source helps to vary the illumination spectrum. The multispectral illumination is coupled to a single fibre and as part of the system control, the illumination wavelengths are selected and synchronised with the detection by the imager and the video data transfer. The resulting raw video data is transmitted in a streaming-data fashion to the embedded processing unit which, in the future, will incorporate increasingly complex image analysis intelligence to assist the surgeon during the operation. Therefore, optimisation of the current implementation is essential in order to support future computation requirements.

Incorporating FPGA technology to surgical systems is an interesting choice when building innovation systems that are cost effective, have low-power consumption, and seek high performance. A multi-stage, FPGA-based customised design using similar image functionality was explored in [2] for the enhanced detection of blood vessels in retinal images. In another example, an FPGA platform was used in an endoscope imaging system [4] to provide a low-cost, high-performance implementation. A FPGA-based controller for robotic-assisted surgical system was developed in [7] to provide real-time control of a robot arms. Similar to our future plans, they aim to build the controller as a single chip, but clearly have different requirements.

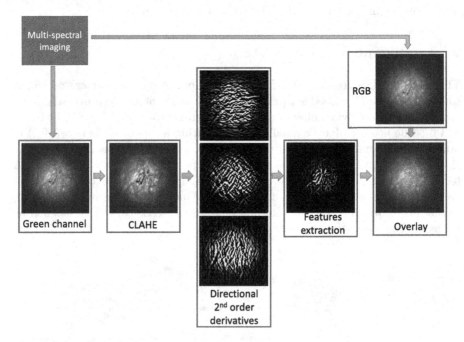

**Fig. 3.** Extraction of tissue features process from real imaging data captured by the multi-spectral imaging system developed by Tyndall Institute.

## 3   Extraction of Tissue Features

A key need is to identify key features in generated images such as in the extraction of tissue features (Fig. 3). Therefore, the proposed system employs the widely-used CLAHE algorithm followed by a features extraction stage. It determines the directional second order derivatives of the enhanced image by computing the eigenvalues of Hessian matrix to decide whether a pixel is of interest or not. Overlying detected features on top of the hyperspectral images helps the surgeons to identify the ROIs. With the aim to incorporate future additional functionality, it is vital to minimise the FPGA resources by mapping effectively the required functionality onto the parallel FPGA resources and employing system level optimisations to produce the smallest footprint.

## 3.1 Image Acquisition

With conventional micro cameras, data is acquired with a rolling electronic shutter at a frame rate of 100 frames per second (FPS). By experimentation of the detection of blood vessels, it was determined that only the green channel needed to be extracted, because it has unique representations of the dark background and the bright retinal blood vessels. Each pixel stores a charge proportional to the light intensity and is converted to a digital value between 0 to 255 within the imager.

## 3.2 CLAHE

CLAHE is applied to enhance the contrast of each pixel based on its spatial location and neighboring pixels and has been shown to map well to FPGA [3]. A key stage of the algorithm is to divide the image into predefined and equal sized tiles where each tile is independent and does not share pixels with its neighboring tiles. A histogram for each tile is then obtained with 256 bins and clipped to a threshold predefined by the user (Fig. 5). All exceeded amounts are accumulated and redistributed uniformly to each bin which prevents noisy pixels from being enhanced by the Adaptive Histogram Equalization (AHE) process [6].

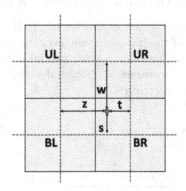

**Fig. 4.** Bi-linear interpolation process

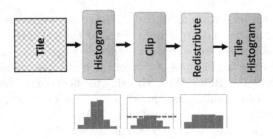

**Fig. 5.** Clipping, redistributing, and accumulating processes.

For each pixel value in the image, a cumulative distribution function (CDF) is generated using the cumulative sum of the redistributed histogram of each tile as below:

$$CDFt(p) = \sum_{n=0}^{p} \frac{h_t(n)}{z} \tag{1}$$

where $p$ pixel in tile $t$, $h_t$ is histogram of tile $t$, and $z$ is the size of the tile. After that, a bi-linear interpolation of each pixel $p$, $I_{new}(p)$, is determined by three other CDFs of pixels from adjacent tiles, as shown in (2) and demonstrated graphically in Fig 4. This interpolation process reduces the impact of any interfering effects that will be generated at the framed boundaries.

$$I_{new}(p) = \frac{s}{s+w}\left(\frac{t}{z+t}cdf_{UL}(p) + \frac{z}{z+t}cdf_{UR}(p)\right)$$
$$+ \frac{w}{s+w}\left(\frac{t}{z+t}cdf_{BL}(p) + \frac{z}{z+t}cdf_{BR}(p)\right) \tag{2}$$

### 3.3 Convolution with Derivatives of Gaussian Kernel

Convolution with the second-order derivative of 2D Gaussian kernel estimates the directional gradients of the image and involves the construction of a Hessian matrix, $H$, of the image. The second-order partial derivative of 2D Gaussian kernels in $x$-direction, $G_{xx}$, $xy$-direction, $G_{xy}$, and $y$-direction, $G_{yy}$, are described in Eqs. (3), (4) and (5) respectively.

$$\frac{\partial^2 G(x,y)}{\partial x^2} = \frac{1}{2\pi\sigma^4}\left[\frac{x^2}{\sigma^2} - 1\right]e^{-\frac{x^2+y^2}{2\sigma^2}} \tag{3}$$

$$\frac{\partial^2 G(x,y)}{\partial xy} = \frac{xy}{2\pi\sigma^6}e^{-\frac{x^2+y^2}{2\sigma^2}} \tag{4}$$

$$\frac{\partial^2 G(x,y)}{\partial y^2} = \frac{1}{2\pi\sigma^4}\left[\frac{y^2}{\sigma^2} - 1\right]e^{-\frac{x^2+y^2}{2\sigma^2}} \tag{5}$$

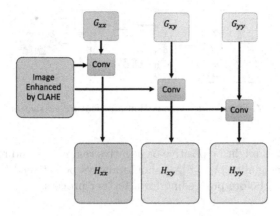

**Fig. 6.** Convolution with second-order derivatives of 2D Gaussian kernel

where $x$ and $y$ are integer values between $[-K, K]$, $K = 4\sigma + 1$ and $\sigma$ is a scaling constant which affects the size and intensity of the Gaussian kernel. Any order derivative of a Gaussian kernel is also separable. This can be computation efficient since separable $(N \times N)$ kernels can be decomposed into horizontal and vertical kernels of size $(N \times 1)$ and $(1 \times N)$ respectively.

### 3.4 Constructing the Hessian Matrix

$H$ is a square matrix which holds the directional second-order derivatives of an image, $I$, such as in Eq. (6). Each directional derivative of $I$ can be determined by the convolution with the directional derivatives of Gaussian kernel (Fig. 6).

$$H = \begin{bmatrix} H_{xx} & H_{xy} \\ H_{yx} & H_{yy} \end{bmatrix} \tag{6}$$

The second-order derivative of $I$ in the $x$-direction $H_{xx}$ is given as Eq. (8) where $H_{xx} = I * G_{xx}$, $H_{xy} = I * G_{xy}$ and $H_{yy} = I * G_{yy}$. The Hessian matrix is symmetric since $H_{xy}$ and $H_{yx}$ are equal.

### 3.5 Eigenvalues of Hessian Matrix

For a given pixel point $(x, y)$, the $H(x, y)$ is a $2 \times 2$ symmetric matrix which has two real eigenvalues. Therefore, determining eigenvalues at point $(x, y)$ can be simplified using linear algebra as the following:

$$H(x, y) = \begin{bmatrix} h_{xx} - \lambda & h_{xy} \\ h_{xy} & h_{yy} - \lambda \end{bmatrix} = 0 \tag{7}$$

where $\lambda = \frac{h_{xx} + h_{yy} \pm \sqrt{(h_{xx} - h_{yy})^2 - 4h_{xy}^2}}{2}$, and $H_{xx}(x, y)$, $H_{xy}(x, y)$, and $H_{yy}(x, y)$ are represented as $h_{xx}$, $h_{xy}$, and $h_{yy}$ respectively. From (7), it can be seen that

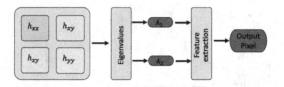

**Fig. 7.** Eigenvalues calculation and feature extraction

the two eigenvalues might be positive or negative real values and might be equal. Therefore, the inequality $|\lambda_2| \geq |\lambda_1|$ should always be satisfied for the purpose of this application before proceeding for a further process.

### 3.6    Feature Extraction or ROI Function

For images with darker features than the background, the edginess function, $F(x, y)$ in (8), is used to discriminate. It uses the eigenvalues of the corresponding Hessian matrix of a pixel (Fig. 7) to produces a value between [0,1], where values close to zeros are associated with the background and vice-versa. This gives,

$$
F(x,y) = \begin{cases} (e^{-\frac{R_B^2}{2\beta^2}})(1 - e^{-\frac{S^2}{2c^2}}) & \lambda_2 > 0 \\ \\ 0 & otherwise \end{cases}
\tag{8}
$$

where $R_B = \lambda_2/\lambda_1$, $S = \sqrt{\lambda_2^2 + \lambda_1^2}$, $\beta = 0.5$, and $c = 15$ are used. We only implemented the traditional Hessian multi-scale filtering in [2] since the improved Hessian multi-scale enhancement filter requires calculations that involve all pixels of the image which impact the overall throughput and memory usage.

## 4    FPGA-Based Image Processing System Architecture

The AMD-Xilinx's Kria KV260 AI board and associated Vitis HLS 2021.2 toolset was used for initial implementation and design exploration. To optimise the image processing implementation, the data flow (DF) optimization was employed as it leads to solutions with lower memory usage and is applied by adding the DATAFLOW pragma in HLS. This ensures flawless data transfer from one function to the other and will support seamless integration of future, real-time functionality, as yet undefined.

Each processing step inside the system has to be linked to the next and/or previous processing step by internal streaming interfaces which will act as FIFO channels after C-synthesis. When using FIFOs, it is important to avoid deadlock, which can occur when depth is not specified correctly. A baseline system architecture was therefore established to allow stable system functionality and

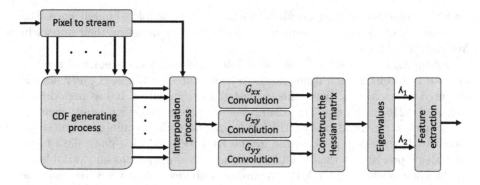

**Fig. 8.** Proposed FPGA-based image processing system architecture

then used as a reference design to evaluate the effectiveness of the applied optimisation techniques.

The baseline image processing system architecture (Fig. 8) comprises cascading processing elements (PEs) connected by streaming interfaces. The CLAHE is organised into the CDF generating processes, comprising large look-up tables (LUTs) which is connected to interpolating processes. The convolution process is applied as one PE, but it has small internal FIFO channels which help the separable convolution and border replication loops to be in-line when specifying the INLINE pragma in the DF optimisation flow. Finally, the Hessian matrix, determination and sorting of the eigenvalues, and the feature extraction functions, are combined into one PE, and termed the feature extraction process.

### 4.1    Experimental Setup

Vitis HLS 2021.2 is used for resource estimation and exporting RTL designs of the IP core while for place and route, we used Vivado 2021.2. For on-chip power, we used linux command "platformstats" and "timeit" package for timing analysis. The target FPGA platform is the Kria KV260 AI board (XCK26-SFVC784-2LV-C). For CPU/GPU evaluation, we used the Jetson Nano development kit which has a 1.43 GHz Quad-core ARM A57 as the CPU and 128-core Maxwell as the GPU. We chose to operate on 5W mode, and we used OpenCV/OpenCV-Cuda 4.1.1 implementations realised using Python on Jupyter notebook. For power analysis, we used "jetson-stats" package while for time analysis, we used "timeit" package. Both are imported as Python code to measure the performance for OpenCV implementations.

## 5    Evaluation

This section provides details of the baseline design and changes in resource utilisation and throughput after system- and algorithmic-level optimisations are applied. These are critical to ensure that sufficient FPGA real estate is available for future improved image analysis functionality and possible AI intelligence. The performance of the optimisations were investigated by assessing their impact in Matlab (Sect. 5.3).

As the CMOS sensor will be 240 × 240 pixels and the system will need to operate at 100 FPS, each frame needs to be executed in 10 ms. If every pixel is executed for each clock cycle, this suggested a design with a 160 ns period time will need 9.216 ms for one 240 × 240 frame to satisfy the design requirements.

Loops are pipelined using PIPELINE pragma with the minimum initiation interval (II) to satisfy period time by the HLS tool. Floating-point data types with single precision is the default for mathematical operations and variables in the baseline design. For CLAHE, the image is divided into a 8 × 8 tile grid size, giving 64 independent regions. For the convolutions, we specify $\sigma$ to be 2 which gives a (19 × 19) filter size, based on Sect. 3.3.

## 5.1   Baseline Design

The main hardware units in the FPGA are comprised of: a dedicated processing DSP48 (DSP) blocks including a 25-bit x 18-bit multiplier, a 48-bit adder and a 48-bit accumulator; a block RAM (BRAM) unit with 36 Kbits of data, configured as either two independent 18 Kb RAMs, or one 36 Kb RAM; a single bit flip-flip (FF) unit with pre-set/pre-clear functionality and; a 5-bit Lookup Table (LUT) which can be configured as logic, memory, or a shift register.

The baseline design of Fig. 8 was coded into three main functions, namely the CLAHE, convolution and the feature extraction processes. FIFOs were implemented as different dataflow objects. The resource breakdown resulted from the synthesis is given in Table 1.

**Table 1.** Utilization estimates of baseline design on the Kria KV260 SOM involving a Zynq UltraScale+ (% of the resource is listed)

| Process | BRAM | DSP | FF | LUT |
|---|---|---|---|---|
| FIFO | 12 (4.2%) | 0 (0.0%) | 2836 (1.2%) | 2695 (2.3%) |
| CLAHE | 26 (9.0%) | 76 (6.1%) | 6179 (2.6%) | 26689 (22.8%) |
| Convolutions | 57 (19.8%) | 565 (45.3%) | 10209 (4.4%) | 40141 (34.3%) |
| Feature ext, | 0 (0.0%) | 58 (4.6%) | 1043 (0.4%) | 5811 (5.0%) |
| Total | 95 (32.0%) | 699 (56.0%) | 20267 (8.7%) | 75336 (64.3%) |

The convolution process has the highest resource allocation as a lot of processing is required. It uses the majority of DSP blocks and in addition, a large amount of BRAMs in order to implement the buffers used for the FIFOs and the efficient separable convolution processes. FIFOs consume almost 4.2% of BRAMs since a large depth is specified to avoid deadlock issues which can cause FIFOs with a small depth size between these loops and functions to be filled and thus blocking writing or reading to the FIFOs.

## 5.2   Convolution Optimisations

In this section, optimisations were identified at the system level and algorithmic level with the aim of reducing the FPGA resources. At algorithmic level, we focused around exploiting common coefficients to employ common factor optimisation (CFO) to reduce the computational complexity [1,9] and also change the order of the computation (re-ordering).

**Hardware Sharing:** With flip-flops readily available in both the programmable logic and DSP48 blocks, pipelining can be used to increase the speed beyond that required and folding then applied to reduce the resources usage. This optimisation is available within the Vitis tools and was employed in the convolution function by applying feature II of pipelined loops. The unroll function produces multiple copies of the same function which are then folded onto one PE, leading to a reduction in the resources. This reduces the number of DSPs to 15%, FFs to 6%, and LUTs to 38% of the baseline design. However it also results in a reduction in the clock rate well below the desired value, in this case 27 MHz.

**Common Factor Optimisation:** The Hessian matrix requires the computation of three second-order directional derivatives of enhanced image (Fig. 9) requiring $3N$ multiplications and $3(N-1)$ additions and associated row buffers. The coefficients of $(N \times N)$ Gaussian kernels are determined by Eqs. (3), (4) and (5) and can be decomposed into $(1 \times N)$ horizontal and $(N \times 1)$ vertical kernels. These coefficients will be fixed for the convolution process. If we expand the horizontal convolution expression in X direction, then for $N$ is 19, this gives,

$$h_{xxh}x_n = h_{xxh1}x_1 + h_{xxh2}x_2 + h_{xxh3}x_3 + h_{xxh4}x_4 + h_{xxh5}x_5 + h_{xxh6}x_6$$
$$+ h_{xxh7}x_7 + h_{xxh8}x_8 + h_{xxh9}x_9 + h_{xxh10}x_{10} + h_{xxh9}vx_{11} + h_{xxh8}x_{12} + h_{xxh7}x_{13}$$
$$+ h_{xxh6}x_{14} + h_{xxh5}x_{15} + h_{xxh4}x_{16} + h_{xxh3}x_{17} + h_{xxh2}x_{18} + h_{xxh1}x_{19}$$
$$(9)$$

This will require 19 multiplications and 18 additions. However, we can exploit the separability and symmetrical proprieties of Gaussian kernels and eliminate zero values. For the specific $xx$ direction, $h_{xxh6} = h_{xxh7}$ and $h_{xxh8} = 0$. Exploiting this and exploiting the symmetry in Eq. (9), we can reorganise this specific computation into Eq. (10) as follows:

$$h_{xxh}x_n = h_{xxh1}(x_1 + x_{19}) + h_{xxh2}(x_2 + x_{18}) + h_{xxh3}(x_3 + x_{17})$$
$$+ h_{xxh4}(x_4 + x_{16}) + h_{xxh5}(x_5 + x_{15}) + h_{xxh6}(x_6 + x_{14} + x_7 + x_{13})$$
$$+ h_{xxh9}(x_9 + x_{11}) + h_{xxh10}x_{10}$$
$$(10)$$

This optimisation reduces the computation by 50% as only eight multiplications and sixteen additions are needed. When this is applied to the other horizontal and vertical directional convolutions, $h_{xy}$ and $h_{yy}$, it reduces the number of DSPs by 50% compared to baseline process in Table 2 while still providing a throughput of 114 FPS. The figures for this revised implementation are listed as **CFO** in Table 2.

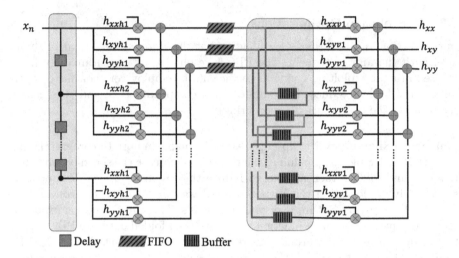

**Fig. 9.** Baseline separable convolution design for three different kernels combined

**Re-ordering:** The separable 2D convolutions can be decomposed into a horizontal followed by a vertical 1D-convolution each involving $N$ multiplications and $N - 1$ additions. The baseline design computes the horizontal followed by the vertical 1D-convolution, requiring the intermediate storage of $(3(N - 1))$ buffers of length equal to an image row (Fig. 9), corresponding to $(N - 1)$ buffers for each of the three different intermediate results produced by the horizontal convolutions. However, if we reverse the order of operation such that we start with vertical convolution, this will require only $(N - 1)$ buffers since enhanced pixels coming from CLAHE process are shared between the different directional derivatives (Fig. 10). For $(19 \times 19)$ kernels, the number of BRAMs are reduced from 54 to 18 which more than 60% saving in convolution process. This **Reorder** design provides a 40% overall reduction in the baseline design in Table 2.

## 5.3    Combined Designs

In this section, we explore more about combined optimisations that would eventually build efficient designs that achieve high performance with minimal resource usage.

**Combined:** A more efficient design can be achieved by combining a number of these algorithmic optimisations. We first apply the **Re-order** optimisation to save in BRAMs usage and then the **CFO** option to reduce the complexity of the convolution function. This provides an additional saving in DSPs usage. The combined design (shown as **Combined** in Table. 2) achieved a 114 FPS which fulfils the design requirement of 100 FPS and with a lower BRAMs and DSPs resource usage. However, we expect a higher throughput after hardware implementation due to high-level optimisations by the Vivado tool.

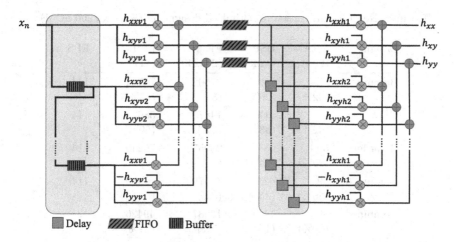

**Fig. 10.** Re-ordered separable convolution implementation for three kernels

**Combined$^+$:** Another obvious optimisation is to trade-off wordlength against resolution due to the small size of the original image. It is clear that a floating-point representation is unnecessarily large for circuit parts of the processing chain. For this reason, we changed the data type for the **Combined** design from 32-bit floating-point to 18-bit fixed-point arithmetic in the convolution only. This is organised into a 10-bit integer with the remaining 8 bits used for the fractional part.

Sufficient performance quality or quality of results (QoR) was ensured by assessing experimentally the visual impact and also measuring the structural similarity index measure (SSIM) and image quality degradation by peak signal-to-noise ratio (PSNR). Our results indicate that the 18-bit fixed-point representation scored on average 0.985 SSIM index and 40dB PSNR value compared to 32-bit floating-point results. The resource utilization labelled as **Combined$^+$** is presented in Table 2 with the biggest saving is in DSP units where the 5 DSPs of the floating-point can be reduced to a single DSP for the 18-bit fixed-point representation. There is also been a small reduction in the number of flip-flops and LUTs needed. As expected, there has only been a minimal change in throughput, 121 FPS, due the consistent use of pipelining.

### 5.4   Implementation Comparison

It is worth considering the performance issues when compared to a GPU implementation. For this reason, the same design was implemented on GPU and initial results generated and compared to the best FPGA realisation. In the GPU realisation, all optimisations were applied to ensure a high quality design. For example, conditional statements used for sorting eigenvalues and in feature extraction function had to be implemented solely using OpenCV-Cuda commands as it does not have ready-to-use functions for this. This allowed the GPU implementation to have a very fast execution compared to CPU.

**Table 2.** Resource utilization of optimized designs on (Kria KV260 SOM)

| Design | BRAM (288) | DSP (1248) | FF (234240) | LUT (117120) | FPS |
|---|---|---|---|---|---|
| Baseline | 95 (32%) | 699 (56%) | 20507 (8%) | 76704 (65%) | 114 |
| CFO | 95 (32%) | 417 (33%) | 14879 (6%) | 58623 (50%) | 114 |
| Re-order | 59 (20%) | 684 (54%) | 25055 (10%) | 76240 (65%) | 114 |
| Combined | 59 (20%) | 422 (33%) | 19479 (8%) | 59480 (50%) | 114 |
| Combined$^+$ | 59 (20%) | 142 (11%) | 13687 (5%) | 49426 (42%) | 121 |

The resulting performance figures are shown in Table 3. As expected, the GPU outperforms the CPU. However, the optimisation implemented in mapping the design to FPGA has resulted in higher throughput when compared to the GPU. The solid FPGA performance is largely achieved due to small image size. The smaller size has resulted in an effective utilisation of the on-board FPGA resources and avoided having to undertake off-chip memory accesses which would compromised the performance. Use of the efficient design allows a throughput rate that is nearly 1.4× as fast as the GPU. The lower power performance of the FPGA device comes to the fore, but the overall System-on-Module (SoM) power consumption results in comparable GPU FPS/W figure. This would be much better if we use the single FPGA figure.

**Table 3.** Throughput and power comparison

| | Image size | Jetson nano developer kit | | Kria vision AI starter kit | |
|---|---|---|---|---|---|
| | | ARM A57 (CPU) | Maxwell (GPU) | Zynq UltraScale+MPSoC (FPGA) | |
| | | | | Baseline | Combined$^+$ |
| Time (ms) | 240 × 240 | 20.50 | 12.10 | 8.73 | 8.26 |
| FPS | 240 × 240 | 48.85 | 82.41 | 114.4 | 121 |
| FPS/W | 240 × 240 | 17.0 | 29.42 | 30.59 | 33.15 |

# 6   Conclusions

The paper presents details of an FPGA implementation of an intelligent surgical imaging system based on a 'chip on tip' camera system. The key challenge is to be able to implement a low power embedded processing unit to be able to enhance the image quality and in the future, provide increased intelligence.

Results were presented on the implementation of the contrast limited adaptive histogram equalization to suppress the contrast of each pixel based on its neighbouring values, convolution procedures using the derivatives of Gaussian and the construction of the Hessian matrix of each pixel with the eigenvalues used by a ROI function. We are able to demonstrate savings in DSP processor resources by up to 80% without a non-discernible loss in image quality. The work to date has been important in ensuring that available FPGA real estate is created so that the user can incorporate future functionality. Future work is targeted at providing much more intelligence into the embedded system which will provide detection capability for the surgeon. This will focus around building up a knowledge of existing operations and providing embedded training on the device.

# References

1. Bailey, D.G.: Design for Embedded Image Processing on FPGAs. Wiley, Hoboken (2011)
2. Elbalaoui, A., Fakir, M., Taifi, K., Merbouha, A.: Automatic detection of blood vessel in retinal images. In: 2016 13th International Conference on Computer Graphics, Imaging and Visualization (CGiV), pp. 324–332 (2016). https://doi.org/10.1109/CGiV.2016.69
3. Honda, K., Wei, K., Arai, M., Amano, H.: CLAHE implementation and evaluation on a low-end FPGA board by high-level synthesis. IEICE Trans. Inf. Syst. **E104D**(12), 2048–2056 (2021). https://doi.org/10.1587/transinf.2021PAP0006. Publisher Copyright: Copyright 2021 The Institute of Electronics, Information and Communication Engineers
4. Liu, X., Li, L.: FPGA-based three-dimensional endoscope system using a single CCD camera. In: 2015 IEEE International Conference on Information and Automation, pp. 614–618 (2015). https://doi.org/10.1109/ICInfA.2015.7279360
5. Pizer, S., Johnston, R., Ericksen, J., Yankaskas, B., Muller, K.: Contrast-limited adaptive histogram equalization: speed and effectiveness. In: 1990 Proceedings of the First Conference on Visualization in Biomedical Computing, pp. 337–345 (1990). https://doi.org/10.1109/VBC.1990.109340
6. Pizer, S.M., et al.: Adaptive histogram equalization and its variations. Comput. Vis. Graph. Image Process. **39**(3), 355–368 (1987)
7. Taghizadegan, A., Piltan, F., Sulaiman, N.B.: Design high frequency surgical robot controller: design FPGA-based controller for surgical robot manipulator simscape modeling. Int. J. Hybrid Inf. Technol. **9**(5), 431–474 (2016)
8. Wäny, M., Voltz, S., Gaspar, F., Chen, L., Tecnopolo, A.L.M.: Ultrasmall digital image sensor for endoscopic applications. In: Proceedings of International Image Sensor Workshop, pp. 1–3 (2009)
9. Woods, R., McAllister, J., Lightbody, G., Yi, Y.: FPGA-Based Implementation of Signal Processing Systems. Wiley, Hoboken (2008)

# Hardware-Aware Optimizations for Deep Learning Inference on Edge Devices

Markus Rognlien, Zhiqiang Que(ID), Jose G. F. Coutinho$^{(\boxtimes)}$(ID), and Wayne Luk

Department of Computing, Imperial College London, 180 Queen's Gate, London, UK
jgfc@imperial.ac.uk

**Abstract.** AI solutions, such as Deep Learning (DL), are becoming increasingly prevalent in edge devices. Many of these applications require low latency processing of large amounts of data within a tight power budget. In this context, reconfigurable embedded devices make a compelling option. Deploying DL models to reconfigurable devices does, however, present considerable challenges. One key issue is reconciling the often large compute requirements of DL models with the limited available resources on edge devices. In this paper, we present a hardware-aware optimization strategy for deploying DL neural networks to FPGAs, which automatically identifies hardware configurations that maximize resource utilization for a given level of computation throughput. We demonstrate our optimization approach on a sample neural network containing a combination of convolutional and fully connected layers, running on a sample FPGA target device, achieving a factor of 3.5 reduction in DSP block usage without affecting throughput when using *performance* mode. When using the *compact* mode, a factor of 7.4 reduction in DSP block usage is achieved, at the cost of 1.8 times decrease in throughput. Our approach works completely automatically without the need for human intervention or domain knowledge.

**Keywords:** Field-programmable gate array · High-level synthesis · Meta-programming · Particle physics

## 1 Introduction

While traditionally reserved for compute-intensive cloud based applications, breakthroughs in hardware capabilities and efficient algorithms have led to AI solutions, such as Deep Learning (DL), becoming increasingly ubiquitous in lightweight edge devices. The clear utility of moving the implementation of DL inference as close as possible to the data source and end user has already been demonstrated with applications like wearable technology, manufacturing and agriculture, highlighting the beginnings of a significant paradigm shift (Bierzynski et al. 2021).

FPGAs make a compelling option for deploying DL models to edge devices due to their extreme parallelization capabilities as well as excellent power efficiency. However, the combination of increasingly high compute demands of modern DL models and the inherently restricted hardware resources of reconfigurable

© The Author(s), under exclusive license to Springer Nature Switzerland AG 2022
L. Gan et al. (Eds.): ARC 2022, LNCS 13569, pp. 118–133, 2022.
https://doi.org/10.1007/978-3-031-19983-7_9

edge devices presents a clear challenge. If the model that one is attempting to realize in a designated reconfigurable device requires compute resources exceeding the amount available, one is left with three main options:

1. The size, and thereby computing cost, of the model can be compressed with both pruning and quantization (Duarte et al. 2018), which requires expertise and effort to prevent degrading the inference performance and accuracy;
2. The targeted device can be replaced by another device with a larger hardware budget, which leads to additional monetary cost and possibly increase in power consumption;
3. The synthesized design can be configured to share (reuse) hardware resources within each DL layer. The use of such a "reuse factor", $n$, for a given design, would allow for a roughly $n$-fold reduction in DSP block usage, but accompanied by a corresponding increase in the initiation interval (II) of the realized design (Duarte et al. 2018). In other words, with this method, resource utilisation is decreased while maintaining the original accuracy, however computation throughput would be reduced by roughly a factor of $n$.

While using a single universal reuse factor across all layers of a DL neural network would result in the aforementioned throughput penalty, previous works (Que et al. 2021) have demonstrated that reuse factors for each layer of a neural network can be set independently. More specifically, this work demonstrates that the careful selection of layer-wise reuse factors can be performed in order to balance the IIs of each layer of the deployed model, thereby potentially reducing the hardware requirements of the design considerably without any changes to its throughput.

Previous efforts to balance IIs using reuse factors relied on the time and attention of human programmers with domain knowledge. This work aims to entirely automate this balancing process. To the best of our knowledge, this is the first work that automatically determines a balancing configuration of reuse factors for a neural network model with heterogeneous layers on FPGAs. Our method will help accelerate the deployment of DL models in edge devices, enabling more efficient usage of limited hardware resources. In particular, this work provides the following key contributions:

**C1.** An approach that automatically balances the IIs of each computation stage by iteratively modifying their individual sharing levels to reduce resource utilisation while minimising performance degradation (Sect. 3);
**C2.** The implementation of our approach using the Artisan Metaprogramming Framework (Vandebon et al. 2021), HLS4ML (Fahim et al. 2021) and Xilinx Vivado HLS (Sect. 3.1);
**C3.** An evaluation of our approach under different settings for a sample neural network (Sect. 4).

## 2    Background

### 2.1    Neural Networks

Out of all methods falling under the large umbrella of Artificial Intelligence and Machine Learning, none have been nearly as influential and widely employed as the neural network, often called Deep Learning (DL). Though recent break-throughs in the domain of DL have utilized more advanced techniques to achieve impressive results, the basic mechanisms forming the foundation of neural networks are simple. The vast majority of neural networks can be divided into *layers* (see Fig. 5), which transform one vector representation of a data sample, known as tensors, into another (possibly of different dimensions). Mathematically, these layers can be generally formalized as affine transformations (a tensor multiplication and an addition) followed by pointwise non-linearity. Simply having a sufficient number of appropriately large layers provide neural networks with the ability to approximate *any* function (Hornik et al. 1989), making them conceptually simple, yet powerful function approximators.

*Fully connected* (alternatively *linear* or *dense*) layers denote layers where every element in the output tensor is dependent on every element in the input tensor. *Convolutional* layers, on the other hand, found in Convolutional Neural Networks (CNNs) greatly save on memory and computation costs by allowing each element in the output tensor to only be affected by a local neighborhood of elements in the input tensor and by reusing the *weights* by which these parameters interact for the computation of each element.

From a computational standpoint, this layer-wise view of neural networks allows us to treat them like computations consisting of stages which have to be performed sequentially, but which internally are highly parallelizable.

### 2.2    Deep Learning on Edge Devices

Because of their typically resource-demanding nature, DL applications have traditionally been considered as confined to dedicated hardware accelerators in central cloud systems. Continued innovation in the capabilities of lightweight devices along with strategies for compressing and improving the efficiency of DL models have challenged this notion, expanding the frontier of AI applications to the edge. The prospect of enabling real-time AI inference of collected data, without the need for constant communication with a central server present obvious benefits in applications ranging form wearable health devices to autonomous vehicles.

A central challenge when deploying DL models to edge devices is ensuring sufficient compute capabilities, particularly with respect to parallelization, in order to achieve acceptable responsiveness. Another challenge is power efficiency, as both battery life and thermal considerations typically weigh heavily in their design specifications. Hence, reconfigurable devices, such as FPGAs, lend themselves particularly well to addressing these challenges, making them an exciting tool in the deployment of AI at the edge (Bierzynski et al. 2021).

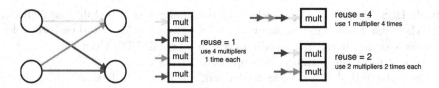

**Fig. 1.** (Source: https://fastmachinelearning.org/hls4ml/_images/reuse_factor_paper_fig_8.png) The figure shows how increasing the reuse factor of a computation can reduce the amount of hardware required at the cost of increased processing time.

## 2.3 Parallelization Optimizations Using HLS

There are many previous studies focusing on parallelization optimizations using HLS (High-Level Synthesis) tools. MPSeeker (Zhong et al. 2017), a rapid performance/area estimation framework, is proposed to explore various fine-grained and coarse-grainded parallelism options for FPGA-based accelerators at an early design stage without invoking HLS tools. The work in (Li et al. 2015) proposes resource-aware throughput optimization using HLS for multi-loops. The work (Oppermann et al. 2019) presents SkyCastle, a resource-aware multi-loop scheduler, for HLS-based kernels composed of multiple, nested loops.

*Reuse factors* (Duarte et al. 2018) can be used to control the number of times each computational unit should be reused in a given stage of the program, as shown in Fig. 1. For the neural network used in this work, each of the 6 layers has its own independent reuse factor which represents the number of time a multiplier is used in the computation. In the case where all reuse factors are set to 1, every single multiplication that needs to be performed over the course of the program translates to a single multiplier unit on the FPGA. In the case where the reuse factors are set to $R$, each multiplier unit performs $R$ multiplications per run of the program, and only $\frac{1}{R}$ of multipliers are needed with an increased IIs. By adjusting the reuse factors of individual layers, it is possible to approximately balance the IIs of the layers, resulting in equivalent throughput at potentially much lower resource costs or a higher throughput with similar resource costs (Que et al. 2021).

## 3   Approach

### 3.1   Design Flow

Figure 2 illustrates our design-flow, which automatically translates a Deep Learning Neural Network Architecture to an optimized RTL design, which we explain next.

First, we employ the HLS4ML tool (Fahim et al. 2021) to convert the Tensorflow model to the corresponding C++ code, using 16-bit fixed point precision for both weights and activations, which can be synthesized to hardware using Xilinx

Vivado HLS. The initial C++ code version is configured to be fully parallelized, with the reuse factor for each layer set to one. Because this initial code disables resource sharing, it can potentially overmap on small FPGA devices, and thus can benefit from our optimisation approach.

Once the initial C++ code is derived, we start the feedback loop cycle and generate different C++ versions based on the original version, where we experiment with different reuse factors for each layer. We use the Artisan meta-programming framework (Vandebon et al. 2021) to manage different C++ versions, including cloning the original version, setting reuse factors based on the optimization algorithm (see Sect. 3.2), running the Vivado HLS tool on the cloned version, and interpreting the corresponding HLS reports.

The optimization algorithm is heuristic-based and iterative, keeping track of the designs that offer the best trade-off (Pareto points), while discarding all other versions. The optimization algorithm operates using two modes: *performance mode* and *compact mode*, which govern how aggressive the algorithm is with reducing the hardware resource requirements. The performance mode attempts to reduce space while preserving close to original performance, while compact mode can offer substantial savings but at a greater hit in performance. The optimization algorithm also allows to control the maximum number of iterations, which corresponds to how exhaustive the algorithm should operate in cases where it does not converge earlier.

Once the algorithm terminates, it outputs the RTL design with the optimized reuse factors for each layer. The Verilog code can be further processed to generate the bitstream to configure the FPGA device.

### 3.2   Optimization Algorithm

This section provides a high-level overview of how the proposed method balances IIs using reuse factors. The basic idea of the algorithm centers on maintaining piecewise linear estimates of how the IIs of the individual layers vary with their reuse factors. The method iteratively selects the most balanced configuration of reuse factors, according to these estimates, to simulate, and uses the result of this simulation to further refine its estimates. Below follows a high-level step-by-step overview of the main stages of the algorithm (see Algorithm 1).

1. A design using a reuse factor of 1 for all layers is synthesized, followed by a design using a user-specified reuse factor, $\lambda$, for all layers. The layer with the highest increase in II between these two syntheses is designated as the *anchor* layer. (Lines 1–4).
2. For a fixed anchor reuse factor (initially 1), linear interpolation is used to estimate the anchor's II at this reuse factor. This II becomes the *target* for this part of the balancing process, shown as a red line in Fig. 3. (Line 8)
3. For each other layer, the reuse factor which results in an II closest to the target based on linear interpolation is selected. This is illustrated by the dashed blue line in Fig. 3. (Lines 9–16)

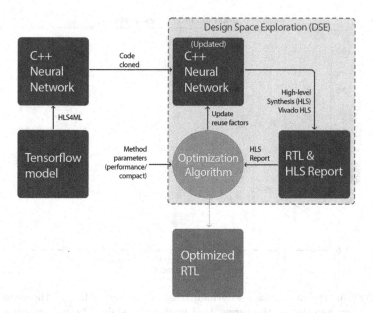

**Fig. 2.** The diagram illustrates the design-flow and the main feedback loop proposed in this project.

4. An error metric is then calculated as the negative sum of relative deviations from the highest estimated II. This metric is an estimate of the amount of "wasted resources" due to II bottlenecking and is shaded red in Fig. 4.
5. Steps 2–4 are repeated for every anchor reuse factor up to a user-defined maximum, M. As evident from line 7 of Algorithm 1, increasing this parameter expands the search space of our method, enabling more aggressive increases in reuse factors, leading to more hardware efficient designs at the cost of reduced throughput.
6. The configuration of reuse factors which has the minimal estimated error, as defined in step 4, is synthesized, reporting IIs for all layers. These values are used to refine the II estimators for the method's next iterations. (Lines 18, 22, 26)
7. Steps 2–6 are repeated until one of three things happen (Lines 19, 23, 28):
   (a) The configuration suggested for synthesis has been suggested before;
   (b) The set of IIs reported by the synthesis have been reported before;
   (c) The method runs for a user-specified maximum number of iterations.

Note that in addition to the specification of the M-parameter, dictating whether the method runs in performance (when M = 1) or compact mode (when M ≥ 2), this algorithm relies on two user inputs which can affect the quality of the solution: $\lambda$ and the maximum number of iterations. The $\lambda$ parameter defines the range over which initial estimates for II gradients will be computed, and should be of the same order of magnitude as the expected optimal reuse factors. A value of $\lambda = 10$ is used in this work for this reason. The maximum number of

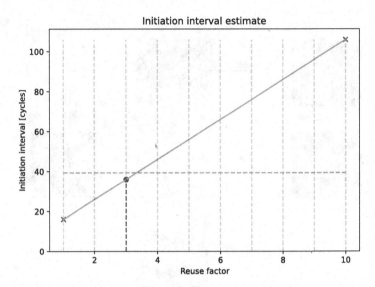

**Fig. 3.** An illustration of how an optimal reuse factor (according to the estimate) is selected to get as close to the target (red line) as possible. The red crosses indicate previous synthesis data for this layer and the solid blue line represents the model's estimates of IIs for all reuse factors. The dotted blue line indicates the integer reuse factor, in this case 3, which maps to the II closest to the target. (Color figure online)

iterators places an upper bound on the computation time of the algorithm, but might cause the algorithm to terminate before convergence has occurred. We used a value of 10 for this parameter, but the iteration limit was never invoked during any of our evaluation.

## 4    Evaluation

### 4.1    Experimental Setup

In order to evaluate the performance of our method, we employ a neural network designed to be deployed across numerous edge devices in the processing pipeline of the Large Hadron Collider. This particular network, shown in Fig. 5, classifies fundamental particles based on their jet substructure, and contains a combination of convolutional and fully connected layers of various sizes, allowing us to evaluate our method's performance in a heterogeneous environment. The network was specified and trained on the same dataset (training (60%), validation (20%), and testing (20%)) as (Duarte et al. 2018) using Tensorflow 2.91, and converted to a C++ DL kernel using HLS4ML 0.6.0. This work splits the whole model into several layers and utilizes a layer-wise hardware architecture (Duarte et al. 2018; Tridgell et al. 2019; Nakahara, 2020) which maps all the layers on-chip. It is flexible and able to take full advantage of the customizability of FPGAs. In addition, the design implements a coarse-grained pipeline to further increase the design throughput.

**Algorithm 1.** Balancing Optimization Algorithm

---

**Input:**

    $k$                                                      ▷ C++ DL kernel with $N$ layers

    $M$                     ▷ resource efficiency level (high = more efficient)

    $\lambda$                                                 ▷ initiation parameter

    *max_iterations*                 ▷ maximum number of iterations

**Output:**

    $C$                  ▷ optimized reuse factors for each layer $[r_1, r_2, ..., r_N]$

1:  $D \leftarrow \emptyset$
2:  $D \leftarrow D \cup$ hls_synth$(k, [1, 1, 1..., 1])$
3:  $D \leftarrow D \cup$ hls_synth$(k, [\lambda, \lambda, \lambda, ..., \lambda])$
4:  $anchor \leftarrow$ **argmax**$\{D[i, \lambda] - D[i, 1],\ i \in 1..N\}$
5:  $iter \leftarrow 0$
6:  **repeat**
7:     **for** $m \leftarrow 1..M$ **do**
8:         $ii_{target} \leftarrow$ ln_interpolation$(D[anchor, :], m)$
9:         **for** $layer \leftarrow 1..N$ **do**
10:             **if** $layer \neq anchor$ **then**
11:                 $E[m,\ layer] \leftarrow$ **argmin**$\{$
                         $|ii_{target} -$ ln_interpolation$(D[layer, :], r)|,$
                         $r \in \mathbf{N}$
12:                 $\}$
13:             **else**
14:                 $E[m,\ layer] \leftarrow m$
15:             **end if**
16:         **end for**
17:     **end for**
18:     $C \leftarrow$ **argmin**$\{$error_estimate$(E[m, :]), m \in 1..M\}$
19:     **if** previously_synthed$(C)$ **then**
20:         **return** $C$
21:     **end if**
22:     $result \leftarrow$ hls_synth$(k, C)$
23:     **if** $result \in D$ **then**
24:         **return** C
25:     **end if**
26:     $D \leftarrow D \cup result$
27:     $iter \leftarrow iter + 1$
28: **until** $iter == max\_iterations$
29: **return** $C$

---

This project was then synthesized, with reuse factors for all layers set to 1, forming an unoptimized baseline for later comparison. Our method was then applied, utilizing Artisan 1.0.7 and Vivado HLS 2019.2 to produce optimized designs for two different parameter settings: *performance* and *compact*, respectively. As previously mentioned, the performance mode ($M = 1$) aims to reduce the hardware resource requirements with only zero to minor reductions in throughput, while the compact mode ($M \geq 2$), works more aggressively to

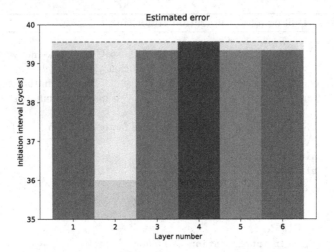

**Fig. 4.** An illustration of how the estimated error for a given configuration of reuse factors is computed. The IIs corresponding to the reuse factors are estimated from interpolation, and the un-normalized error is then found by computing the negative deviations from the highest of these II estimates, shown here as the area shaded light red. The y-axis has been truncated to highlight this process. (Color figure online)

reduce DSP block usage at the expense of performance. The second synthesis parameter, $\lambda$ was set to 10 for both runs. We evaluate both settings in the following subsections.

### 4.2   Performance Mode

By setting the M-parameter of the optimization algorithm to 1, the search space of valid reuse factor configurations is restricted to the set for which the lowest reuse factor of any layer is 1. This ensures that the total II of the full network does not drastically increase, if at all.

After synthesizing the two cases of all reuse factors being 1 and all being 10, the method converges after two iterations of the algorithm in performance mode. The initial synthesis where all reuse factors are 1 as well as the two configurations suggested by the algorithm are shown in Fig. 6. The synthesis where all reuse factors were set to 10 is excluded from this and similar plots, as adjusting the scale of the y-axis to fit the results of this simulation would make it difficult to discern differences in the remaining groups of bars.

The proposed method came very close to finding the optimal configuration with its first suggestion, setting every reuse factor to its optimal value apart from that of layer 5. Examining why this happened highlights a key aspect of how the algorithm works. Looking at Fig. 7, we can see the algorithm's estimate of how the II of layer 5 varies with respect to its reuse factor both before and after synthesizing its first suggestion. The algorithm under-estimates the II of layer

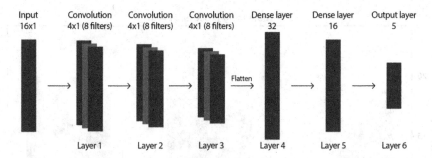

| Input 16x1 | Convolution 4x1 (8 filters) | Convolution 4x1 (8 filters) | Convolution 4x1 (8 filters) | Dense layer 32 | Dense layer 16 | Output layer 5 |

**Fig. 5.** An overview of the structure of the neural network optimized and synthesized for an FPGA to evaluate our approach. The network consists of 6 total layers, 3 1D-convolutions followed by 3 linear layers of shrinking size. The activation function following the first five layers is ReLU, and since the network aims to solve a classification problem, the output activation function used is SoftMax.

5, but uses the information it gains from the penultimate synthesis to arrive at the optimal reuse factor.

## 4.3   Compact Mode

If the balanced solution obtained with *performance* mode does not fit the target device and a decrease in throughput can be tolerated, the value of M can be increased ($M \geq 2$) to enable the *compact* mode which explores configurations with larger reuse factors.

For instance, setting M to 2 expands the search space to configurations where the smallest reuse factor of any layer is no larger than 2. In this case, the algorithm makes a total of 5 suggestions before converging. These suggestions, in addition to the initial synthesis of all reuse factors set to 1, can be seen in Fig. 8.

While the algorithm using the *performance* mode terminates due to the algorithm suggesting a configuration of reuse factors which has been previously suggested and synthesized, the *compact* mode terminates because two consecutive syntheses yield identical IIs for all layers. This early stopping criterion was implemented in order to prevent fruitless gradual decrements of a single reuse factor when the algorithm believes it is close to an optimal solution, when in reality it already has one. Figure 9 illustrates how the II of layer 6 varies with its reuse factor. Were it not for this early stopping criterion, the algorithm would continue performing these marginally tweaked and expensive syntheses until a major drop to an II of 24 cycles would occur at a reuse factor of 40, proving that an II of 35 was indeed the best II in this particular instance.

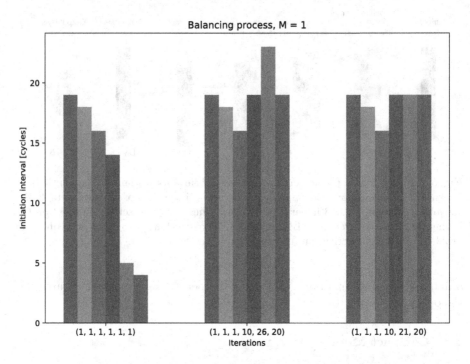

**Fig. 6.** An overview of the configurations of reuse factors suggested by the *performance* mode algorithm along with the base case of all reuse factors set to 1. Each of the three groups of 6 bars represent a single synthesis. The heights of the bars correspond each layer's II using the configuration of reuse factors in brackets below each group of bars.

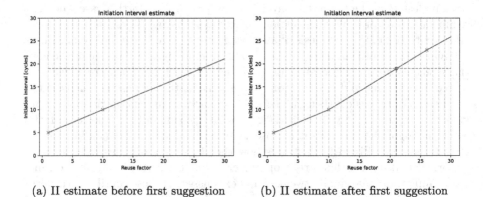

(a) II estimate before first suggestion        (b) II estimate after first suggestion

**Fig. 7.** These figures illustrate how the model uses information from simulations to improve its estimates and give better suggestions. The first plot shows how the model estimates the relationship between the II and reuse factor of layer 5 based on the two initial simulations. The model under-estimates the gradient when extrapolating from a reuse factor of 10, and suggests a reuse factor of 26. When the synthesis result informs the model of its under-estimate, it finds the optimal reuse factor.

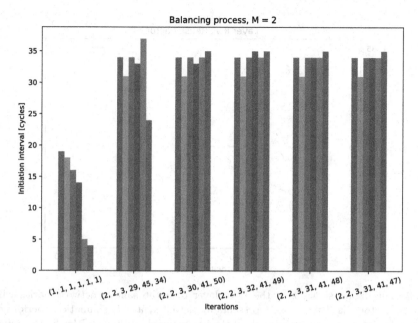

**Fig. 8.** Configurations of reuse factors suggested by the algorithm in *compact* mode. Each of the groups of 6 bars represent a single synthesis. The heights correspond to the IIs using the reuse factors in brackets below each group.

## 4.4 Comparison Between Performance and Compact Modes

Table 1 shows II and latency, as well as DSP block, FF and LUT usage, for the unoptimized design as well as designs optimized by the algorithm running in both performance and compact mode. By looking specifically at the number of DSP blocks used by each of the designs, we can see that the sample network studied in this work would not fit on the sample target device, requiring more than three times the available DSP blocks. By applying the performance mode of the method outlined in this work, the DSP block usage was reduced by a factor of 3.5. This allows the network to fit the target device without any decrease to the throughput compared with the original design, as is evident from the identical II. Besides minor increases in FF and LUT resource usage, the balancing of IIs by increasing reuse factors inevitably incurs an increase in latency.

If we wanted to realize the sample network shown in Fig. 5 in an FPGA with even fewer available DSP blocks, such that the performance mode design would not fit, we could apply the more aggressive compact mode of the method. In this case, the DSP block usage was further decreased by a factor of 2.1. This, however, forces the method to further increase both the latency and the II.

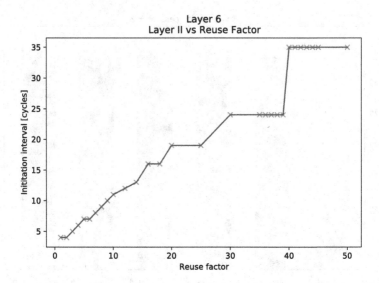

**Fig. 9.** This figure shows how the II of layer 6 in the sample network varies with its reuse factor. Each red cross represents an actual synthesis simulation (performed independently of any execution mode of the balancing algorithm). (Color figure online)

**Table 1.** Performance and resource usage comparison between the unoptimized and optimised versions automatically derived by our approach (performance and compact modes, respectively). The rightmost column represents the case where all reuse factors are set to 4 (discussed in Sect. 4.5). Resource usage percentage in brackets corresponds to the proportion of available resources used (*Xilinx Artix A200*).

|         | Unoptimized    | Performance    | Compact        | Homogeneous <4> |
|---------|----------------|----------------|----------------|-----------------|
| II      | 20             | 20             | 36             | 67              |
| DSPs    | 2,269 (310%)   | 642 (87%)      | 308 (42%)      | 737 (100%)      |
| Latency | 45             | 88             | 150            | 87              |
| FFs     | 45,954 (17%)   | 51,398 (19%)   | 52,729 (20%)   | 49,387 (18%)    |
| LUTs    | 100,525 (75%)  | 108,248 (80%)  | 108,291 (80%)  | 118,586 (88%)   |

## 4.5   Comparison with State-of-the-Art

Duarte et al. (2018) uses reuse factors to trade increased IIs, and thus decreased throughput, for reduced hardware requirements when deploying a neural network to an FPGA. Unlike our approach, which allows the reuse factor of each layer of the network to be set independently, Duarte et al. (2018) uses a single homogeneous reuse factors for all layers. If this restriction of a singular reuse factor were imposed on the sample network used for evaluation in this paper, a reuse factor of 4 would need to be applied to all layers in order to fit within the resource constraints of our chosen target device. As shown in the rightmost column of Table 1, this would lead to a factor 3.4 decrease in throughput when compared to the design produced by our method in addition to requiring more DSP blocks.

Que et al. (2021) balanced the IIs of the layers of a Recurrent Neural Network (RNN) by modifying the reuse factors of each layer independently. However, this was done manually using expert knowledge about the tools being used, the specific properties of the network being synthesized and the target device. Without this knowledge, a naive strategy for finding an optimal configuration of reuse factor would be to synthesize designs using a singular reuse factor, $n$, across all layers in some plausible range $1 \leq n \leq N$, and then identifying an optimal configuration by setting the reuse factor of each layer based on the results of this simulation. As the highest reuse factor explored by our method in this evaluation is 50, covering this design space with a brute force approach would require 50 such syntheses. In our evaluation, each synthesis of a relatively small neural network takes approximately 10 min, thus the synthesis alone would take more than 8 h of compute time to derive the optimal solution with the naive method. Our method in its performance mode required only 4 such syntheses, rather than 50, while the compact mode, navigating a larger search space, required only 7. As the computation time spent by the algorithm itself (that is, time not spent on synthesis) is on the order of milliseconds and therefore negligible in this context, our method achieved a factor 7–13 speedup of the DSE process compared to a naive approach, enabling greatly accelerated iteration.

## 4.6  Further Work

As our method exclusively extracts II data from the HLS report, it is not able to fully exploit all available DSP blocks on the target device. A future extension to the method could use additional available data, such as latency and resource usage, to produce the configuration of reuse factors for a given DL model which maximizes throughput given the resource constraints imposed by the target device and a latency constraint manually specified by the user.

As explained in Sect. 3.2, we require a user-specified reuse factor, $\lambda$, to obtain an initial estimate of the gradient of each layer's II with respect to its reuse factor. It is possible that a heterogeneous configuration of reuse factors could provide more useful information. One extension might therefore be to compute such a configuration using the IIs resulting from the first synthesis, which should give some information about suitable orders of magnitude of the reuse factors in the final solution.

Though our method's performance has only been evaluated for one sample network, the heterogeneous nature of this network suggests that the method generalizes well across different types and sizes of neural network layers. Seeing as our method makes no assumptions about the implementations of these layers, other than that they are highly parallelizable stages of a computation, further work could be done to evaluate our method on the synthesis of other non-DL programs consisting of similarly parallelizable stages.

Finally, another method for addressing a resource-constrained environment is to perform quantization. Further work will examine how our II-balancing method can be combined with quantization schemes for further hardware reductions.

## 5 Conclusion

This paper has outlined a method for automatically balancing the initiation intervals (IIs) of sequential stages of a computation to iteratively modify reuse factors for each stage. For one particular algorithm setting, this method reduced the computational hardware requirement to realize a neural network by a factor of 3.5 without affecting throughput. It was demonstrated that the use of this method allowed the neural network to fit within the hardware resources of a designated target device, which otherwise would have required more than three times the available resources. If one wanted to target an even smaller device, a more aggressive parameter setting of the algorithm was shown to decrease the DSP block requirement by a factor of 7.4, while II increased by a factor of 1.8. In contrast to previous efforts to balance IIs using reuse factors, the balancing algorithm proposed in this paper is completely automatic.

In contrast to previous related works using one reuse factor for all layers, the use of multiple reuse factors in our method facilitated a factor of 3.4 increase in throughput from the same resources. Our approach is automatic and can achieve a factor of 7.5–13 speed improvement over a naive exploration of the same search space of reuse factors.

**Acknowledgements.** The support of the UK EPSRC (grant number EP/V028251/1, EP/L016796/1, EP/S030069/1 and EP/N031768/1) and AMD is gratefully acknowledged.

## References

Bierzynski, K., et al.: AI at the edge. 2021 EPoSS White Paper (2021)

Duarte, J., et al.: Fast inference of deep neural networks in FPGAs for particle physics. J. Instr. **13**(07), P07027 (2018)

Fahim, F., et al.: hls4ml: an open-source codesign workow to empower scientifc low-power machine learning devices. arXiv (2021)

Hornik, K., Stinchcombe, M., White, H.: Multilayer feedforward networks are universal approximators. Neural Netw. **2**, 359–366 (1989)

Li, P., et al.: Resource-aware throughput optimization for high-level synthesis. In: Proceedings of the 2015 ACM/SIGDA International Symposium on Field-Programmable Gate Arrays, pp. 200–209 (2015)

Nakahara, H., et al.: High-throughput convolutional neural network on an FPGA by customized JPEG compression. In: IEEE 28th Annual International Symposium on Field-Programmable Custom Computing Machines (FCCM). IEEE (2020)

Oppermann, J., et al.: SkyCastle: a resource-aware multi-loop scheduler for high-level synthesis. In: 2019 International Conference on Field-Programmable Technology (ICFPT), pp. 36–44. IEEE (2019)

Que, Z., et al.: Accelerating recurrent neural networks for gravitational wave experiments. arXiv (2021)

Tridgell, S., et al.: Unrolling ternary neural networks. ACM Trans. Reconfigurable Technol. Syst. (TRETS) **12**(4), 1–23 (2019)

Vandebon, J., et al.: Enhancing high-level synthesis using a meta-programming approach. IEEE (2021)

Zhong, G., et al.: Design space exploration of FPGA-based accelerators with multi-level parallelism. In: 2017 Design, Automation & Test in Europe Conference & Exhibition (DATE), pp. 1141–1146. IEEE (2017)

# IPEC: Open-Source Design Automation for Inter-Processing Element Communication

David Volz$^{(\boxtimes)}$ ⓘ, Christoph Spang ⓘ, and Andreas Koch ⓘ

Embedded Systems and Applications, Technical University of Darmstadt,
Karolinenplatz 5, 64289 Darmstadt, Germany
volz@esa.tu-darmstadt.de

**Abstract.** With growing FPGA capacities, the complexity of realizable systems-on-chip grows as well. State-of-the-art FPGA accelerators encompass many heterogeneous processing elements that often require efficient Inter-PE communication, as well as with external interfaces, e.g., to the host or memory. While the toolflows and languages to create *individual* processing elements have improved considerably in recent years, the composition of multi-PE SoCs on FPGAs, including the required custom interconnects and the creation of powerful APIs for a host to *interact* with these complex accelerators, has been a largely manual and error-prone ad-hoc process. The IPEC system described here aims to automate much of this effort by offering the system architect selected powerful primitives to easily describe even advanced SoC compositions. Compared to traditional manual approaches, the length of the required descriptions has been reduced by up to two orders of magnitude for the real-world designs examined here. For easy usability, the open-source IPEC system employs a domain-specific language embedded in Python.

**Keywords:** Automated on-chip interconnect · Task parallelism · Processing elements · TaPaSCo · FPGA design automation

## 1 Introduction

Reconfigurable logic devices such as FPGAs have been less affected by Moore's Law slowing down, and continue to offer larger capacities with each new generation. However, apart from specialized applications such as ASIC emulation, actually putting all of that reconfigurable space to good use, e.g., for improved computing performance, remains challenging.

Construction of individual PE improved significantly due to advances in HLS and new hardware construction languages, but the assembly of a complete SoC leveraging many heterogeneous PE and distributed memory still takes considerable effort.

Some aspects of this complexity have been addressed by abstraction frameworks such as TaPaSCo [9] and others, as discussed in Sect. 3. These systems

© The Author(s), under exclusive license to Springer Nature Switzerland AG 2022
L. Gan et al. (Eds.): ARC 2022, LNCS 13569, pp. 134–149, 2022.
https://doi.org/10.1007/978-3-031-19983-7_10

can automate much of the lower-level aspects of the SoC construction process, and provide concise and efficient APIs for interacting with the host, hiding many intricacies of the underlying mechanisms.

What is still lacking is support for more easily describing systems of many *parallel interacting* PEs. While the connections can be created using tools such as Xilinx IP Integrator, this is a laborious process when using the GUI. It is possible to automate that process with Tcl scripts, but manually creating these scripts is similarly tedious and highly error-prone, especially for complex designs.

As an alternative to existing work, we contribute the *Inter Processing Element Communication* (IPEC) framework, for automatically synthesizing complex systems of interacting PEs. IPEC descriptions are formulated at higher abstraction levels than IP Integrator and described in a concise DSL embedded into Python. The toolflow then leverages the existing TaPaSCo framework to create the lower-levels of the SoC, and also provides automated hardware/software integration.

These high-level descriptions allow an easy scaling of architectures, and thus enhance the portability of the same base-architecture across different device sizes. By creating custom interconnect structures, the area and performance overheads of using a general-purpose NoC can be optimized.

Even in its initial form described here, IPEC already enables higher productivity hardware designs by raising the abstraction level and degree of automation over existing solutions. But its underlying technologies, such as the IPEC Intermediate Representation (IIR) used to internally represent entire accelerator-heavy SoCs with their communication and synchronization mechanisms, forms the basis for more advanced SoC-level optimization steps in further development.

Section 2 describes the fundamental ideas, protocols, and components IPEC builds upon. Section 3 gives an overview over related work. Section 4 discusses the primitives provided by IPEC, while Sect. 5 shows how the user can integrate them into a design. Section 6 demonstrates IPEC for two different use-cases. Section 7 concludes with future work.

## 2    Fundamentals and Terminology

**Processing Elements (PEs)**, in the context of IPEC, describe a computing unit that can be instantiated multiple times. Depending on the individual use-case, a design may either consist of homogeneous or varying purpose heterogeneous PEs. A PE may have access to local and global memories and may be interconnected to other PEs. For use with TaPaSCo, PEs are packaged as IP-XACT blocks [8].

**Task Parallel System Composer (TaPaSCo)** provides a toolflow to automatically integrate user provided PEs into a *composition*, a set of interconnected PEs, which in the next step can be synthesized onto an FPGA [9]. TaPaSCo uses the notion of a *task* from the heterogeneous computing model, which decomposes large computations into smaller tasks that can run concurrently. Tasks can be started on a PE from the host using the TaPaSCo API, or from other PEs [10].

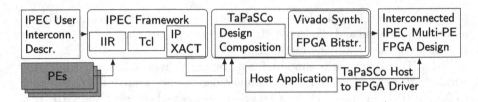

**Fig. 1.** IPEC Toolflow: User-provided Python-based interconnect descriptions are converted into an IPEC Intermediate Representation (IIR), compiled into Tcl, and packed as IP-XACT core. TaPaSCo gets this core definition and creates the composition, which is synthesized onto FPGA.

The **Advanced eXtensible Interface (AXI)** is part of the AMBA (Advanced Microcontroller Bus Architecture) specification and is a freely-available, open standard for the connection and management of functional blocks in a system-on-chip (SoC) [1]. It is available in older and newer versions and also includes a lightweight and streaming option.

**On-Chip Interconnect Topology** Existing on-chip Interconnect Topologies are often regular structures such as a ring, star, or fully meshed interconnect. As part of this work, we will focus on user-defined and potentially irregular topologies, with direct connections between PEs.

**IPEC's Toolflow** is outlined in Fig. 1. The user first provides the design's PE and a high-level Python IPEC interconnect description to the IPEC framework, which then auto-generates the interconnects in Tcl and packages the multi-PE design as a single transparent IP-XACT core. This IPEC core is then supplied to the existing TaPaSCo toolflow, which builds, synthesizes, and loads the bitstream onto an FPGA.

## 3    Related Work

Different existing tools assist the user in generating FPGA designs comprised from multiple accelerators. As part of this section, we will focus on those tools, which also include active support for inter-PE communication.

**TaPa** follows a *Task Parallel* approach like TaPaSCo, but focusses more on High-Level Synthesis (HLS) [3]. It generates PEs by applying HLS to the compute kernels of an OpenCL program. The PEs are placed on the System on Chip (SoC) and connected to a *shared ring network*. Each PE can put data onto the network and peek at or pull from other PEs. TaPa provides C++ structs to describe data exchanges between PEs. Using them from within a kernel will result in the corresponding ring network accesses at runtime. Since all communication takes place on the shared ring network, this can pose a *bottleneck* if many PEs are active at the same time and try to communicate.

**ESP** generates a system from HW tiles [7]. A tile can be a processor, memory, accelerator or auxiliary function. The processor and accelerator tiles include a first level cache and a DMA engine for accessing the caches of other tiles, while memory tiles only include a last level cache. DMAs are routed over a mesh network connecting all tiles. However, a potentially more efficient *direct communication* between accelerators is *not supported*.

**GENIE** (GENeric Interconnect Engine) enables the user to connect compute elements (CEs) according to user defined connection tables [16]. Hardware for splitting and merging connections is generated automatically. It uses a custom *routed streaming* protocol, which includes addressing by giving each slave an ID. However, it only generates interconnect structures for its own protocol and requires that CEs support it.

**Archborn** provides a Tcl abstraction layer, which enables the user to concisely create PE and Memories, then connect them using busses [14]. The user can attach PE to a bus, which in turn can be connected to create an NoC. However, the user has to manually create these structures and the framework does not include conversion between protocols.

**Cascabel** is a TaPaSCo extension, which enables on-device dynamic dispatch [10]. It replaces the default TaPaSCo scheduler with one that can process launch requests from host and PEs. However, it can only launch one task at a time, each with a limited number of task parameters. Already running PEs *cannot communicate directly*.

A key limitation of the provided frameworks is that they mostly rely on fixed protocols and interconnect topologies (e.g., mesh, star, ring). While this does make sense for ASICs, the large multiplexers are often slow on FPGAs. In contrast, IPEC generates *custom interconnect structures* matching the communication patterns of a specific application.

# 4 Capabilities

With TaPaSCo and other task parallel frameworks, the fundamental abstraction is that of a *task*, which is submitted to one PE and processed in its entirety. IPEC, on the other hand, uses *task groups* as the fundamental abstraction. A *task group* comprises multiple tasks, which can exchange data using shared memory or connections. Figure 2a shows such a task group as a Data-Flow Graph (DFG).

Each of the PE A to F represent one task of the entire group. Each task, in turn, runs on a PE optimized for it. The host launches a task group together with the necessary input parameters and is notified of its completion by using the interrupt signal of a designated PE, usually either the first or last one in the DFG. PEs can share data only along the edges of the DFG, this means that, e.g., PE D has no means of communicating with PE C. Note that the DFG is a directed graph, but which may contain cycles.

## 4.1 Connections

Every PE has one or more ports to send data to or receive data from other PE's ports and memory. IPEC supports three protocols from the AXI4 family for the ports: AXI4, AXI4 Lite, and AXI4 Stream. Additionally, connecting individual

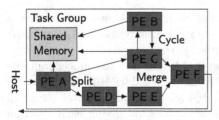

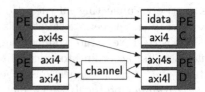

(a) Possible data-flow graph of a task group: After launching a task group from the host, the PEs (A - F) communicate during computation. Each edge represents an individual connection.

(b) Sample topology between the ports of PEs (A - D): IPEC is flexible regarding a port's fan-in, fan-out, and protocol. Routing resources can be reduced by consolidating connections into channels. Connecting individual signals is also supported.

**Fig. 2.** A sample data-flow graph and topology, which can be mapped using IPEC.

wires is possible as well. Using IPEC, the user can create arbitrary connections between ports, e.g., as shown in Fig. 2b.

A single master port can have multiple outgoing connections to other slaves, while a single slave can have multiple incoming connections from other masters. After specifying all connections, IPEC automatically generates the corresponding hardware and connections further described in Sect. 5.5. Interconnects are created automatically when needed. For ports with many incoming or outgoing connections, the design is automatically optimized by creating a hierarchical interconnect structure. With address-based protocols like AXI4 and AXI4 Lite, a master can send data to individual slaves by using an address map (described in greater detail in Sect. 5.6). AXI4 Stream masters, on the other hand, broadcast data to all of their slaves. AXI4 Stream slaves include a FIFO in order to act as a buffer to avoid slowing-down the master in case a slave is not ready yet.

Furthermore, connecting ports with mismatching protocols is supported, but may require the user to specify a conversion protocol. Converting AXI4 to AXI4 Lite is done automatically, while converting an AXI4 Stream to AXI4 requires the user to specify a hardware module to do the conversion.

In order to save routing resources, connections between different ports can be grouped to form a *Channel*. A Channel can have multiple input ports, which are arbitrated onto a single connection. On the other end, the data is forwarded to the single addressed slave, or broadcast in the case of streams.

## 4.2 Memory

One advantage of FPGAs is the availability of distributed memory and customizable memory systems such as [11]. To exploit distributed memory, PEs can each have a local BRAM attached, which can also be made accessible to other PEs. Since BRAM on most modern FPGAs is dual-ported, IPEC exposes both ports to the user, who can then decide whether to give a single PE exclusive access

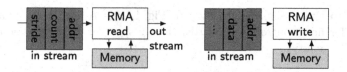

**Fig. 3.** Shared memory accesses using AXI4 Stream, require RMA converters, which are auto-generated by IPEC. An RMA read has up to three parameters determining which data words to return. An RMA write has at least one data packet, but will write additional data to successive memory addresses.

to a port for minimum latency, or share it among multiple PE. Furthermore, IPEC treats all types of memory identically, including BRAM, DRAM, HBM, and register files. In the case of off-chip memory, IPEC delegates generating the memory controller to TaPaSCo, but will create the necessary interconnects for merging all connections accessing the same memory. PEs can perform their memory accesses via AXI4, AXI4 Lite, and AXI4 Stream. For AXI4 Streams, the required Remote Memory Access (RMA) converter units, as shown in Fig. 3, are created automatically.

**RMA Read.** The PE has an address stream connected to the RMA unit and a data stream back from the RMA unit. A read request contains up to three parameters: the address, number of elements to read and the stride between successive elements. After receiving a read request, the RMA unit will read the data from memory and broadcast it to all receivers of the stream.

**RMA Write.** The PE has a combined address and data stream connected to the RMA unit. A write request contains at least two parameters: the address and the data. Sending more than one data packet will write to successive addresses.

Data stored inside a PE and shared memory is persistent across launches, meaning it is still available when the next task or task group is started. However, it falls to the user to ensure that, if a later task requires data from a previous one, the new task or group is launched on the specific PEs that can physically access that memory.

### 4.3   Dispatch - Starting PEs

Since a task group consists of multiple tasks, and therefore involves multiple PEs, there has to be a way to start all PEs belonging to the same task group. We discuss the two possibilities shown in Fig. 4.

**Software Dispatch.** Task groups can be launched under host control by assigning each involved PE a unique ID. The host can then individually launch the tasks in a group using the identified PEs. While very flexible, software dispatch has a relatively high communication overhead, as each task requires two PCIe transfers. In the example at the top of Fig. 4, PEs A and B are launched as group under host control. Afterwards, their respective tasks can communicate using IPEC facilities.

**Hardware Dispatch.** Instead of being launched under host control, IPEC can configure PEs to be launched on-chip, without host intervention. Therefore, PEs are fitted with a *Stream Starter*, which accepts new launch requests, including the required parameters, from an AXI4 Stream. This allows arrangements as shown in the left part of Fig. 4, where only PE C is host-launchable by its ID. The PE D is then launched on-chip over IPEC links. In the example, PE D can receive additional data from and return its result to PE C over additional streams. The Stream Starter blocks until its controlled PE becomes idle again. Note that hardware dispatch requires some care from the user, as in some cases, such as circular structures, there is the risk of deadlocks.

**Locks for Stream Synchronization.** To prevent multiple PE from interfering with each other, including deadlocks, individual stream connections can be blocked using a lock. Locks contain an accumulator register connected to an AXI4 Stream slave. Each incoming packet increments the accumulator or applies a simple binary operation with the data field of the packet. This way, accumulators can realize *atomic operations* across multiple concurrently executing PEs. Additionally, the lock is linked with a channel and blocks all communication over the channel if the accumulator is non-zero. This allows the realization of different synchronization schemes such as semaphores, and mutexes.

## 5    Using IPEC to Simplify SoC Implementation

This section details how the user can create compositions using the previously discussed functionalities. For ease of use and to make it more accessible to users inexperienced in hardware development, IPEC is controlled by high-level *Python* descriptions. We chose Python specifically for lowering the hardware designer's entry barrier. With IPEC, not only single-PE but multi-PE HLS designs become feasible without the need for Tcl or any HDL knowledge to interface with existing toolflows. Together with TaPaSCo's HLS support, the user can now easily generate a multi-PE SoC with custom interconnect structures.

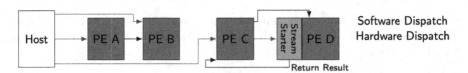

**Fig. 4.** IPEC supports both host software and on-chip hardware dispatch. With software dispatch, the host starts PEs individually. With hardware dispatch, PEs have a Stream Starter attached to their configuration registers, which allows other PEs to start tasks without host intervention.

**Listing 1.1.** Python code for an introductory example of an IPEC composition.

```
1   pea = PEA(ID=1)
2   peb = PEB()
3   pec = PEC()
4   hbm = HBM()
5   c = Channel(pea.maxis0,peb.config)
6   lock = Lock(c)
7   Channel(peb.maxis,pec.config)
8   Channel(pec.maxis,peb.config)
9   Channel(pea.maxis1,pec.maxis1,lock)
10  for i in range(0, 10):
11      ped = PED(ID=i+1)
12      bram = BRAM('16K')
13      Channel(ped.maxi0, bram.port0)
14      Channel(ped.maxi1, hbm.saxi)
```

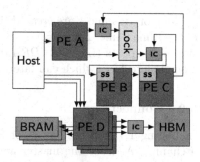

**Fig. 5.** Corresponding block design: PE B and PE C form a cycle started by PE A through a lock. Each PE D has its own BRAM and a connection to shared HBM.

As shown previously in Fig. 1, using Python syntax, the user writes a script instantiating all PEs, memories, and connections between them. Our library then converts the given description into an intermediate representation, from which the necessary converters and interconnects can be automatically inferred and the address map is computed. Finally, from the extended intermediate representation, an IP-XACT core containing all resources is created. For maximum automation, IPEC is integrated into TaPaSCo. However, it can also be used in a stand-alone manner in other design flows. Listing 1.1 is a simple introductory example for using IPEC to describe the block design shown in Fig. 5. More complex real-world use-cases will be discussed in Sect. 6.

## 5.1 Device, PEs and Memory

When using IPEC, PEs can be instantiated by calling a Python constructor via its identical name. To this end, IPEC reads the user's TaPaSCo hardware cores directory and automatically creates a Python class for every PE type found. Note that IPEC adheres to TaPaSCo's tenet of being language agnostic. Thus, while the actual cores might have been created using Verilog HDL, Chisel, HLS, Bluespec, or any other design flow, this no longer plays a role in their IPEC composition. The code in Listing 1.1 creates the PEs PE A (Line 1), PE B (Line 2), PE C (Line 3), and multiple instances of PE D (Line 11). Each PE object contains member attributes for every interface the PE exposes with the same name and protocol, thus making it easy for the user to reference a specific PE port in the IPEC script. Other hardware modules are created similarly, for example the yellow lock in Fig. 5 results from Line 6 in Listing 1.1.

In the case of PE A and PE D, the constructor includes the ID parameter, thus making the PEs host-launchable using the TaPaSCo API. PE B and PE C, on the other hand, are equipped with a PE Stream Starter created implicitly by connecting an AXI4 Stream to master to their configuration registers. They can thus be launched on-chip without host intervention.

Memory instances are created similar to PEs by calling a Python constructor of the same name. *BRAM* creates one block of BRAM of the specified size with two access ports (Line 12). *DRAM* and *HBM* aggregate all connected ports to a single interface, which can later be connected to a memory controller.

## 5.2   Connections

In Listing 1.1, different ports of PEs and memory are connected by creating a channel. At least one master and one slave is to be specified per channel. If multiple masters are part of a channel (Line 9), IPEC creates an interconnect to arbitrate them onto a single connection. If multiple slaves are present in a channel, the resulting interconnect will *broadcast* to all slaves for the case of the slaves being AXI4 Streams, or unicast to the single specific slave as addressed by AXI4 and AXI4 Lite interfaces. Multiple channels connected to the same port are handled analogously. E.g., all PE D instances are connected to the same HBM in Line 14. When creating the lock in Line 6, IPEC splits the given channel and routes it through the lock.

## 5.3   Locks - Deadlock Avoidance

Locks offer a way to synchronize the execution of PEs, or prevent a deadlock. In Fig. 5, PE A can start a cycle, which contains PE B and PE C, with PE B starting PE C as it finishes, and vice versa. If PE A restarts PE B before this cycle is over, PE C will wait for PE B to finish, which, in turn, waits for PE C to finish, causing a deadlock. To prevent this, we add a lock in Line 6.

The channel in Line 9 connects PE A and PE C to the accumulator part of the lock, allowing them to block the second channel through the lock. This second channel allows PE A to start PE B, if the accumulator register is 0. After PE A starts PE B, it increments the accumulator of the lock by one, thus blocking any of its *own* future attempts of starting PE B. PE C's way to start PE B (Line 8), on the other hand, is not blocked by the lock and it can still restart PE B. When no more iterations between PE B and PE C are required, PE C will reset the lock, thus re-enabling PE A to launch PE B again, and start a new processing cycle.

## 5.4   IPEC Intermediate Representation

For improved efficiency, the IPEC framework does not immediately generate the corresponding hardware when the Python call is processed. Instead, the calls construct the IPEC Intermediate Representation (IIR, see Fig. 1) in the background, which is then processed in its entirety to generate the interconnects. The IIR is graph-based and comprises *cells*, *ports*, and *connections*:

**Cells** are hardware modules available to IPEC as IP-XACT cores. While all cells have ports to express their connection points, IIR distinguishes between *PEs, Memory, Stream Operations, Interconnects,* and *(AXI) Converters.*

**Ports** encapsulate all the low-level physical signals of a Cell associated with a specific protocol into one user accessible object. IPEC differentiates between AXI4, AXI4 Lite, AXI4 Stream, Clocks, Resets, Interrupts, and raw input and output signals. Address based protocol ports are part of the address map generation.

**Connections** are point to point connections between ports. IPEC generates a Tcl script from IIR, which, when used from within the context of the Xilinx IP Integrator, *imports*, *creates*, and *configures* every referenced IP and the *connections* between them to generate an IP-XACT core.

## 5.5  Interconnect Generation

When the IIR is constructed, the protocols of connected ports may not match. Ports may even have multi-protocol fanouts. This is resolved by first inserting generic interconnects which lack all protocol information. Afterwards, protocol information, such as type, data width, and address width, is *propagated* through the connection graph, starting from each port with a known protocol. When different protocol information is propagated to the same port, IPEC selects a common "super" protocol on the master side, or a common "sub" protocol on the slave side. As an example, in Listing 1.1, the data width of the lock is not specified. If multiple masters propagate different data widths to the same slave having an unknown data width, then the *widest* data width of all masters is selected for the slave. Conversely, if multiple slaves connect to a single master, the narrowest data width is selected. The user can control this process by specifying the protocol manually at key points, and then leave it to IPEC to infer the remaining protocol parameters. After protocol propagation, IPEC inserts *converters* between each pair of ports with mismatching protocol specifications. Finally, each generic cell is replaced by one of the IP-cores that is available to IPEC and has the required properties. While these capabilities are similar to those in Xilinx Vivado, they allow IPEC to parameterize generic user IP cores like the lock as needed.

## 5.6  Address Map Generation

In contrast to AXI4 Streams, AXI4 and AXI4 Lite require assigned addresses for communication. Thus, each master has an address space containing the address segments of every slave it is connected to. IPEC automatically creates these address maps for each master by inserting the slaves in the order specified by the user into the masters address space. IPEC may leave parts of the address space unassigned to ensure each slaves' address segment starts at an aligned address divisible by its own size to allow more efficient address decoding.

## 5.7  Advantages of Embedding IPEC in Python

IPEC profits from being a Domain-Specific Language *embedded* into a high-level language, namely Python. This is exploited in Listing 1.1 by using a *for*-loop to concisely create multiple PEs, BRAM, and the connections between them. Note that only a single HBM instance is created (Line 4), which has *multiple* connections created in Line 14. IPEC will create an interconnect block *merging* all of the individual links.

While these abstractions could be implemented in Tcl, which is directly supported by Vivado, we chose Python to accommodate non-hardware designers, who can use it in combination with *HLS* to employ reconfigurable computing.

## 6    Evaluation

This section discusses two *real-world* case studies which successfully leverage IPEC. Both projects initially relied on the Xilinx *IP Integrator* GUI to manually create communication structures between PEs, before being migrated to IPEC. For both use-cases, other approaches would either not provide sufficient bandwidth (e.g., a single global shared memory), or require more FPGA resources (e.g., an NoC in soft-logic). The final composition when using IPEC is identical to the previous manually created composition. Since the design, and therefore the performance is identical, the focus of this study will thus be on the *productivity gains* achievable using IPEC, as compared to the Xilinx IP Integrator GUI. As simple measure for the productivity gains, we compare the lines of IPEC Python code with the number drag-and-drop user actions required in the GUI, which is reflected by the number of corresponding Tcl lines automatically created by the IP Integrator tool. In our experience, the number of Tcl lines is a good estimation for the number drag-and-drop operations, ignoring grouping commands.

By using IPEC, it becomes much easier to perform design space exploration by varying parameters of a composition, or to scale an IPEC design up or down to target different FPGAs.

### 6.1    Case Study I: neoDB Database System

Many modern Data Base Management Systems (DBMSs) use *multi-versioning* to enable consistency and high parallelism for both long-running analytical queries (reads), and low-latency update transactions (writes) [18]. In this scheme, the DBMS holds multiple versions of the same tuple linked with timestamps to determine which single version is the current one (*visible*) to a given transaction or query. This *visibility check* requires loading tuples and comparing their timestamp against the timestamp of the ongoing query.

In practice, the number of active versions can reach several hundred millions [12], resulting in many entries being evicted from fast memory to cold storage. Thus, in today's DBMSs, analytical queries may be slowed by high latency memory accesses when checking tuples for visibility.

neoDB is a next-gen DBMS based on PostgreSQL that uses FPGA-accelerated Near-Data Processing (NDP) to address many traditional bottlenecks [2]. The example employed as use-case for IPEC performs visibility checks

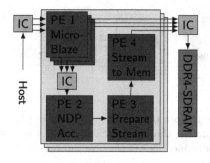

**Fig. 6.** System composition of neoDB. Configuration connections are not shown for clarity.

**Listing 1.2.** IPEC code for NeoDB

```
1  dram  = DRAM()
2  for i in range(0,2): # 0..1
3    pe2 = NDP_Accelerator(ID=2)
4    for j in range(0,16): # 0..15
5      pe1 = MicroBlaze(ID=1)
6      Channel(pe1.maxis, pe2.saxis)
7      Channel(pe1.maxi, dram.saxi)
8    pe3 = Stream_Preparation(ID=3)
9    pe4 = Stream_to_Memory(ID=4)
10   Channel(pe2.maxis, pe3.saxis)
11   Channel(pe3.maxis, pe4.saxis)
12   Channel(pe4.maxi, dram.saxi)
```

on the FPGA in NDP-fashion to determine the visible records. These can then be returned back to the host, or be forwarded to further NDP accelerators on the FPGA. In both cases, the results are written back to host memory.

The neoDB composition examined here comprises four types of PE working together to perform an NDP-operation. MicroBlaze softcores load tuples from memory and perform the visibility checking, forwarding only the visible tuples over an AXI4 Stream. Next, a specialized NDP accelerator continues to process the visible tuples, using a complex data analytics operation in the actual system. The third PE transforms the analytics accelerator results in preparation for writing them to host memory, which is performed by the final PE. These four PE types form a *cluster*, which can be replicated on larger target FPGAs. The host only interacts with the first PE of each cluster, launching parallel tasks on multiple softcores.

Figure 6 shows an example of a composition for this architecture, including multiple clusters each containing multiple softcores and an analytics accelerator each. Listing 1.2 shows the IPEC code describing this composition, having two clusters and 16 MicroBlaze softcores per cluster. The Tcl script to generate the composition contains almost 1,000 lines, each line representing one manual and error prone action the user performed when using the Xilinx IP Integrator. Even when using TaPaSCo to create much of the low-level infrastructure, more than 200 Tcl lines remain just to realize the inter-PE communication patterns. IPEC can express these in just 12 code lines and allows to flexibly balance the different processing pipeline parts to match throughputs across stages.

Furthermore, in the future, neoDB will require far more complex communication topologies, as well as support for fast atomic operations for synchronization. IPEC already supports both of these functionalities.

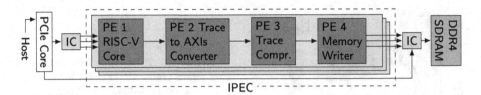

**Fig. 7.** System Diagram of the Fuzzing Accelerator. Note that a fuzzing cluster of PE 1–4 can be replicated on larger chips for higher fuzzing throughput. Since PE 2–4 are only configured and started by the host once, their connections to the host interconnect are omitted for clarity.

## 6.2 Case Study II: Hardware Fuzzing Accelerator

Fuzzing is an automated method for finding vulnerabilities in applications using a large number of computer generated test cases as input [15]. A black-box fuzzer will randomly create such test cases and then externally observe the program for unexpected behavior. In contrast, gray-box and white-box fuzzers indirectly or directly obtain the program-internal state. Control flow information helps guiding test case generation towards higher coverage, thereby increasing the chance to actually find unintended program states or vulnerabilities [13].

Traditionally, software-based fuzzing frameworks such as AFL++ [5,6] are used to perform this fuzzing-process. A program is iteratively executed and monitored for any still undiscovered and possibly hazardous state. In software, the monitoring aspect is typically realized by statically or dynamically inserting new tracing instructions into the program. When fuzzing a program in a non-native ISA, an emulator has to be employed.

Alternatively, the process of patching, emulating program execution, and monitoring program states can be accelerated on an FPGA. In this manner, a potentially large number of ISA-native processor cores may execute the program with higher efficiency than emulation could achieve. Also, the program state can be monitored via dedicated hardware blocks without the need for special instructions. Beyond uncompressed monitoring, dedicated hardware may also generate and continuously update a condensed trace of the program execution and finally write it into the FPGA's DDR-SDRAM. This coverage information then guides the host in its generation of new and tighter test cases.

In its current version, the fuzzer is limited to executing baremetal-only applications without the capability of including any non-statically linked libraries. Even with these limitations, though, it is suitable to demonstrate IPEC's capabilities.

The fuzzing accelerator is organized into clusters, each holding four communicating PEs as shown in Fig. 7. The first PE contains the processor core and a tracing interface. Depending on the specific core's capabilities, the Real-Time Lightweight Integrity enForcement intErface (RT-LIFE) [17] or the RISC-V Trace (interface) Specification [4] are used to monitor the instruction stream. The raw trace output is hardwired to the second PE, which transforms the trace

**Listing 1.3.** IPEC code for 25 fuzzing clusters.

```
1   dram  = DRAM()
2   for i in range(0,25):  # 0..24
3     pe1 = RISC_V_Core_PE(ID=i*4+1)
4     pe2 = Converter_PE(ID=i*4+2)
5     pe3 = Compressor_PE(ID=i*4+3)
6     pe4 = MemoryWr_PE(ID=i*4+4)
7     Channel(pe1.o_data, pe2.i_data)
8     Channel(pe2.maxis, pe3.saxis)
9     Channel(pe3.maxis, pe4.saxis)
10    Channel(pe4.maxi, dram.saxi)
```

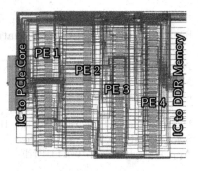

**Fig. 8.** Resulting block design.

into an AXI4 Stream. The trace is compressed in the third PE. Finally, the fourth PE writes the compressed tracing information into the FPGA's DDR-SDRAM. Each PE communicates with the next one via a hardwired connection, or an AXI4 Stream, while the last PE is connected to DRAM.

The block design for a system containing 25 fuzzing clusters requires a total of 2,000 lines of Tcl to describe, each representing one user interaction with the GUI. Even with the automation already provided by TaPaSCo, up to 600 *additional* design elements have to be manually formulated just for the inter-PE communication, requiring a line of Tcl for each element. The IPEC automation reduces this description to just 10 lines, shown in Lisitng 1.3. The resulting block design with 25 fuzzing clusters is shown in Fig. 8, highlighting the error-proneness of the manual process.

Scaling the number of fuzzing clusters up or down becomes trivial when using IPEC. Combined with the existing TaPaSCo framework, this enables a high degree of portability and very simple design space exploration.

As a result, IPEC allowed to explore compositions with a varying number of fuzzing clusters, and to select the composition yielding the highest wallclock throughput, i.e. fuzzing jobs-per-time, by trading-off parallelism and achievable clock frequency for different FPGAs.

# 7   Conclusion and Future Work

IPEC provides a solution for building complex SoCs with many interconnected accelerator units. For the two real-world use-cases discussed here, the tool already has significantly improved designer productivity and will enable much more comprehensive design space explorations than feasible using the traditional manual approaches.

Future work on IPEC will build on the existing foundations. Specifically, we will examine high performance off/on-chip task dispatch using the hardware structures introduced in this work, and extending its capabilities to start a predefined set of multiple PEs with a single launch command, including some form of on-device scheduling to maximize utilization of available PEs.

IPEC will be released as open-source software under the GNU LGPL v3 license at https://git.esa.informatik.tu-darmstadt.de/ipec/ipec.

**Acknowledgements.** The authors acknowledge the financial support by the Federal Ministry of Education and Research of Germany in the project "Open6GHub" (grant number: 16KISK014).

Part of this research work has been funded by the German Federal Ministry of Education and Research and the Hessian Ministry of Higher Education, Research, Science and the Arts within their joint support of the National Research Center for Applied Cybersecurity ATHENE.

# References

1. ARM: Amba specifications (2022). https://developer.arm.com/architectures/system-architectures/amba/specifications. Accessed 4 Jan 2022
2. Bernhardt, A., et al.: neodb: in-situ snapshots for multi-version dbms on native computational storage. In: Proceedings of ICDE (2022)
3. Chi, Y., Guo, L., Lau, J., Choi, Y.k., Wang, J., Cong, J.: Extending high-level synthesis for task-parallel programs. In: 2021 IEEE 29th Annual International Symposium on Field-Programmable Custom Computing Machines (FCCM), pp. 204–213 (2021). https://doi.org/10.1109/FCCM51124.2021.00032
4. Div.: RISC-V trace specification (2021). https://github.com/riscv/riscv-trace-spec
5. Div.: Afl++ github repository (2022). https://github.com/AFLplusplus/AFLplusplus. Accessed 5 Jan 2022
6. Fioraldi, A., Maier, D., Eißfeldt, H., Heuse, M.: AFL++: combining incremental steps of fuzzing research. In: 14th USENIX Workshop on Offensive Technologies (WOOT 2020). USENIX Association (2020)
7. Giri, D., Chiu, K.L., Eichler, G., Mantovani, P., Carloni, L.P.: Accelerator integration for open-source SoC design. IEEE Micro **41**(4), 8–14 (2021). https://doi.org/10.1109/MM.2021.3073893
8. Group, S.S.W.: IEEE 1685–2009 - IEEE Standard for IP-XACT, Standard Structure for Packaging, Integrating, and Reusing IP within Tool Flows (2022). https://standards.ieee.org/standard/1685-2009.html. Accessed 10 Jan 2022
9. Heinz, C., Hofmann, J., Korinth, J., Sommer, L., Weber, L., Koch, A.: The TaPaSCo open-source Toolflow. J. Signal Process. Syst. **93**(5), 545–563 (2021). https://doi.org/10.1007/s11265-021-01640-8
10. Heinz, C., Koch, A.: Supporting on-chip dynamic parallelism for task-based hardware accelerators. In: Applied Reconfigurable Computing. Architectures, Tools, and Applications (ARC) (2021)
11. Lange, H., Wink, T., Koch, A.: Marc ii: a parametrized speculative multi-ported memory subsystem for reconfigurable computers. In: ACM Proceedings Design, Automation, and Test in Europe (DATE). ACM (2011)
12. Lee, J., et al.: Hybrid garbage collection for multi-version concurrency control in sap hana, pp. 1307–1318 (2016). https://doi.org/10.1145/2882903.2903734
13. Liang, H., Pei, X., Jia, X., Shen, W., Zhang, J.: Fuzzing: state of the art. IEEE Trans. Reliabil. **67**(3), 1199–1218 (2018). https://doi.org/10.1109/TR.2018.2834476

14. Ma, S., Ding, H., Huang, M., Andrews, D.: Archborn: an open source tool for automated generation of chip heterogeneous multiprocessor architectures. In: 2015 International Conference on ReConFigurable Computing and FPGAs (ReConFig) pp. 1–6 (2015). https://doi.org/10.1109/ReConFig.2015.7393293
15. Oehlert, P.: Violating assumptions with fuzzing. IEEE Secur. Priv. 3(2), 58–62 (2005). https://doi.org/10.1109/MSP.2005.55
16. Rodionov, A., Biancolin, D., Rose, J.: Fine-grained interconnect synthesis. ACM Trans. Reconfigurable Technol. Syst. 9(4) (2016). https://doi.org/10.1145/2892641
17. Spang, C., Meisel, F., Koch, A.: RT-LIFE: portable RISC-V interface for real-time lightweight security enforcement. In: International Conference on Embedded Computer Systems: Architectures, MOdeling and Simulation (SAMOS). Springer, Heidelberg (2021)
18. Özcan, F., Tian, Y., Tözün, P.: Hybrid transactional/analytical processing: a survey, pp. 1771–1775 (2017). https://doi.org/10.1145/3035918.3054784

# Light-Weight Permutation Generator for Efficient Convolutional Neural Network Data Augmentation

Bowen P. Y. Kwan[1(✉)], Ce Guo[1], Wayne Luk[1], and Peiyong Jiang[2,3]

[1] Department of Computing, Imperial College London, London, UK
{pyk12,c.guo,w.luk}@imperial.ac.uk
[2] Centre for Novostics, Hong Kong Science Park, Hong Kong SAR, China
[3] Li Ka Shing Institute of Health Sciences, The Chinese University of Hong Kong,
Hong Kong SAR, China
jiangpeiyong@cuhk.edu.hk

**Abstract.** Permutation is a fundamental way of data augmentation. However, it is not commonly used in image based systems with hardware acceleration due to distortion of spatial correlation and generation complexity. This paper proposes Restricted Permutation Network (RPN), a scalable architecture to automatically generate a restricted subset of local permutation, preserving the features of the dataset while simplifying the generation to improve scalability. RPN reduces the spatial complexity from $O(Nlog(N))$ to $O(N)$, making it easily scalable to 64 inputs and beyond, with 21 times speed up in generation and significantly reducing data storage and transfer, while maintaining the same level of accuracy as the original dataset for deep learning training. Experiments show Convolutional Neural Networks (CNNs) trained by the augmented dataset can be as accurate as the original one. Combining three to five networks in general improves the network accuracy by 5%. Network training can be accelerated by training multiple sub-networks in parallel with a reduced training data set and epochs, resulting in up to 5 times speed up with a negligible loss in accuracy. This opens up the opportunity to easily split long iterative training process into independent parallelizable processes, facilitating the trade off between resources and run time.

## 1 Introduction

A Convolutional Neural Network (CNN) is well-known for its ability to process and model images for a wide range of applications. Its success is tied to the availability of large datasets for training the CNN models.

However, obtaining a sufficiently large dataset for training is not always practical. It may require manual labelling of training samples by experts, and data harvesting can be difficult. The US-HHS Influenza activity level is recorded weekly in 10 regions of mainland US, even 10 years worth of data would only be $10 \times 520$ data points [1]. Lack of data could also be a problem for inference. Image classification relying only on a single image can be error-prone, for example suffering from adversarial attack. Unlike video classification where consecutive frames can be used to classify the same given object to improve accuracy, there is usually no multiple representation of a particular object in an image dataset.

Data augmentation is a commonly used approach for computer vision applications to enlarge an existing dataset. Research [2–4] showed that randomized data obtained by permutation of the original images are still useful in training and inference for image classification and time-series prediction tasks. However, there are three major challenges hindering the potential of such method.

The first challenge is the spatial correlation distortion for inference. Permutation would inevitably destroy the spatial correlation of the original image. The generated image would have very different features compared to the original image, reducing the classification accuracy.

The second challenge is having inconsistent features for training. As different permutations would have different underlying features, using random permutations to train a network would make the feature to be learnt inconsistent during training. It would be more difficult for the model to converge, leading to longer training time, and reducing the accuracy.

The third challenge is the data generation complexity and memory footprint. The routing algorithms for existing permutation generators are often very complicated. It is not easy to figure out the required control for a particular permutation. The generated data also need to be stored, increasing the data storage requirement and memory transfer bottleneck.

This paper introduces a novel architecture to automatically generate permutations of the original image efficiently. The key idea is to apply **restricted local** row permutation by swapping neighbouring rows of the original image. The architecture has 3 major features, each addressing one of the above challenges:

(a) Minimal spatial correlation distortion of images. Local row-swapping can preserve the feature of the original image, reducing the drop in accuracy when using the permuted image for inference.
(b) Automatic generation of a pre-defined set of permutations. By generating a deterministic set of permutations, the underlying characteristic of the image can be maintained consistently within each set of permutations for training.
(c) Simple and scalable structure. Hardware can be simplified and optimized to efficiently generate a deterministic set of local row permutations, reducing its complexity. It allows the permutation to be generated on the fly on FPGA, reducing data storage and transfer between the FPGA and its host.

This paper also proposes the **ensemble method** to make use of the augmented data based on row permutation. For inference using existing models, several permuted images would be fed to the model. The overall result would be obtained by majority voting (for classification task) or averaging (for time-series prediction task) of the individual results. To benefit from the augmented data for training, an ensemble of networks would be used, similar to the random forest method. Each set of permutations would be used to train one sub-network, and the result of all sub-networks would be combined to determine the overall outcome. As the training of an individual sub-network is independent of other sub-networks, this opens up the opportunity to train the sub-networks in parallel, reducing the overall training time. The boosting effect of the ensemble method can also improve the overall accuracy even though each sub-network may have lower accuracy, providing another possibility to trade-off accuracy for training time required.

The major contributions of this paper are:

1. RPN (Restricted Permutation Network), a simple and scalable parametric design for efficient hardware implementations of restricted permutations.
2. Illustration of the generated permutation as a valid and effective data augmentation technique for applications such as deep learning training.
3. An ensemble method to use augmented data for both inference and training to improve accuracy while reducing training time.

## 2 Background

### 2.1 Data Augmentation

Data augmentation is a common approach to synthesise new training samples for deep learning models. Conventional image processing techniques have been used widely for data augmentation, such as applying additive noise [5], reflections and colour perturbation [6], skew, rotation and scaling [7]. Despite providing simple generation methods, it is difficult to generate diverse data samples based on image processing while preserving the ground truth label.

Deep Generative Models, such as Generative Adversarial Networks (GANs) [8], are alternatives for data generation. The generator and discriminator of GAN play a two-player minimax game during training. The generator tries to generate images similar to the given image, while the discriminator tries to identify the generated one from the given images. To preserve the temporal dynamics of time-series models, TimeGAN [9] is proposed to generate images utilizing temporal correlations. A Bayesian data augmentation method [10] is also proposed based on GAN, using one generation model and two discriminative models. It treats the synthetic data points as instances of a random latent variable drawn from a distribution learnt from the given set of annotated training data, iteratively generating new data points. With proper training, GAN can produce very diverse images, however, the training process is usually time-consuming, and fine-tuning is required to generate images of different sizes.

### 2.2 Permutation Generation Network

Beneš network [11] and butterfly network [12] are both recursively defined networks that are used for signal permutation. The major drawback is the low scalability of the networks due to implementation difficulty caused by routing the interleaving wires between each stage, reducing the operating frequency and input size. A Beneš network with arbitrary input size [13] is proposed to relax the constraint of having $2^n$ input ports, reducing unnecessary resources consumed by unused ports. However, the connection is more complex, making the design much less regular, thus more difficult to implement. Another difficulty is

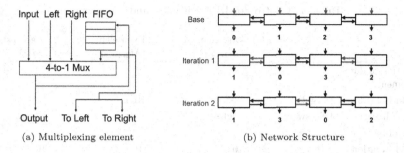

(a) Multiplexing element                    (b) Network Structure

**Fig. 1.** Architecture of the restricted permutation network

determining which permutation to produce. A hardware indexing system [14] is proposed to map each index to a specific permutation. However, the method is not very scalable as there is a factorial growth of available permutations.

## 3   Accelerator Architecture

The two key features of the permutation generated by the proposed Restricted Permutation Network (RPN) are:

1. Local row permutation
2. Restricted and pre-determined permutation

The key idea of the RPN is to generate permutations by swapping neighbouring rows of the original image. This ensures each row of the permuted image would at most be 1 row away from its original position, persevering mostly the original spatial correlation. A pre-determined set of permutations can be chosen to simplify the control of the network, avoiding any data collision and congestion.

The RPN has 3 parameters, $N$, $k$, and $d$. $N$ is the length of the network, defining the range for permutation, as well as resource usage. $k$ refers to the number of stages, trading off resources for reduced latency. $d$ is the group size, defining the maximum displacement of each element, and also the available permutations before repeating.

### 3.1   Network Structure

The RPN consists of a single layer of $N$ multiplexing elements. As shown in Fig. 1a, each element is a 4-to-1 multiplexor with a FIFO. The elements are only connected to their neighbours, forming a 1 dimensional chain. This provides a compact design with simple routing. Figure 1b shows a network with $N = 4$. Each element is responsible for handling the value of one row. Each row of the original image is being fed to the input port of the corresponding multiplexing element. The original image would be output without permutation done in the base iteration, and it would also be stored in the FIFO.

For each permutation iteration, the multiplexing unit can either output the FIFO value, indicating no swapping done, or the value from its left or right

**Table 1.** Control for RPN with odd and even swap

|  | Left Edge ($M_0$) | Odd element ($M_{2m+1}$) | Even element ($M_{2m+2}$) | Right Edge ($M_N$) |
|---|---|---|---|---|
| Direction of data movement |  |  |  |  |
| – Odd iteration | Right | Left | Right | Left |
| – Even iteration | No swap | Right | Left | No swap |
| Control bits |  |  |  |  |
| – Odd iteration | 01 | 10 | 01 | 10 |
| – Even iteration | 11 | 01 | 10 | 11 |
| Control signal | Toggle | Toggle | Toggle | Toggle |
| Generation | bit 1 | both bits | both bits | bit 0 |

neighbour. The output value would be stored in the FIFO to be used in the next iteration to generate the next permutation.

As the row permutation has to be done without replacement, i.e. each row has to appear exactly once in the permuted image, swapping has to be done in pairs. When the multiplexing element $M_i$ outputs the value from its right neighbour $M_{i+1}$, $M_{i+1}$ has to output the value of its left neighbour, $M_i$.

For input image of size $R \times C$, the length of network, $N$, is set as the number of rows of the image, $R$, to allow permutation to be done on every row, while the FIFO depth is set to $C$, which is the length of each row.

### 3.2   Permutation Selection

To simplify the control signal generation while keeping the diversity of permutations, odd and even swap is implemented.

The red arrows in Fig. 1b indicate the data flow. For the base case, the image comes in from the input, and is output without any permutation. For iteration 1, $M_0$ swaps with $M_1$, and $M_2$ swaps with $M_3$. For iteration 2, edge element $M_0$ and $M_3$ remain unchanged, while $M_1$ swap with $M_2$.

A generalized swapping algorithm and the corresponding control is shown in Table 1. Elements swap with its left and right neighbour alternatively in consecutive iterations. Edge element would remain its value every other iteration as it only has one neighbour to swap with.

The odd and even swap greatly simplifies the control of RPN. For any iteration, there is no need to compute the corresponding control for individual elements, or store a predefined set of control signals. The control signals are generated simply by toggling the initial control bits.

With such a simple generation method, when using $N$ elements in the network, $2N$ permutations can be generated before repeating. Every row would be at most $j$ rows away from its base position in the $j^{th}$ permutation, restricting the permutation to be relatively local. The permutation order is fixed and deterministic, facilitating the identification and grouping of the augmented data within the same permutation.

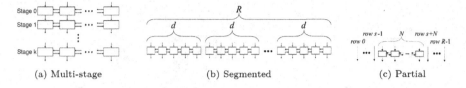

Fig. 2. Available configurations for restricted permutation network

### 3.3 Further Optimization

Simple modifications can be made to address different design specifications and constraints, further optimizing the network for specific applications as shown in Fig. 2.

*Multi-stage configuration* - For a fully pipelined design with only a few permutations required, $k$ networks with the FIFO removed can be cascaded to form a $k$-stage network. All $k$ permutations can be produced within a pipeline, speeding up the generation $k$ times while reducing the memory requirement. $k$ offers the trade off between resource usage and latency.

*Segmented configuration* - To better preserve the local spatial correlation for large images, multiple smaller RPNs can be used instead of using one for the entire image. By grouping every $d$ adjacent rows, the maximum displacement of each row is limited from $R$ to $d$, while reducing the non-repeating permutations from $2R$ to $2d$. $d = 5$ is chosen to balance the preservation of local correlation and available permutations.

*Partial configuration* - Another optimization to reduce resource usage and memory requirement is permuting only a subset of rows. By setting $N < R$, only $N$ adjacent rows of the image would be permuted, while the remaining $R - N$ rows are unchanged. The resultant permutations would still be valid permutations preserving the local spatial correlation, with only $N/R$ of resources used. $N$ is used to balance resource usage and available permutations.

Each of the three configurations addresses a different type of design specification. The implementation of the modifications is independent of each other, giving the flexibility for users to apply more than one optimization to the same design. For example, configuring the RPN to have multiple stages applying only on a selected set of adjacent rows, with segmented configuration, achieving a multi-stage partial segmented design.

## 4  Evaluation

### 4.1  Effect of Using Different Permutations

Experiments are conducted to show the effect of using RPN for both training and inference on image classification and time-series prediction tasks.

*i. Inference* - To test the quality of images generated by RPN, images of different maximum displacement ($d$) are tested with DeepVariant [15] to classify

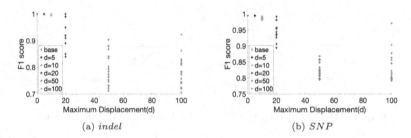

(a) *indel*                              (b) *SNP*

**Fig. 3.** Image classification accuracy with permutation of different maximum displacement. The F1-score is the harmonic mean of precision and recall of a classifier. It ranges
from 0 to1, with a higher score indicating a better classifier.

the type of genetic variant. DeepVariant first compiles rows of DNA sequences
into pileup images, then uses CNN for image classification. Two different types of
variants, indel and SNP, are being tested. Each image consists of 100 independent
rows of DNA sequences with 221 characters each. DNA sequences are taken from
the publicly available HG002 Illumina WGS reads, with the Genome in a Bottle
small variant benchmarks for HG002. 1193 images are used for each test. For each
displacement case, 20 permutations are randomly selected to test for accuracy.

As seen in Fig. 3, the F1 scores of both indel and SNP drop and get more
diverse as $d$ increases. Small values of $d$ restrict row swapping to be take place
locally, preserving the original spatial correlation of the image, thus leading to
higher accuracy of classification. For large values of d, the accuracy can still be
maintained at a high level for some images. This is because some permutations
could retain the original correlation despite having a global swap, for example
flipping the entire image upside down. However, in general, the spatial correlation
is getting more distorted as $d$ increases. This leads to diverse result of accuracy as
$d$ increases. By a reasonable choice of $d$ ($d < 10$), the F1 score can be maintained
above 0.97, showing that the RPN provides high quality augmented data.

$d$ can be adjusted using the segmented configuration of RPN, as shown in
Fig. 2b, balancing the need to preserving spatial correlation for inference of image
classification and available permutations.

***ii. Training*** - As mentioned in [2], CNNs trained with random permutation
are less accurate compared to the ones trained with the original dataset due to
the inconsistency in underlying features of images with different permutations.
This issue can be addressed by only using images with the same permutation to
train the CNN model.

To test the dataset generated by RPN, CNNs, each trained with different
permutation sets, are compared to the CNN trained with the original dataset for
time-series prediction task, DL4Epi [1]. DL4Epi uses RNN to capture long term
correlation and CNN to fuse information of the US-HHS dataset. It consists of
weekly influenza activity levels for the 10 districts of the mainland U.S. measured
using the weighted ILI metric. As the order of the 10 districts is independent,
permuting the rows should give the same information.

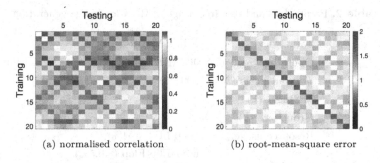

(a) normalised correlation          (b) root-mean-square error

**Fig. 4.** Training result of time-series prediction with permuted dataset

The original training set and all 19 augmented datasets generated by the RPN are used to train different CNN models. The best model for each permutation is used here.

The normalised Pearson correlation score and root-mean-square error ($rmse$) of the CNNs are shown in Fig. 4a and 4b respectively. The x-axis indicates the permutation set of the training dataset (with 1 being the original dataset), and the y-axis represents the permutation set for testing data. The correlation scores are normalized by the baseline CNN trained with the original dataset. Red in Figure 4a means the CNN outperforms the baseline system, white refers to similar performance and blue indicates worse. Along the diagonal of the grid, the cells are mostly white or red, indicating when tested with the dataset of the same permutation, most models can perform as well as the baseline. The same trend is also shown for $rmse$, with minimal error along the diagonal.

Despite having the same high quality data compared to the original set, all the generated set are significantly different, as shown by the decrease in correlation and increase in error when training and testing set mismatch, indicated by the elements not on the main diagonal. It shows that models trained by different permutation sets would capture significantly different spatial correlation of the images. This helps introducing diversity to the network ensemble when different permutation of the data is used to train the individual network of the ensemble.

### 4.2   Comparison to Existing Data Augmentation Methods

The RPN is compared against common data augmentation method for images, Generative Adversarial Network (GAN) [9], and addition of white Gaussian noise [5]. Software code runs on a 6-core Intel Core i7 at 2.6 GHz, with 16 GB RAM. The parameters and details of the RPN used are listed in Table 2.

*i. Image Quality and Accuracy* - Figure 5a shows the comparison of the accuracy of images with Gaussian noise addition and RPN images. Structural Similarity Index Measure (SSIM) is used to quantify the effect of the noise addition. SSIM ranges from 0 to 1, the higher value indicates the more similar the new image is compared to the original one.

**Table 2.** Parameters and resource usage of RPN for image generation

| Target device | Xilinx Virtex-7 FPGA |
|---|---|
| Operating frequency | 400 MHz |
| # Input ports ($N$) | 200 |
| # Stages ($k$) | 1 |
| Group size ($d$) | 5 |
| Resource usage | 6660 LUT (∼1%)<br>6687 Flip-Flop (∼0.5%) |
| Power consumption | 1.12 W |

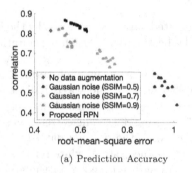

(a) Prediction Accuracy

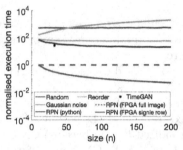

(b) Speed up of RPN compared to other image generation methods

**Fig. 5.** Comparison of software data augmentation and RPN

As the effect of noise is the same for different datasets, the variance of the noise is selected by a sweep for mean SSIM of different noise magnitudes over 300 images of the US-HHS dataset. To achieve SSIM of 0.5, 0.7, and 0.9, the variance of the Gaussian noise added are 0.8, 0.5, and 0.25 respectively.

As seen in the figure, images generated by RPN in general preserves the high correlation and low root-mean-square error. The accuracy of Gaussian noise images worsens as noise increases. For actual hardware implementation, depending on the choice of precision, it can be difficult to inject exactly the required amount of noise to achieve the desired SSIM. This leads to another uncertainty in the data augmentation.

RPN is a simple and robust data augmentation method, as it can generate images without having to analyze the dataset in advance, and the quality of the generated images is independent of the precision used in the system.

***ii. Generation Complexity and Performance*** - Different software row permutation generation methods are being tested with TimeGAN and Gaussian noise addition using Python built-in functions to augment images of size $n \times n$.

The speed up of RPN is plotted in Fig. 5b, using the RPN full image generation as the normalisation reference. For full image generation, the FPGA implementation of RPN is 21 times faster than the software version of RPN for

**Table 3.** Comparison of the restricted permutation network and existing permutation architecture

| | Beneš network | Butterfly network | RPN single stage | RPN multi-stage |
|---|---|---|---|---|
| Diameter | $2log(N) + 1$ | $log(N) + 2$ | 1 | $k$ |
| Basic unit | $2 \times 2$ switch | $2 \times 2$ switch | 4–1 MUX | 4–1 MUX |
| # element | $2log(N)$ | $Nlog(N) + N$ | $N$ | $kN$ |
| Congestion (Worst Case) | Fixed(1) | Variable ($\sqrt{N}$) | Fixed(1) | Fixed(1) |
| Connection distance (max) | $N/2$ | $N/2$ | 1 | 1 |
| Latency | $C$ | $C$ | $C$ | $C/k$ |
| Permutation exploration | All | All | $2d$ | $2d$ |
| Memory requirement | None | None | $N$ FIFO of size $C$ | None |

$n = 200$, and over 100 times faster than other software augmentation methods, such as random permutation and Guassian noise addition. For convolution computation, it would only add 10 extra cycles for $d = 5$. This is a negligible overhead added to the time taken to complete the entire 2D convolution of the image. It shows that the architecture is best used as a lightweight parametric library element for pre-processing of FPGA applications.

TimeGAN is 28 times slower than RPN for $n = 33$. It also requires at least hours to train and the generation does not scale with different image sizes, making it the least flexible way of data augmentation among the methods compared.

*iii. Data Storage and Transfer* - The generation of TimeGAN involves the generation of a random seed, while the Gaussian noise is also generated randomly. To keep track of the augmented dataset, the dataset must be stored in memory, resulting in a larger memory footprint.

For the permutation method, the data augmentation is reproducible given the permutation order. With odd-even swap, the permutation set is pre-determined and can be computed on the fly. No extra storage is needed while unblocking the data transfer bottleneck to the FPGA.

## 4.3  Comparison to Existing Permutation Architectures

The RPN is compared against two most common permutation networks, Beneš network and butterfly network in Table 3.

Apart from reducing the network complexity from $Nlog(N)$ to $N$, the connection among elements is also greatly simplified by reducing the connection distance. Both Beneš and Bufferfly networks connect elements across the stages, with a maximum of $N/2$ elements apart, creating a lot of wire interleaves, as shown in Fig. 6a. The interleaving problem worsens as input size $N$ increases. This imposes difficulties in routing, leading to reduced operating frequency and possible input size.

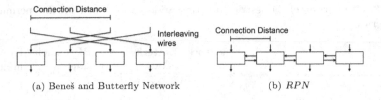

(a) Beneš and Butterfly Network                (b) *RPN*

**Fig. 6.** Illustration of simplification done on RPN

RPN addresses the problem of interleaving wires by only connecting elements within the distance of 1, i.e. the neighbouring elements. This leads to a more compact design, improving the scalability and regularity of the architecture, as shown in Figure 6b. RPN can easily be scaled to any $N$, while Beneš and Bufferfly networks only work best for $N$ being powers of 2, with place and route become significantly more difficult when $N > 64$.

## 5   Applications

To benefit from data augmentation with permutation, the ensemble method is used for both DeepVariant inference and DL4Epi training to improve the accuracy while reducing training time. As there is no other published hardware that implements the target applications, RPN results are compared to the software counterpart. The parameters and details of the RPN used are shown in Table 4. RPN serves as a lightweight parametric add-on for pre-processing of FPGA applications, adding only a negligible amount of hardware resource and power consumption on top of the main application.

**Table 4.** Parameters and resource usage of RPN for DeepVariant and DL4Epi

| Target device | Xilinx Virtex-7 FPGA | Xilinx Virtex-7 FPGA |
|---|---|---|
| Operating frequency | 400 MHz | 400 MHz |
| Target application | DeepVariant (Inference) [15] | DL4Epi (Training) [1] |
| # Input ports ($N$) | 100 | 10 |
| # Stages ($k$) | 1 | 1 |
| Group size ($d$) | 5 | 10 |
| Resource usage | 3336 LUT ($\sim$0.5%) | 342 LUT ($\sim$0.05%) |
|  | 3325 Flip-Flop ($\sim$0.2%) | 339 Flip-Flop ($\sim$0.02%) |
| Power consumption | 0.665 W | 0.233 W |

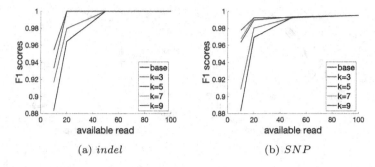

(a) *indel*                          (b) *SNP*

**Fig. 7.** Image classification accuracy with permutation of different available reads

## 5.1   Inference

For image classification tasks, the decision is made based on a single image. Unlike video classification that consecutive frames can be used to identify the same object, it is difficult to do the same for image classification to generate different images from just 1 image.

Permutation provides a convenient way to generate multiple images from just 1 image to improve the accuracy of image classification with ensemble method, for example, majority voting or weighted sum. Local permutations are preferred to preserve the spatial correlation of the original image.

The effect of using permutation ensemble is shown using DeepVariant. Despite having high accuracy, it is very difficult to retrain the network based on different scenarios, as it requires months of training with lots of data. The following are 2 cases that DeepVariant suffers from loss in accuracy.

***i. Fewer Reads Available*** - A common problem for genetic variant call is not having enough reads for a particular position. This would mean having fewer rows with data in the image.

To simulate the effect of having fewer available reads, only every $i^{th}$ row of the image is kept, then the image is padded with rows of zeros at the bottom. Permuted images are generated by the segmented RPN, with $d = 5$, $N = 100$.

As seen in Fig. 7, the F1 scores drop as the number of reads reduces. The recall is still maintained in a high level, indicating very few false negatives (FN). The drop in accuracy is caused by the increase in false positives (FP). The model can still identify most true positives (TP) correctly with different permuted images but with less precision, each having different FP. Majority voting is used to identify the TP and rule out FP. Combining the result of permuted images, in general, F1 scores can be improved by 5%. Having more permuted images could keep improving the combined result. However, 3 images in total (base case with 2 permuted images) would be a good trade off between accuracy improvement and resources to generate the additional results.

***ii. Shorter Reads Available*** - The read length of the dataset is dependant on the samples and the DNA sequencer. Having shorter reads means the compiled image has fewer columns. Ideally, the network should be retrained according to

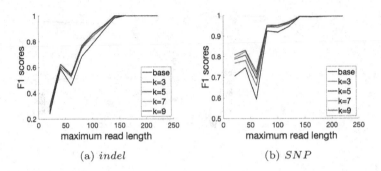

(a) *indel*                    (b) *SNP*

**Fig. 8.** Image classification accuracy with permutation of different maximum read length

the read length. However, due to the difficulty to retrain the network and for flexibility of the system to take input of slightly different sizes, zero padding is used to make up the size of the image to $100 \times 221$. However, having a shorter read would means more zero padded columns at the 2 ends of the image.

The effect of reduced read length is shown in Fig. 8. As the read length is around 100–150 for the HG002 dataset, there is no drop in F1 scores until the maximum read length drop to below 150. The F1 scores of both indel and SNP keep dropping as maximum read length reduces.

The results show that DeepVariant maintains very high precision, i.e. having very few FP, with reducing read length. The drop in F1 scores is caused by the increase in FN, as it fails to identify the presence of genetic variant. This also applies to the result of the permuted images. All of them have very few FP, and each identifies different TP.

Based on such feature, instead of using majority voting to determine the TP, the union of the results is used. As each of the permuted images covers a slightly different set of TP, the union of TP greatly reduces the FN. Although it would also lead to the increase of FP, it is not causing a problem as the union set of FP is still very small compared to the TP, about 5 FP in 700 TP. Figure 8 shows the combined result of 3, 5, 7, 9 permuted images. It can be seen that the combined result in general increases the F1 scores by 0.1. The combined result keeps improving as more permuted images are used. However, further improvement is not as obvious. Using 3 images in total (base case with 2 permuted images) would be a good trade off between improvement in accuracy and resources to generate the additional results.

## 5.2   Training

As different permutations have different spatial correlations, using all generated images with different permutations to train one network is not ideal.

The augmented dataset can benefit an ensemble of networks, each trained with a particular set of permutations. Results of the sub-networks can be com-

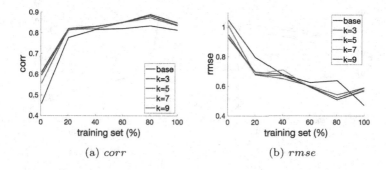

(a) *corr*                              (b) *rmse*

**Fig. 9.** Combined time-series prediction with partial training dataset

bined to determine the overall result. The ensemble diversity brought by permutation would improve the accuracy compared to individual sub-network.

As the training of each sub-network is independent of each other, they can be trained in parallel. By using the ensemble method, accuracy can be restored by combining the results of different sub-networks. This relaxes the accuracy requirement of each sub-network, leading to further opportunities to speed up training, for example, reducing the training set and reducing the training epoch.

The idea of an ensemble of networks trained with permutations of data is tested with DL4Epi. Permuted images are generated by RPN with $d = 10$, $N = 10$. The result of time-series prediction is combined by taking arithmetic mean.

*i. Reduced Training Set* - Figure 9 shows the effect of reducing the training set. Reducing the training dataset would reduce *corr* and increase *rmse*. To compensate for the reduction in network accuracy, results of multiple networks are combined to improve the quality of the prediction. In general, having 3 sub-networks increases *corr* by around 0.05 and reduces *rmse* by 10%. Further increase in the number of sub-networks does not show significant improvement.

Having 5 networks, each trained with 20% of the original training set, has similar performance compared to the baseline network trained with the entire dataset. This can be seen as successfully augmented the dataset 5 times for training. It indicates the potential to speed up the training time by 5 times when the networks are trained in parallel.

However, the improvement brought by combining sub-networks is not limitless. The combined result appears to converge beyond 5 networks used. This would imply that the base network still has to be reasonably accurate, otherwise even with the improvement brought by permuted dataset and ensemble, the overall performance of the network would not be of acceptable quality. For example, in the DL4Epi case, training with 1% of training dataset resulted in $corr = 0.46$, with the best combined result being 0.61, which is still far worse than the base network trained with 20% training set.

*ii. Reduced Training Epoch* - The rate of improvement for network training diminishes as the network converges after training with more epochs. Instead of training a more accurate network with more epochs, multiple networks, each

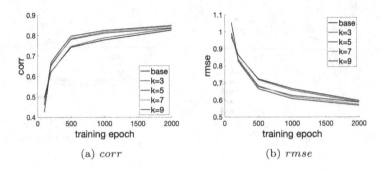

(a) *corr*                                    (b) *rmse*

**Fig. 10.** Combined time-series prediction with reduced epoch

trained with fewer epochs, can be combined to speed up training by training in parallel.

Figure 10 shows the effect of reducing the training epoch. For the base case, training the network with 500 epochs can already achieve 0.75 for *corr*. However, it takes another 1500 epochs to further increase it by 0.05. The same applies to *rmse*, having 500 epochs reduces the error from 1 to 0.7, but a further reduction of 0.1 would require 1500 more epochs.

By combining the results from 5 networks each trained with 500 epochs, the overall result is comparable to the baseline network trained with 2000 epochs. Although the total training time to train all 5 networks appears to be 25% more than the baseline, the ensemble method provides the possibility to split the training task, and spread the computation load among different devices in parallel. The 5 networks can be trained on different devices in parallel, achieving a 4 times speed up. Instead of having one long iterative process that can not be easily parallelized to utilize the existing resources, the ensemble method opens up the opportunity to speed up training by trading resources for time.

In order to properly apply the ensemble method, the epoch used has to be carefully determined so that each sub-network is of reasonable quality. For instance, combining multiple networks trained with only 1 epoch would not be improved by the ensemble method, as the networks are not useful at this point. A more appropriate time to terminate training is when the gain from each epoch has drastically dropped over a few epochs, which would indicate the network has already learnt a significant amount of features from the dataset, and would take much longer to further improve.

## 6   Conclusion

This paper presents a novel scalable architecture to automatically generate restricted local permutation efficiently, preserving the spatial correlation of the original image while reducing memory footprint and transfer. The Restricted Permutation Network, RPN, is fully pipelined with deterministic and regular latency, making it a perfect light weight parametric library element for data augmentation for FPGA applications. Together with the ensemble method, permuted images can improve accuracy and training time for CNN inference and training, improving the accuracy of image classification by around 5%, and speeding up training by 4 to 5 times with a negligible drop in accuracy. Future work includes automating parametric analysis and extending the RPN architecture to cover other permutation applications.

**Acknowledgement.** The support of the Croucher Foundation, the UK EPSRC (grant number EP/V028251/1, EP/L016796/1, EP/S030069/1 and EP/N031768/1) and Xilinx is gratefully acknowledged.

# References

1. Wu, Y., Yang, Y., Nishiura, H., Saitoh, M.: Deep learning for epidemiological predictions. In: SIGIR (2018)
2. Ivan, C.: Convolutional neural networks on randomized data. CoRR (2019)
3. Um, T.T., et al.: Data augmentation of wearable sensor data for Parkinson's disease monitoring using convolutional neural networks. In: ICMI (2017)
4. Iwana, B.K., Uchida, S.: An empirical survey of data augmentation for time series classification with neural networks. In: ICPR (2020)
5. Akbiyik, M.E.: Data augmentation in training CNNs: injecting noise to images. In: ICLR (2020)
6. Krizhevsky, A., Sutskever, I., Hinton, G.E.: ImageNet classification with deep convolutional neural networks. In: NIPS (2012)
7. Simard, P., Steinkraus, D., Platt, J.: Best practices for convolutional neural networks applied to visual document analysis. In: ICDAR (2003)
8. Goodfellow, I.J., et al.: Generative adversarial networks. In: NIPS (2014)
9. Yoon, J., et al.: Time-series generative adversarial networks. In: NIPS (2019)
10. Tran, T., Pham, T., Carneiro, G., Palmer, L.J., Reid, I.D.: A bayesian data augmentation approach for learning deep models. CoRR (2017)
11. Beneš, V.E.: Mathematical Theory of Connecting Network and Telephone Traffic. Academic, New York (1965)
12. Cooley, J.M., et al.: An algorithm for the machine calculation of complex fourier series. Math. Comp. **19**, 297–301 (1965)
13. Jumandi, Z., Samsudin, A., Budiarto, R.: Optimized arbitrary size networks. In: ICTTA (2004)
14. Butler, J.T., Sasao, T.: Hardware index to permutation converter. In: IPDPS (PhD Forum) (2012)
15. Poplin, R., et al.: A universal SNP and small-indel variant caller using deep neural networks. Nat. Biotechnol. **36**, 983–987 (2018)

# Real-Time Embedded Object Tracking with Discriminative Correlation Filters Using Convolutional Features

Michal Danilowicz[ID] and Tomasz Kryjak[✉][ID]

Embedded Vision Systems Group, Computer Vision Laboratory,
Department of Automatic Control and Robotics,
AGH University of Science and Technology, Krakow, Poland
{danilowi,tomasz.kryjak}@agh.edu.pl

**Abstract.** Object tracking is an essential element of visual perception systems. It is used in advanced video surveillance systems (AVSS), autonomous vehicles, robotics, and many more. For applications such as autonomous robots, the system must be implemented on some embedded platform with limited computing performance and power. Furthermore, sufficiently fast response is required from the tracking system in order to perform some real-time tasks. Discriminative Correlation Filter (DCF) based tracking algorithms are popular for such applications, as they offer state-of-the-art performance while not being too computationally complex. In this paper, an FPGA implementation of the DCF tracking algorithm using convolutional features is presented. The ZCU104 board is used as a platform, and the performance is evaluated on the VOT2015 dataset. In contrast to other implementations that use HOG (Histogram of Oriented Gradients) features, this implementation achieves better results for $64 \times 64$ filter size while being able to potentially operate at higher speeds (over 467 fps per scale).

**Keywords:** Discriminative correlation filter · Object tracking · FPGA · Real-time image processing

## 1 Introduction

Object tracking is one of the basic tasks of computer vision. In general, it can be described as determining the objects' positions in consecutive frames. Tracking is used in many civilian applications (autonomous vehicles, advanced surveillance, robotics, human-computer interfaces) and military applications (air defence, targeting systems, missile control systems). Depending on what data the tracking system has and what we expect at the output, there are several subtypes of this problem. We can assume tracking of only one object (VOT – Visual Object Tracking) or several (MOT – Multiple Object Tracking), and decide whether it is necessary to reidentify the object after it has been lost (long-term vs. short-term tracking). It is also important if we track classes of objects known in advance

L. Gan et al. (Eds.): ARC 2022, LNCS 13569, pp. 166–180, 2022.
https://doi.org/10.1007/978-3-031-19983-7_12

(model-based tracking) or whether we should be ready to track any arbitrarily indicated fragment of an image. A final distinction is whether we only use the current and previous frames (casual tracker), or whether we also have access to future frames of the image (for example, post-processing of a video surveillance camera recording).

This paper addresses the issue of single object, short-term, model-free and online tracking, which is the premise of the *short-term challenge* of the VOT Challenge [16]. In addition to the effectiveness of the task itself in predicting the displacement of an object between successive frames, another very important parameter of the tracking system is the processing speed. If the time between successive predictions of the tracking system is too long, it may result in a too large change in the position or appearance of the object, resulting in poor performance. Moreover, in some systems, the energy efficiency is also crucial. Examples are solutions for autonomous vehicles in the broad sense.

In recent years, the use of convolutional networks for the generation of image features in computer vision algorithms has become increasingly popular. These features usually allow algorithms to achieve greater efficiency than the image itself or the so-called *hand-crafted features* like HOG (Histogram of Oriented Gradients) or Colour Attributes [10]. However, convolutional networks, particularly deep networks, require a lot of computing power to work in real-time. It is helpful to use platforms that support parallel computing, such as FPGA (*Field-Programmable Gate Array*) or GPU (*Graphics Processing Unit*). Specifically, the first one provides the ability to obtain high processing speed and low energy consumption, thanks to the possibility of optimising the computational architecture and precision of calculations to a specific algorithm. Quantisation of neural networks, i.e. reduction of the number of bits in the representation of processed data and model parameters, allows for a significant reduction of computational and memory complexity of algorithms with little loss of performance [3,21].

In this paper, a hardware implementation of the deepDCF tracking algorithm is presented. Using the FINN compiler for neural network acceleration and parallel computations in FPGA devices we were able to achieve an average processing speed of 467,3 fps (frames per second) per scale at $64 \times 64$ filter size.

The main contributions of this paper include:

- Optimisation and analysis of a deepDCF tracking algorithm for implementation on an embedded computing platform and evaluation on the VOT2015 dataset.
- Implementation of a tracking system based on correlation filters using convolutional network features. The system outperforms other similar approaches in tracking performance and speed.

To our knowledge, no paper has been published in which the deepDCF algorithm has been implemented in an FPGA.

The remainder of this paper is organised as follows. Section 2 describes object-tracking methods using correlation filters. Section 3 discusses the state-of-the-art of implementing correlation filters on embedded FPGA platforms. Section 4 presents the evaluation of the software model, the quantisation process of the convolutional network, and the hardware implementation. The last section contains a discussion of the results obtained and directions for further research.

## 2   Object Tracking with Correlation Filters

In this section, we present the first algorithm in the correlation filter family – MOSSE (Minimum Output Sum of Squared Error) [4], and its subsequent improvements that have been implemented on embedded platforms. It should be noted that there are also other modifications to the algorithm, such as SRDCF (Spatially Regularized Discriminative Correlation Filters), however, they have a much higher computational complexity and are therefore currently not considered for implementation on embedded vision platforms.

The following algorithms share a simple concept. The tracked object model is initialised in the first frame of the video sequence. In subsequent tracking frames, a filter response is obtained by correlating the current object model with a part of the image around the last known object position. The location of the maximum correlation value in the response is used to predict the new object's position. Also, the model is updated taking into account the new, potentially changed, appearance of the object.

### 2.1   MOSSE

The goal of the MOSSE algorithm is to find an optimal filter $w \in \mathbb{R}^{M \times N}$ (where $M \times N$ is the size of the filter and the tracked region) which is defined by the following LS (*Least Squares*) regression problem:

$$\arg \min_{\hat{w}} \sum_{i=1}^{N} ||\hat{w}^* \odot \hat{x}_i - \hat{y}_i||^2 \tag{1}$$

where $\odot$ means element-wise multiplication, $\hat{\ }$ hat denotes a discrete Fourier transform (DFT) of some signal and $*$ is a complex conjugate. The problem is defined in the frequency domain because using the FFT algorithm (Fast Fourier Transform) and the convolution theorem, the computational complexity of the correlation can be lowered from $\mathcal{O}(M^2N^2)$ to $\mathcal{O}(MNlogMN)$. The training set consists of $(x_i, y_i)$ pairs, where $x_i \in \mathbb{R}^{M \times N}$ is a grayscale image patch centered around the target object in the first frame. The samples are generated by aplying random affine transformations to the initial object's appearance. For regression targets $y_i \in \mathbb{R}^{M \times N}$, a discrete two-dimensional Gaussian is used.

The problem (1) has a closed-form solution given by:

$$\hat{w} = \frac{\sum_{i=1}^{N} \hat{y}_i^* \odot \hat{x}_i}{\sum_{i=1}^{N} \hat{x}_i^* \odot \hat{x}_i} \tag{2}$$

The prediction of object's position is done by computing filter response in pixel coordinates space by using inverse, discrete Fourier transform (IDFT):

$$g = \mathcal{F}^{-1}(\hat{w}_{t-1}^* \odot \hat{x}_t) \tag{3}$$

After every prediction, the filter is updated using a running average to address changes in the object's appearance:

$$\hat{a}_t = \eta \hat{y}^* \odot \hat{x}_t + (1 - \eta)\hat{a}_{t-1} \tag{4}$$

$$\hat{b}_t = \eta \hat{x}_t^* \odot \hat{x}_t + (1 - \eta)\hat{b}_{t-1} \tag{5}$$

where $\hat{w}_t = \frac{\hat{a}_t}{\hat{b}_t}$ (element-wise division), and $\eta \in [0, 1]$ is a learning rate parameter.

## 2.2 KCF

The correlation filter tracker was further improved by considering tracking as a linear ridge regression problem [13,14]. The method is called KCF (Kernelized Correlation Filter) and the goal is to find a linear function $f(z) = w^T z$ which minimises the error between samples $x_i \in \mathbb{R}^d$ and regression targets $y_i \in \mathbb{R}$:

$$\epsilon = \sum_i (f(x_i) - y_i)^2 + \lambda ||w||^2 \tag{6}$$

An interesting conclusion from these works is, that if data matrix $X$ is circulant, the regression problem (6) is equivalent to the MOSSE filter (1) for one sample ($n = 1$). The advantage of such representation of the problem (6) is a possibility to solve it in some nonlinear space $\varphi(x)$ using the *kernel trick* [19]. In brief, a kernel function $\kappa(x, z)$ must be defined which acts as a dot product in non-linear space $\varphi(x)$. For that purpose, a so-called *kernel correlation vector* is computed:

$$k^{xz} = \exp\left(-\frac{1}{\sigma^2}\left(||x||^2 + ||z||^2 - 2\mathcal{F}^{-1}\left(\sum_l^C \hat{x}_l^* \odot \hat{z}_l\right)\right)\right) \tag{7}$$

For tracking, the filter is initialised by:

$$\hat{\alpha} = \frac{\hat{y}}{\hat{k}^{xx} + \lambda} \tag{8}$$

Prediction:

$$\mathbf{f}(z) = \mathcal{F}^{-1}(\hat{k}^{xz} \odot \hat{\alpha}) \tag{9}$$

Update:

$$\hat{\alpha}_t = (1 - \eta)\hat{\alpha}_{t-1} + \eta\hat{\alpha} \tag{10}$$

$$\hat{x}_t = (1 - \eta)\hat{x}_{t-1} + \eta\hat{x} \tag{11}$$

The algorithm offers an improvement in tracking performance compared to MOSSE with a little extra computational complexity that comes from the need to compute the kernel correlation vector (7). Computing the IDFT $\mathcal{F}^{-1}$ and DFTs $\hat{x}_l^*$ is necessary in the MOSSE algorithm anyway and the exponent function operation can be for example stored in LUTs (Look Up Tables) on the target hardware platform.

## 2.3  DSST

Scale estimation in the tracking system is typically done by predicting the filter at multiple scales. In that case, the object scale corresponds to the largest correlation score obtained. In the paper [8], the concept of DSST (Discriminative Scale Space Tracking) is presented. The method uses an additional correlation filter dedicated to predicting the change in scale. Training and prediction samples $\mathbf{x} \in \mathbb{R}^{S \times D}$ are constructed by generating one-dimensional feature vectors $x_s \in \mathbb{R}^D$ of the object for several scales $s \in [1, S]$. Each vector is extracted from an image patch of size $\beta^n H \times \beta^n W$ centered around the object's position. $\beta > 1$ is a scale factor parameter (typically around 1.01) and $n \in \left\{ \lfloor -\frac{S-1}{2} \rfloor, \dots, \lfloor \frac{S-1}{2} \rfloor \right\}$.

This solution to scale prediction has shown better performance while also reducing computational complexity compared to estimating the filter in multiple scales.

## 2.4  Convolutional Features

Another improvement to the MOSSE algorithm was to use multidimensional image features [9,14] like histograms of oriented gradients (HOG) or generated by a convolutional neural network. Such algorithms are often called DCF (*Discriminative Correlation Filters*). In such a case, for initialisation, update and prediction, multidimensional samples $x \in \mathbb{R}^{[C \times H \times W]}$ are used, as well as $D$ filters, each for one feature channel.

$$\hat{w}^l = \frac{\hat{y}^* \odot \hat{x}^l}{\sum_{l=1}^{C} \hat{x}^{l*} \odot \hat{x}^l} \tag{12}$$

$$\hat{a}_t^l = \eta \hat{y}^* \odot \hat{x}_t^l + (1 - \eta)\hat{a}_{t-1}^l \tag{13}$$

$$\hat{b}_t = \eta \sum_{l=1}^{C} \hat{x}_t^{l*} \odot \hat{x}_t^l + (1 - \eta)\hat{b}_{t-1} \tag{14}$$

$$g = \mathcal{F}^{-1}\left( \sum_{l=1}^{C} \hat{w}_{t-1}^{l*} \odot \hat{x}_t^l \right) \tag{15}$$

In the paper [6], the *deepDCF* algorithm is presented which utilises a convolutional network to generate image features in the DCF framework. A vgg-2048 [5] model trained for the classification task was used on the ImageNet [11] dataset. The image features $x$ in Eqs. (12)–(15) are generated by the network after applying a preprocessing consisting of scaling the image to a fixed size (in [6], a $224 \times 224$ window was used) and normalisation. The output features are then multiplied by a Hann window before applying them to the tracking algorithm.

Only by using convolutional features (in fact, only the first layer), the simple DCF algorithms gave better tracking performance than more complicated

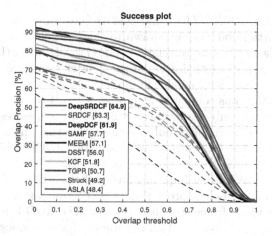

**Fig. 1.** The comparison of tracking performance of correlation filter based algorithms on the OTB-50 dataset (source: [6]).

methods. The comparison on the OTB-50 dataset [23] with other state-of-the-art tracking algorithms, including other correlation filter methods, is shown in Fig. 1. It is worth mentioning that the KCF and DSST algorithms can be applied regardless of the feature extraction method as long as the features are spatially correlated.

## 3   Previous Work

The implementation of correlation filters in FPGA devices has been addressed in a number of research papers. The paper [22] presents the implementation of the DCF + DSST algorithm on the Zynq ZedBoard platform (xc7z020clg484-1). The architecture implemented with the Vivado HLS tool offers image processing with a resolution of 320 × 240 at an average rate of 25.38 fps. An FPGA implementation of the **HOG** generation presented in the article [12] is used as image features. The authors analyse the basic computational steps of the algorithm: SVD (Singular Value Decomposition), QR decomposition (used in feature dimensionality reduction) and the determination of the two-dimensional discrete Fourier transform. The architecture of the QR decomposition algorithm has been optimised and uses 2.3 times less computational resources. The SVD computation has been accelerated nearly 3.8 times with respect to the known FPGA implementation [18], but consumes about twice as many computational resources. The authors did not provide information about the tracking performance after applying the proposed optimisations.

The authors of the article [24] implemented a three-scale KCF algorithm based on HOG features using the Vivado HLS tool. They used the Zynq ZCU102 MPSoC platform and achieved 30 fps for a 960 × 540 resolution. A brief analysis of the parallelisation of HOG feature generation operations by using the

*PIPELINE, ARRAY_PARTITION* and *DATAFLOW* directives of the HLS tool was performed. Attention was also drawn to the possibility of parallelising the computation of kernel feature correlation (Eq. (7)), detection (Eq. (9)) and filter update (Eq. (8)). No optimisation of the Fourier transform calculation was performed, and the function available in the HLS library was used. The effectiveness of the algorithm was compared with other state-of-the-art methods on the UAV123 set, however, only a selected part of the test sequences was used. The comparison is not very reliable if only for the reason that the authors obtained a better result with the KCF algorithm than with SRDCF, which is directly a better algorithm in other comparisons in the literature [7].

The work [17] presents an implementation of the KCF + DSST algorithm using the Vivado HLS tool. A processing rate of 25 fps was achieved, although it is not clear for which frame size and filter size. The HOG features were used. Only a qualitative (visualisation of sample frames from the sequence) evaluation of the tracking performance on sequences prepared by the authors and selected from the OTB set was presented. No quantitative evaluation and comparison with other methods or implementations in view of the applied optimisations was provided.

The publication [15] describes the implementation of the MOSSE algorithm in one scale on the Zynq UltraScale+ MPSoC ZCU104 platform. The Verilog hardware description language was used, which generally allows for lower FPGA resource requirements (for example, for the dot product operation [3]). Filter initialisation procedure was implemented on the processing system of the platform due to iterative operation and the need to implement affine transformations. The two-dimensional discrete Fourier transform was implemented by utilising two Xilinx FFT modules for one-dimensional signals and a BRAM to transpose the data. The system operates on a real-time video stream at 60 fps for $64 \times 64$ filter size.

The paper [25] presents a single scale KCF + HOG algorithm on the ZYNQ-7000 (xc7z100ffg900-2) platform implemented in Vivado HLS. A simpler linear kernel function was used and the filter update mechanism was abandoned in favour of lower computational complexity. An evaluation of the tracking efficiency of the implemented system was performed based on a set of own 5 sequences containing drones. No comparison of effectiveness with state of the art on common benchmarks was provided. A processing speed of 41 fps was obtained.

In the work [20], the authors describe an FPGA implementation of the DCF + DSST filter on the XC7K325T FPGA device. The system achieves processing speed of 153 fps on 33 image channels (one grayscale and 32 HOG) with filter size of $32 \times 32$. However, the paper does not include any evaluation results of the tracking performance. Also, no implementation details are mentioned (HLS or VHDL, Verilog).

The works presented in this section mostly lack evaluation of tracking quality and comparison to other implementations. All described hardware implementations are using HOG or greyscale features, which impacts processing speed or tracking performance. Additionally, most implementations utilise HLS (High Level Synthesis) tools for development, which introduces resource usage overhead compared to hardware description languages approaches like VHDL or Verilog. This issue was discussed in detail in [3] in the case of dot product computation.

In this paper, we present the use of convolutional features to achieve higher tracking performance with less computational complexity than HOG feature-based solutions, which further allows for higher processing speed.

## 4 The Proposed CF Implementation

The main concept of this paper is to prove that choosing a convolutional network as a feature extractor for correlation filter tracking not only gives better performance than HOG features, but also can be efficiently accelerated on FPGA to achieve high processing speeds. The work started with the Python implementation of a software model of the deepDCF algorithm. The environment was chosen mainly due to the presence of libraries suitable for testing and training neural networks such as PyTorch. It was also possible to use the official evaluation tools for the VOT Challenge, which are available in Python. In addition, it was possible to use the Brevitas tool, which is a wrapper for the PyTorch library and performs neural network calculations, with a fixed precision (for instance, 8 bits or even 1 bit).

### 4.1 CNN Quantisation Using Knowledge Transfer

First, the quantisation of the convolutional layer generating features for the filter was performed. For this purpose, the PyTorch library was used to implement learning on the ImageNet set. The training was organised in the knowledge transfer style, i.e. it assumes the presence of a teacher model performing the computation in full precision and a quantised student model. The teacher model was the first layer (including maxpooling and ReLU (Rectified Linear Unit)) of the VGG11 network, pre-trained for the classification task on the ImageNet set. In preliminary experiments, it was noted that reducing the precision in the representation of weights and activations to four bits did not introduce a large increase in learning error. Additional experiments could be conducted to test the effect of different degrees of quantisation of the feature-generating network on tracking quality. Furthermore, the architecture of the student was identical to that of the teacher. The student model was also initialised with the weights of the teacher model. The cost function was the mean square error between the features returned by the teacher model and the student model, while the training was carried out with the SGD (Stochastic Gradient Descent) algorithm with parameters $learning\_rate = 0.01, momentum = 0.9, weight\_decay = 10^{-4}$.

### 4.2 Software Model Evaluation on VOT2015

The VOT (Visual Object Tracking) challenge environment was used to evaluate the tracking performance of the software model. Our results were compared with those of the KCF and DSST algorithms published by the organisers of the VOT challenge 2015 [2]. Accuracy (A) represents the average IoU (Intersection over Union) between the object position returned by the algorithm and the reference position in each image frame (both described by bounding boxes). Robustness (R), on the other hand, is the ratio of frames in which the object was lost to all frames in the tested sequence. The decisive metric in ranking the algorithms in the competition is EAO (Expected Average Overlap), which takes into account both accuracy and robustness. The data is summarised in Table 1.

**Table 1.** The table compares our software model to the state-of-the-art correlation filter tracking algorithms used in FPGA implementations. The **bolded, underlined** model was implemented in hardware and discussed in Sect. 4. The evaluation was done on the VOT 2015 dataset. Arrows denote whether more is better ↑ or less is better ↓ for a given evaluation metric. Using just 8 channels of convolutional features and 3 scales for $64 \times 64$ filter gives better results than KCF and DSST filters on HOG features used in current hardware implementations.

| Algorithm | Features | ROI size | A↑ | R↓ | EAO↑ |
|---|---|---|---|---|---|
| deepDCF (multiscale, not precised) (original impl. [6]) | CONV (96 channels float precision) | $224 \times 224$ ($112 \times 112$ filter) | 0.48 | 1.75 | (not given) |
| deepDCF (5 scales) (our implementation) | CONV (32 channels 4bit quantisation) | $224 \times 224$ ($112 \times 112$ filter) | 0.505 | 1.829 | **0.207** |
| deepDCF (5 scales) (our implementation) | CONV (64 channels 4bit quantisation) | $224 \times 224$ ($112 \times 112$ filter) | 0.484 | 1.879 | **0.203** |
| deepDCF (3 scales) (our implementation) | CONV (32 channels 4bit quantisation) | $128 \times 128$ ($64 \times 64$ filter) | 0.494 | 1.92 | **0.184** |
| **deepDCF (3 scales)** (our implementation) | CONV (8 channels 4bit quantisation) | $128 \times 128$ ($64 \times 64$ filter) | 0.491 | 2.082 | **0.183** |
| deepDCF (3 scales) (our implementation) | CONV (16 channels 4bit quantisation) | $128 \times 128$ ($64 \times 64$ filter) | 0.487 | 1.975 | **0.174** |
| DSST (evaluated by VOT commitee) | HOG | $2 \times$ target size (same as filter) | 0.54 | 2.56 | **0.17** |
| KCF (evaluated by VOT commitee) | HOG | $2.5 \times$ target size | 0.48 | 2.17 | **0.17** |
| deepDCF (3 scales) (our implementation) | CONV (4 channels 4bit quantisation) | $128 \times 128$ ($64 \times 64$ filter) | 0.456 | 2.611 | **0.145** |

The results in Table 1 confirm that the use of features from a single convolutional layer instead of HOG provides better results. The thesis is further strengthened by the fact that the mechanisms of better and faster scale prediction (DSST) and nonlinear regression (KCF) can also be used with convolutional features, which is one of the directions of our further work. In addition, an interesting finding is that it was possible to reduce the channels used by the filter to eight (in the deepDCF work there were 96 channels originally) without a significant decrease in tracking performance. The difference becomes only significant when the number of channels is reduced to 4.

## 4.3   Multichannel MOSSE Filter Implementation on FPGA

Based on the software model, the deepDCF algorithm was implemented in the SystemVerilog hardware description language. The work started with the analysis of the project [15], in which the single-channel MOSSE algorithm was implemented. The solution used as a video source a 4K video stream fed to the programmable logic (PL) through an HDMI port. The first change was to switch to communication between the PL and the processing system (PS, ARM-based in the considered device) to send image data and receive the new object's position. This makes hardware debugging easier because one can easily verify intermediate data like image features and current filter coefficients using DMA in PYNQ environment. The input images are cropped by the PS and the ROI is send to the PL via DMA transfer. However, it is also possible to restore the original video source by adding a module that crops the object from the image and scales it to the desired size. This is one of our future steps.

The top-level diagram is shown in Fig. 2. DMA communicates with the PS through the memory-mapped AXI interface and provides AXI Stream ports to send video to the convolutional network module and to receive the filter response. The task of the PS is to read a video frame, crop an image patch at the current position of the object, and send this fragment to the PL. The image is processed by the convolutional network and the filter module, which finally returns the object's position displacement and any possible change in scale.

The FINN [3,21] tool was used to implement the trained convolutional layer in the FPGA. This is an experimental environment from AMD Xilinx for implementing neural networks in selected MPSoCs[1]. The tool is based on the finn-hlslib library [1] in which basic modules are defined, and a compiler that transforms the network architecture description from Brevitas to a graph composed of these basic modules. FINN also offers the generation of a processing system driver to communicate with the FPGA, but this feature was not used in this project.

The schematic of the DCF multichannel filter module is shown in Fig. 3. All channels of a given DCNN feature pixel are fed in parallel to the module input. The BRAM modules were used as read-only memories for the Hann window parameters and for the two-dimensional Gaussian distribution pre-calculated in the software model. The input feature channels are split into parallel Channel filter modules, each implements Eqs. (12)–(15) for its channel. For the prediction step (logic highlighted in green in the diagrams), the filter responses from each channel are summed, and then the inverse Fourier transform (Eq. (15)) is computed. The prediction is followed by the filter update step (logic highlighted in red), for which the sum of the energy spectrums over all input channels must

---

[1] In previous FINN versions, Alveo boards were also supported (up to v0.7).

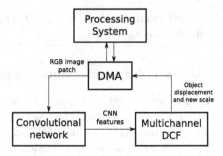

**Fig. 2.** Top level diagram of the implemented design. The image patch containing the tracked object is prepared by the Processing System by cropping and resizing the video frame. It is sent to the Programmable Logic via DMA (Direct Memory Access) module which streams the data to the convolutional network module generated by FINN. The tracking is done in the Multichannel DCF module which outputs the predicted object displacement back to the DMA.

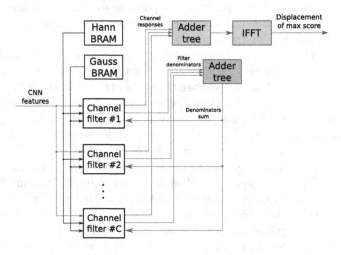

**Fig. 3.** Diagram of the main filter module. One of the advantages of the algorithm is the possibility of full parallelisation among channels. Hann BRAM and Gauss BRAM are used as read-only memory for storing pre-computed windowing function and the Gaussian distribution.

be computed (Eq. (14)). Since each filter channel is updated independently, the sum from the red adder tree is returned to the Channel filter module.

The Channel filter module is part of the design proposed in [15] with some modifications. The schematic is shown in Fig. 4. Although object features of size 64 × 64 are processed for prediction (this is also the size of the filter), a wider image context is sent to the module because the update must be performed on a new object position. For this purpose, the entire wider image context is written to BRAM in parallel. After the prediction is completed (i.e., after the responses from

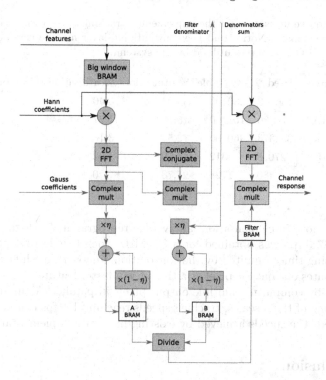

**Fig. 4.** Diagram of the module responsible for a single input feature channel. It implements multichannel DCF filter Eqs. (12)–(15). Logic responsible for update and prediction are highlightened in red and green respectively. Because the filter needs to be updated at the new, predicted object location, a wider context of the object features must be saved in the Big window BRAM.

the individual channels are summed up and the IFFT is calculated), the position of the feature patch is known and needs to be read from Big window BRAM.

To implement the two-dimensional Fourier transform, the IP provided by Xilinx was used to calculate the one-dimensional transform of each row of input data. These results are then stored in BRAM, from which they are read column-wise into a second one-dimensional transform module.

The hardware implementation was validated using the software model and yielded the same results on sequences from the VOT2015 set. The FPGA resource consumption of the system implementation for an eight-channel $64 \times 64$ filter is shown in Table 2. We used 32-bit fixed point precision in the calculations required by the filter and the system currently operates in one scale.

**Table 2.** Resource utilisation for the implemented tracking system with 64 × 64 filter and 8 feature channels. Notice that the convolutional layer module uses only a small portion of all FPGA resources utilised by the system.

| Resource | Used | Available | % utilisation | % utilisation (CNN only) |
|----------|------|-----------|---------------|--------------------------|
| LUT | 156663 | 230400 | 68,00 | 5,40 |
| LUTRAM | 15436 | 101760 | 15,17 | 1,77 |
| FF | 334373 | 460800 | 72,56 | 3,18 |
| BRAM | 270,5 | 312 | 86,70 | 1,92 |
| DSP | 480 | 1728 | 27,78 | 0 |

For the above implementation, an average reprogrammable logic processing speed of **467.3 fps** was obtained for a 375 MHz clock (single ROI processing). The processing time is limited by the convolutional network module, which currently computes one output pixel at a time. Even faster feature extraction could be achieved by computing multiple output pixels in parallel. Assuming sequential processing of the 3 scales, tracking speeds reaching 150 fps can be expected, which exceeds the speeds achieved by existing hardware implementations.

## 5    Conclusion

In this paper, we presented a real-time FPGA implementation of deepDCF tracking algorithm. We evaluated the performance of the proposed solution and compared it with other similar approaches on the VOT2015 benchmark. The use of convolutional features in correlation filter-based object tracking offered an improvement in comparison to the often used HOG features. Next, we implemented the proposed method in a SoC FPGA device, which allowed us to take advantage of the computation parallelisation and quantisation. We also demonstrated that the models generated by the FINN compiler can be successfully used with one's own design implemented in a hardware description language.

The used filter size of 64 × 64 offers higher accuracy (EAO 0.183 on the VOT2015 benchmark) than the algorithms implemented on FPGAs in the other articles discussed here while maintaining an average processing speed of 467.3 fps per scale. It is possible to select a larger filter, for example 112 × 112 to achieve even higher tracking quality but at the expense of processing speed. A lower FPGA clock could also be used to achieve lower power consumption depending on the particular application of the tracking system.

As part of future research, we plan to implement sequential processing of several scales or an application of the DSST filter. It is also worth investigating the possibility of using a nonlinear KCF filter by adding a kernel function computation to the existing implementation. We will also investigate the impact of the number of bits in the representation of the filter computation, as this potentially could reduce the FPGA resource consumption. The source code of the implementation is available at https://github.com/mdanilow/MOSSE_ fpga/tree/deep_features.

**Acknowledgment.** The work presented in this paper was supported by the National Science Centre project no. 2016/23/D/ST6/01389 entitled "The development of computing resources organisation in latest generation of heterogeneous reconfigurable devices enabling real-time processing of UHD/4K video stream" and AGH University of Science and Technology project no. 16.16.120.773.

# References

1. Finn-hlslib. https://github.com/Xilinx/finn-hlslib
2. Kristan, M., et al.: The visual object tracking vot2015 challenge results. In: Visual Object Tracking Workshop 2015 at ICCV2015 (2015)
3. Blott, M., et al.: Finn-r: an end-to-end deep-learning framework for fast exploration of quantized neural networks. ACM Trans. Reconfigurable Technol. Syst. (TRETS) **11**(3), 1–23 (2018)
4. Bolme, D.S., Beveridge, J.R., Draper, B.A., Lui, Y.M.: Visual object tracking using adaptive correlation filters. In: 2010 IEEE Computer Society Conference on Computer Vision and Pattern Recognition, pp. 2544–2550 (2010). https://doi.org/ 10.1109/CVPR.2010.5539960
5. Chatfield, K., Simonyan, K., Vedaldi, A., Zisserman, A.: Return of the devil in the details: Delving deep into convolutional nets. CoRR abs/1405.3531 (2014). http:// arxiv.org/abs/1405.3531
6. Danelljan, M., Häger, G., Khan, F.S., Felsberg, M.: Convolutional features for correlation filter based visual tracking. In: 2015 IEEE International Conference on Computer Vision Workshop (ICCVW), pp. 621–629 (2015). https://doi.org/10. 1109/ICCVW.2015.84
7. Danelljan, M., Häger, G., Khan, F.S., Felsberg, M.: Learning spatially regularized correlation filters for visual tracking. In: 2015 IEEE International Conference on Computer Vision (ICCV), pp. 4310–4318 (2015). https://doi.org/10.1109/ICCV. 2015.490
8. Danelljan, M., Häger, G., Khan, F.S., Felsberg, M.: Discriminative scale space tracking (2016)
9. Danelljan, M., Häger, G., Shahbaz Khan, F., Felsberg, M.: Accurate scale estimation for robust visual tracking. In: Proceedings of the British Machine Vision Conference. BMVA Press (2014). https://doi.org/10.5244/C.28.65
10. Danelljan, M., Khan, F.S., Felsberg, M., Van De Weijer, J.: Adaptive color attributes for real-time visual tracking. In: 2014 IEEE Conference on Computer Vision and Pattern Recognition, pp. 1090–1097 (2014). https://doi.org/10.1109/ CVPR.2014.143
11. Deng, J., Dong, W., Socher, R., Li, L.J., Li, K., Fei-Fei, L.: ImageNet: a large-scale hierarchical image database. In: CVPR09 (2009)
12. Hahnle, M., Saxen, F., Hisung, M., Brunsmann, U., Doll, K.: Fpga-based real-time pedestrian detection on high-resolution images. In: 2013 IEEE Conference on Computer Vision and Pattern Recognition Workshops, pp. 629–635 (2013)
13. Henriques, J., Caseiro, R., Martins, P., Batista, J.: Exploiting the circulant structure of tracking-by-detection with kernels, vol. 7575, pp. 702–715 (2012). https:// doi.org/10.1007/978-3-642-33765-9_50

14. Henriques, J.F., Caseiro, R., Martins, P., Batista, J.: High-speed tracking with kernelized correlation filters. IEEE Trans. Pattern Anal. Mach. Intell. **37**(3), 583–596 (2015). https://doi.org/10.1109/TPAMI.2014.2345390

15. Kowalczyk, M., Przewlocka, D., Kryjak, T.: Real-time implementation of adaptive correlation filter tracking for 4k video stream in zynq ultrascale+ mpsoc. In: 2019 Conference on Design and Architectures for Signal and Image Processing (DASIP), pp. 53–58 (2019). https://doi.org/10.1109/DASIP48288.2019.9049203

16. Kristan, M., et al.: A novel performance evaluation methodology for single-target trackers. IEEE Trans. Pattern Anal. Mach. Intell. **38**(11), 2137–2155 (2016). https://doi.org/10.1109/TPAMI.2016.2516982

17. Liu, X., Ma, Z., Xie, M., Zhang, J., Feng, T.: Design and implementation of scale adaptive kernel correlation filtering algorithm based on hls. In: 2021 IEEE International Conference on Signal Processing, Communications and Computing (ICSPCC), pp. 1–5 (2021). https://doi.org/10.1109/ICSPCC52875.2021.9564815

18. Mohanty, R., Gonnabhaktula, A., Pradhan, T., Kabi, B., Routray, A.: Design and performance analysis of fixed-point jacobi svd algorithm on reconfigurable system. IERI Procedia **7**, 21–27 (2014). https://doi.org/10.1016/j.ieri.2014.08.005

19. Schölkopf, B., Smola, A.: Smola, A.: Learning with Kernels - Support Vector Machines, Regularization, Optimization and Beyond, vol. 98. MIT Press, Cambridge (2001)

20. Song, K., Yuan, C., Gao, P., Sun, Y.: Fpga-based acceleration system for visual tracking. CoRR abs/1810.05367 (2018). http://arxiv.org/abs/1810.05367

21. Umuroglu, Y., et al.: Finn: a framework for fast, scalable binarized neural network inference. In: Proceedings of the 2017 ACM/SIGDA International Symposium on Field-Programmable Gate Arrays, FPGA 2017, pp. 65–74. ACM (2017)

22. Walid, W., Awais, M.U., Ahmed, A., Masera, G., Martina, M.: Real-time implementation of fast discriminative scale space tracking algorithm. J. Real-time Image Process., 1–14 (2021)

23. Wu, Y., Lim, J., Yang, M.H.: Online object tracking: a benchmark. In: IEEE Conference on Computer Vision and Pattern Recognition (CVPR) (2013)

24. Yang, H., Yu, J., Wang, S., Peng, X.: Design of airborne target tracking accelerator based on kcf. J. Eng. **2019** (2019). https://doi.org/10.1049/joe.2018.9159

25. Yang, K., Xie, M., An, J., Zhang, X., Su, H., Fu, X.: Correlation filter based uav tracking system on fpga. In: IET International Radar Conference (IET IRC 2020), vol. 2020, pp. 671–676 (2020). https://doi.org/10.1049/icp.2021.0758

# VenOS: A Virtualization Framework for Multiple Tenant Accommodation on Reconfigurable Platforms

Panagiotis Miliadis[1]([✉])[ID], Dimitris Theodoropoulos[2][ID],
Dionisios N. Pnevmatikatos[1], and Nectarios Koziris[1][ID]

[1] Computing Systems Laboratory, National Technical University of Athens,
Athens, Greece
{pmiliad,pnevmati,nkoziris}@cslab.ece.ntua.gr
[2] Telecommunication Systems Institute, Technical University of Crete,
Chania, Greece
dtheodoropoulos@tuc.gr

**Abstract.** As FPGAs provide tremendous improvements in performance
and energy efficiency in a wide range of workloads, cloud infrastructures
increasingly incorporate them in their infrastructure for on-demand application acceleration. However, accelerator development remains challenging, and ways to program, deploy and securely utilize FPGAs are still
difficult to manage both for provider and developer alike. The complexity of such systems is compounded when moving to multi-tenant environments, where cloud providers seek to multiplex tenants on a single
FPGA platform to increase their return of investment. To this end, we
present VenOS, a full-stack framework that enables multiple application
hosting on FPGAs. VenOS exposes a high-level API for developers to easily and securely offload data execution to hardware. Under the hood, it
utilizes a simple -yet efficient- NoC approach for sharing FPGA resources
among tenants, virtualizes memory and I/Os operations and offers strong
data isolation against malicious transactions. Finally, VenOS comprises
a resource manager based on memory segmentation, along with isolation
modules that offer a protection layer between the accelerators and the system. Experimental results suggest that VenOS is a befitting platform that,
despite its ease of use, benefits applications by 1.15x–2x, while introducing a resource overhead of only 11%. Finally, our system scales by up to
3.79x when four accelerators are mapped.

**Keywords:** FPGA · Multi-tenancy · Virtualization · Network-on-chip

## 1 Introduction

FPGAs are now commonly used on data centers and cloud infrastructure for
on-demand acceleration. FPGAs provide more flexibility than their ASIC and
GPU counterparts, while application acceleration on these devices deliver competitive performance at a greatly improved energy efficiency for a wide range of

© The Author(s), under exclusive license to Springer Nature Switzerland AG 2022
L. Gan et al. (Eds.): ARC 2022, LNCS 13569, pp. 181–195, 2022.
https://doi.org/10.1007/978-3-031-19983-7_13

applications. However, typical kernels utilize only a small fraction of the available resources, leading to poor logic and memory utilization. To increase return of investment (RoI), cloud providers seek to host multiple customer kernels on a single FPGA platform [1–3,9]. However, application development remains challenging, and ways to program, deploy and securely utilize FPGAs are still difficult to manage from both provider's and developer's perspectives. To make things worse, additional challenges arise when moving on multi-tenant environments, where fair resource allocation, isolation and protection mechanisms must be introduced to manage FPGA platforms.

State-of-the-art FPGAs offer a large pool of memory and reconfigurable resources. To manage such a large pool, a more dynamic and scalable approach is needed, especially when moving on scale-out environments and more FPGAs are accessible. Moreover, cloud FPGAs are typically used for prototyping developing and accelerator testing, so it is important to facilitate the development and deployment of accelerators, by keeping the already well-known existing environments, without introducing additional concepts to developers. Finally, data and functional isolation are essential when moving on multi-tenant environments, as malicious tenants have the opportunity to interfere with other users on two levels; by either using a malicious accelerator or accessing an FPGA unauthorized memory space from host.

To this end, we propose VenOS, a virtualization framework for multiple tenant accommodation on reconfigurable platforms. VenOS uses a simple - yet efficient NoC to spatially multiplex and fairly share the large pool of reconfigurable and memory resources amongst tenants. VenOS strongly focuses on data and functional isolation of tenants to prevent malicious users to access unauthorized data or interfere with the execution of accelerators. Our work targets the Platform as a Service (PaaS) model, where the system is abstracted by the user, while I/O interface and FPGA resources are virtualized. This model hides unnecessary low-level hardware and platform specific details from developers, who can focus on developing and testing their accelerator.

Our work makes the following contributions:

- We propose VenOS, a novel virtualization framework for accommodating multiple tenants on FPGA platforms. Tenants and memory dies appear as distinct nodes of a network on chip, where the network provides an efficient, fair, flexibile and scalable sharing of FPGA resources.
- We provide strong data isolation mechanisms on two levels; a) on the host machine by proposing a memory segmentation method for managing and allocating FPGA memory address space, and b) on the FPGA by proposing a protection layer that blocks invalid memory requests and malicious or incorrect data for accessing unauthorized address space or polluting the memory and network.
- We provide a quantitative evaluation of VenOS using five real-world applications. Results show that VenOS occupies 11% of FPGA resources and benefits the runtime of accelerators by $1.15\times$–$2\times$, while it scales by up to $3.79\times$ when four accelerators are mapped. Finally, we show that VenOS can adopt differ-

ent topologies, based on system requirements, while the use of a network on chip greatly helps fair sharing of FPGA resources.

The rest of the paper is organized as follows: Sect. 2 discusses the related work on the field of FPGA virtualization and multi-tenancy. Section 3 presents VenOS and provides all necessary details regarding our framework. Section 4 presents the evaluation results, followed by Sect. 5 to conclude the paper.

## 2    Related Work

A considerable amount of research has been done on FPGA virtualization and management of FPGAs on cloud environments. Amazon [2] and Alibaba [1] utilize the Vitis Unified Software Platform [24] to enable application development and deployment on their FPGA instances. By using Vitis, an FPGA platform is divided into static and dynamic regions, where an application can be exchanged at run time with the help of partial reconfiguration. However, there is no support for I/O abstraction or for multi-tenant environments.

Recent surveys give excellent overviews of the work generated by the community. Quraishi *et al.* [20] present a survey of works in the field of FPGA virtualization, review the existing systems based on their architecture and discuss the key objectives of FPGA virtualization. Wulf *et al.* [23] focus on hypervisor-based virtualization of embedded reconfigurable systems, where host and FPGA share the same address space. In this section, we focus on more recent works that virtualize FPGAs on cloud and support multi-tenants environments.

AmorphOS [5] offers two modes to increase FPGA utilization: a) "low latency" where each accelerator operates in a distinct dynamic region, and b) "throughput" where all kernels are synthesized into a single bitstream. Mechanisms for correct checkpoint and resume are required to alternate between the two modes, which introduce development and deployment overheads to tenants. Moreover, AmorphOS dedicates an even share of I/O and memory bandwidth to each tenant. Coyote [10] aims to provide an OS-centric approach, by providing a suite of OS abstractions working with the host OS. They pair each accelerator with a TLB and custom MMU, which unifies the memories of the FPGA and host machine. Coyote aims to make the FPGA part of host's software system.

In Optimus [14], accelerators are organized as leaves of a binary tree, while intermediate nodes control the data flow. Accelerators access the memory through a virtual address space. Meanwhile, they cannot be moved using partial reconfiguration, but Optimus offers time-division multiplexing with mechanisms similar to AmorphOS. Host and FPGA share the same address space, however, a host process cannot access the address space of a vFPGA. Megatron [12] is based on Optimus system to provide virtualization through a hardware TLB, a ring buffer for writing and a software table walker to serve the misses. Moreover, [12] provides a extensive analysis of performance to demonstrate the competitiveness of the customizable translation service.

Vital [26] focuses on maximizing the per-FPGA area utilization, by segmenting the design on multiple smaller bitstreams and accommodating them on vFPGA slots. It targets homogeneous multi-fpga environments and offers an augmented compiler that supports bitstream segmentation and mapping. Hetero-Vital [27] extends the previous work between heterogeneous platforms, mitigates the communication overheads across bitstream segments, but introduces large compilations.

Chen *et al.* [7] enable FPGAs on the cloud by using Linux-KVM, deployed in a modified OpenStack cloud environment. Other similar works [15,16] are based on overlay techniques for virtualization, while CPM [18] focuses on an efficient area sharing methodology amongst tasks by creating a single large bitstream through clever clustering and custom, task-specific partitioning. Synergy [11] propose a runtime-based compiler which integrates suspend and resume mechanisms on accelerators to enable time multiplexing. Finally, RACOS [22] provides a simple and intuitive software interface to load/unload reconfigurable hardware accelerators and perform data I/Os transparently to the user.

Compared to previous work, VenOS takes a more FPGA-centric approach, by implementing a simple network on chip for accommodating multiple tenants and sharing the FPGA resources amongst them. Our work focuses on strong data isolation between accelerators by providing protection mechanisms both on the Host and the FPGA platform. Furthermore, VenOS does not introduce any development overheads to tenants, as it utilizes well-known existing environments. In a few words, VenOS provides a solution for flexible, scalable and fair sharing of FPGA resources, I/O and hardware details abstraction and strong data isolation mechanisms.

On the field of FPGA OSes, BORPH [6,21] offers a homogeneous UNIX interface for both software and hardware processes, by providing native kernel support. ReconOS [13] and Hthreads [19] extend the multi-thread programming model to a FPGA, and provide support for inter-thread communication and synchronization. Meanwhile, LEAP [8,17] provides OS-managed communication channels between different hardware modules and a dynamically partitioning algorithm to share the on-board memory. Unlike these works, VenOS focuses on accommodating multiple tenants on a single FPGA platform, virtualizing FPGA as a set of accelerators, abstracting I/O operations from application developers while providing fair, flexible and scalable sharing of FPGA resources.

## 3    VenOS Framework

In this section, we propose the VenOS framework. At first, we present a high-level view of VenOS architecture and provide information about its implementation. Next, we focus on the two main building blocks: *Memory* and *User Nodes*. We describe their functionality and importance in the overall framework. Finally, we present the resource manager, which is responsible for accommodating the tenants into users nodes and managing the FPGA memory address space.

### 3.1    VenOS Architecture

The VenOS architecture is outlined in Fig. 1. VenOS considers the FPGA as a distinct platform with its own dedicated memory for accelerating specific work-

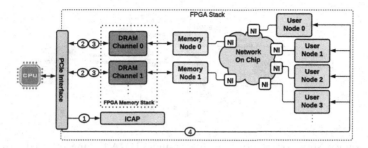

**Fig. 1.** High level view of VenOS architecture. User and Memory Nodes are connected through a network on chip. Host machine is responsible to load (step ①) an accelerator, perform read (step ②) and write (step ③) operations, and configure the user nodes (step ④) to initiate the execution of an accelerator.

loads. The FPGA is connected to the host system through a PCIe interface for transferring data, accessing the ICAP, and controlling User Nodes. Both accelerators from tenants and memory dies are connected through their respective nodes via a network on chip. A User Node is responsible for creating memory requests according to the accelerator it services, and facilitates hardware protection between the VenOS system and the accelerator. Similarly, a Memory Node is responsible for serving the memory requests from different accelerators and route data between its memory and NoC. This offers great flexibility as memory processes are decoupled from compute, while communication between nodes is hidden under the computation of other accelerators. Moreover, the utilization of NoC enables performance scalability, as either memory dies or accelerators from tenants can be added as distinct nodes to the network.

The programming model of VenOS does not deviate from other well-known and established existing tools for FPGAs, such as Vitis. Application developers utilize an easy-to-use OpenCL-like software programming API, which abstracts all low-level hardware and platform details of an FPGA, as well as I/O operations. The integration of a kernel on VenOS system takes place by using a load command (step ①), which performs partial reconfiguration through the ICAP module to reconfigure a user node with the desired bitstream. Read (step ②) and write (step ③) commands are used for transferring data between the host machine and FPGA memories, through the PCIe interface. Finally, developers can initiate the execution (step ④) of their accelerator. In this step, information about memory allocations of the user and metadata are passed on special modules, and control commands are used to initiate the execution of the kernel.

The VenOS architecture can integrate accelerators written on HDL languages, such as VHDL or Verilog, as well as designs developed on HLS. To this end, VenOS does not introduce any increase in the learning curve of application developers, making our platform also ideal for prototyping developing.

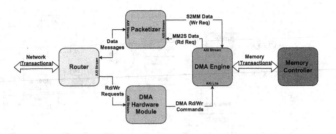

**Fig. 2.** Memory Node Architecture. A Router and a DMA Engine are used for memory and network transactions respectively. The Hardware Driver controls the DMA Engine, while Packetizer converts data to messages and vice-versa.

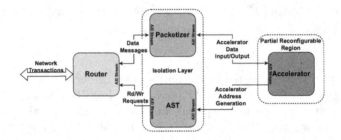

**Fig. 3.** User Node architecture. It operates as a hardware wrapper that hosts the accelerator and provide access to the NoC, through the router. A special Packetizer and an Accelerator Segment Table (AST) module are designed to provide isolation and protection between the accelerator and VenOS system.

### 3.2  Memory Node

*Memory Nodes* are responsible for serving memory requests generated by the accelerators and routing data between the network and FPGA Memory. The components of a *Memory Node* are shown in Fig. 2. The *Router* is responsible for controlling the traffic on the node. The design of the router is directly related to the network topology, which can be easily configured on VenOS architecture based on system requirements. Data messages from both DMA engine and network are directed to *Packetizer*, which converts data into messages and vice-versa.

VenOS offers a lightweight, yet efficient *DMA Hardware Module* that initiates DMA memory transactions, fully decoupled from the CPU. Each accelerator, by sending memory request messages, can indirectly initiate memory transactions to either fetch or store data to a memory bank. The DMA Hardware Module is responsible to control the DMA engine, check its status or interrupts, and assign the starting address and length of the memory transactions. The communication between the driver and the DMA Engine is done by using the AXI4-Lite protocol. Two streaming interface are connected with the Packetizer, each responsible for fetching data into the memory or for exporting them to Packetizer, always depending on the type of the request that the hardware driver serves.

## 3.3   User Node

Accelerators from tenants are mapped on preconfigured regions by using partial reconfiguration, a feature enabled with ICAP. Each partial reconfigurable region employs exactly one tenant, guaranteeing functional isolation among others. Malicious accelerators cannot interfere with other accelerators, as each *User Node* is an autonomous node, while nodes only share the network on chip. To successfully integrate multiple accelerators on VenOS, we have designed a common IP wrapper, which provides a standard interface between the accelerator and the rest of the system. The IP wrapper includes a set of streaming interfaces, responsible for memory operations, as well as for inputs and outputs. This choice offers significant advantages: a) developers can focus on the computational part of their kernel and b) the streaming interface offers better compatibility with the pipeline and dataflow HLS primitives. Figure 3 shows the rest components of the node.

The *Router* is responsible for controlling the traffic on the node. VenOS architecture gives the flexibility to adopt different network topologies, depending on system requirements. Currently, the design of the router is directly related to the topology, and further analysis is left for future work. A novelty of VenOS is that it provides a special hardware module for isolating and preventing accelerators for accessing memory addresses outside the range that users have previously allocated. To enable this feature, we have implemented two modules: a) the *Accelerator Segment Table (AST)* which is responsible for generating valid memory requests, and b) the *Packetizer* which buffers and prevents malicious or incorrect data to access the network. Combined together, they form an isolation layer between each accelerator and the rest of the system. The Packetizer feeds the accelerator with incoming data, fetched only by a valid read request. On the other direction, outgoing data are transmitted into the network only if the AST module determines that the corresponding write request addresses a valid address location in memory. If not, the outgoing data are dropped, in order to not harm the bandwidth of the network and the memory addresses of other tenants.

AST is responsible for generating valid memory request messages, according to the memory operations produced by the associated accelerator. This procedure is depicted in Fig. 4. Rows in AST provide metadata about the variables of the accelerator, such as the starting address, the size of the variable in memory and the bank which is stored. All information is initialized right before the execution of the kernel. To generate a memory request message, an accelerator has to provide the tag of the requested variable, the length of the request and an address offset. The AST module checks whether the variable is part of the program and extracts the necessary information to generate the memory request. A memory request message is divided into four fields: the *Address*, which is calculated by the starting address and the offset, the length of the request, the memory operation, and finally the memory bank which will serve the request. The valid requests are passed into the network, as well as the *Packetizer*, to allow outgoing data accessing the network.

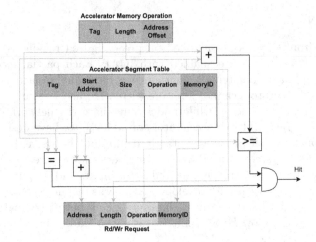

**Fig. 4.** Memory Requests of an accelerator are based on a content addressable memory. Both the Accelerator Segment Table (AST) module and the Packetizer operate as data protection layer by isolating addresses through user's metadata.

### 3.4 Resource Manager

The Resource Manager is responsible for managing and allocating the address space of the FPGA memory and the partial reconfigurable regions across tenants. By using the VenOS API, tenants can allocate or free FPGA memory, request to load a bitstream, or access the FPGA memory address space. To this end, the VenOS resource manager is responsible for providing both functional and data isolation between tenants. While for the former case is sufficient to look for an idle *User Node* on VenOS system and load the accelerator, providing data isolation is more complicated. We implement a memory segmentation method in software, which allocates and manages the FPGA address space between tenants and stores the memory footprint on hash tables. To reduce memory fragmentation, VenOS adopts a best-fit algorithm, which returns the smallest available segment according to the request from tenant.

Figure 5 shows the memory segmentation method as part of the resource manager in VenOS. Tenants submit requests to perform memory operations, such as memory allocation and data transfers between Host and FPGA. For each tenant, a unique userID key is assigned by VenOS and is used as identifier to keep the memory footprint of each tenant. The memory footprint is essential for our protection mechanism, as VenOS allows data transactions only if the requested address and memory block are contained by the memory footprint. So, by keeping the memory footprint for each tenant along with the use of memory segmentation method, VenOS provides strong data isolation against malicious activities, as tenants can only access and manage FPGA address spaces that have been previously allocated.

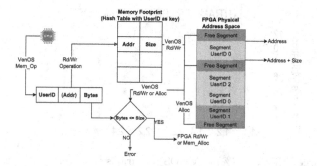

**Fig. 5.** Memory operations in VenOS framework. For memory allocations, VenOS utilize a memory segmentation method, while it keeps a memory footprint for each tenant for read and write commands in FPGA memory.

## 4    Evaluation

### 4.1    Experimental Setup

VenOS is implemented on AlveoU250 Data Center acceleration card using Vitis HLS 2020.2 and Vivado 2020.2 development environments. The FPGA is connected through a PCIe link to a host machine that features a Xeon Gold 5120 CPU running at 2.20 GHz, paired with 252 GB of DRAM. To evaluate VenOS, we use five real-world benchmarks: SHA256 Hashing and AES256 Encryption algorithms from the cryptography IP cores [4], and the 3D-Rendering (3DR) and Face Detection (FD) applications from Rosetta Benchmark [25]. Furthermore, we designed a Pointer Chasing (PC) application that sequentially reads and writes data from/to memory; this corresponds to worst-case DMA patterns and creates a latency bottleneck. We choose a transfer size of 64 bytes from and to memory, that corresponds to the data width of the DDR memory controller.

Unless stated otherwise, in our experiments, we use a simple ring topology to connect all nodes across the FPGA fabric. Other topologies could be implemented at the expense of FPGA resources, but our goal is to evaluate the use of a network on chip on VenOS architecture, and not its topology. The system clock frequency is set at 130 MHz, which drives the DMA hardware Driver, user and memory nodes, as well as accelerators.

### 4.2    Resource Overhead

Performance is not the only metric for consideration when designing a system for accommodating multiple tenants on FPGAs. The resource overhead is just as important, because the overhead created by the system reduces the available reconfigurable resources which can be utilized either from tenants or for multiplexing more of them.

Figure 6 presents the resource utilization overhead of VenOS, on various case scenarios for a varying number of memories and tenants. When VenOS includes

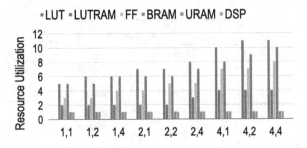

**Fig. 6.** Resource Utilization (%) of VenOS on various case scenarios. Each scenario on x-axis is described as {#Memory,#User} nodes on VenOS system.

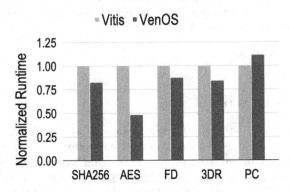

**Fig. 7.** Normalized Runtime of VenOS architecture compared to Vitis (smaller is better).

a single Memory and User Node, it utilizes 5% of LUTs and BRAMs. When multiplexing more tenants, VenOS needs less than 1% of LUTs, BRAM and FFs per *User Node*. Most of resources are for storing the memory footprint and metadata of the tenant before the execution of the accelerator. VenOS needs an extra 2% of LUTs and 1% on both FFs and BRAMs for an additional *Memory Node*, respectively. In an extreme case where 4 Users Nodes are multiplexed with 4 Memory Nodes, VenOS utilize only 11% of the overall resources, leaving the largest part of the reconfigure fabric for the accelerators.

Future FPGAs is likely to offer a larger pool of reconfigurable resources. Therefore, FPGAs can accommodate even more tenants, so the system requires to be scalable in order to integrate them without significant changes. By using VenOS, new user nodes can be mapped to multiplex even a greater number of tenants, while network on chip offers great and easy scalability in order to share the FPGA resources amongst accelerators.

### 4.3   Virtualization Overhead

The first step for evaluating VenOS is to compare it with a complete, mature environment. We choose Vitis framework which is utilized by Alibaba and Ama-

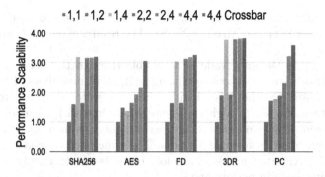

**Fig. 8.** Performance benchmarks of the applications running in VenOS framework, showing the ability of VenOS architecture to scale with respect to the number of accelerators. All results are normalized on the single Memory-User Node scenario. Each scenario on legend is described as {#Memory,#User} nodes on VenOS system.

zon F1 instances. From a such coarse-grain comparison, it is hard to draw exact conclusions, but our goal is to prove that VenOS is a befitting platform for application development both in terms of performance and in terms of ease of deployment. On Fig. 7, we present the results for the five benchmark accelerators on VenOS compared to ones developed on Vitis.

Four out of five applications benefit from VenOS architecture in terms of performance. 3D-Rendering application and SHA256 hashing algorithm present a 1.2× speedup compared with the corresponding application developed on Vitis, while Face-Detection application benefits by 15%. Meanwhile, AES present great improvement, almost 2× against Vitis. The reason is that it has small computation time compared to the communication with the memory, and VenOS can fetch all data into the accelerator with a single memory request, significantly increasing the runtime. The achieved speedup on these applications is attributed to the following reasons: a) VenOS depends on streaming interfaces for fetching data on accelerators, which is way more efficient compared to the memory map used by Vitis and b) each accelerator can initiate indirectly a memory request by using the DMA hardware driver, a module which accelerates the memory request processing time. On the other hand, VenOS introduce performance penalties on pointer chasing application. The accelerator produces a high number of memory operations, which VenOS should validate and transform into memory request messages. This repetitive procedure increases the latency, which also worsens with the use of the network on chip and DMA Engine.

Nevertheless, we can conclude that VenOS does not introduce significant performance penalties. On the contrary, the majority of applications benefit from our system, as they show increased performance compared to Vitis.

## 4.4  Performance Scalability of VenOS Architecture

One of VenOS contributions is that implements a network on chip to offer scalable, flexible and fairly resource sharing of FPGA resources. The first step towards evaluating this choice is to prove that our architecture scales on respect to the number of User and Memory Nodes. The results of our tests are reported on Fig. 8.

When a single Memory Node is accessible through the network, SHA256, FD and 3DR accelerators show significant scalability regardless of the number of compute units. On the other hand, AES accelerator struggles to scale for four compute units, as its high communication time with memory compared to computation, affects negatively the performance, as memory requests from all compute units target a single Memory. The same phenomenon is observed as well with PC accelerator, where all memory requests are serialized and introduce significant overheads in performance.

On the other hand, when more Memory Nodes are accessible through our network, memory requests are distributed amongst them. This distribution of memory requests significantly boosts the performance on both AES and PC accelerators, compared to baseline, specially when the number of Memory Nodes are equal to User Nodes. The other three accelerators present a negligible increase in performance.

VenOS architecture has the advantage of adopting different network topologies based on system requirements. We also implement a crossbar interconnect between the nodes and compared it with the results taken by using Ring topology. The use of a crossbar seems beneficial to AES accelerator where the performance is boosted from 2.17× to 3.07× compared to baseline. This phenomenon is attributed to the fact that crossbar topology helps data and requests to reach faster their respective nodes compared to Ring, significantly reducing the communication time with the Memory. Corresponding results on a much smaller scale are also observed for the other accelerators, pointing out that topology affects the performance of the kernels, always in relation to workload and the type of accelerator. Further analysis is left for future work.

Nonetheless, the choice to base VenOS architecture on NoC is proved beneficial, because the overall performance of our system scales in relation to the number of User Nodes. Meanwhile, accelerators with higher communication time with memory or with a large number of memory requests are significantly assisted from more Memory Nodes, as memory requests can be distributed amongst them and DMA engines perform parallel accesses to FPGA Memory dies.

### 4.5   Interference Among Collocated Accelerators

Finally, we evaluate VenOS when multiple different applications are running in parallel. We introduce *interference*, a metric that shows the percentage drop in the performance of an accelerator when another accelerator is running in parallel, while their memory transactions target the *same* Memory Node. Consequently, we show how accelerators are affected when sharing the resources of an FPGA. The results are shown on Fig. 9, where the interference for each accelerator is reported.

When two accelerators are running in parallel on VenOS system, the maximum observed interference is 29%, reported for two AES accelerators. Moreover,

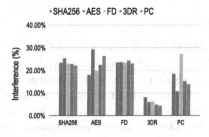
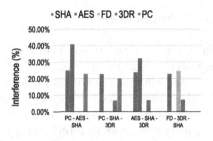

(a) Interference with two Accelerators    (b) Interference with three Accelerators

**Fig. 9.** Performance of collocated accelerators running simultaneously on VenOS architecture, sharing both Memory Node and Network. The results shows the interference between the accelerators and are normalized when the accelerator solely occupies VenOS system (smaller is better).

for the majority of our test cases, we observe an almost 18%–23% of interference between two collocated accelerators. An exception occurs with 3DR application where the interference decreases at 6.5%. We found out that the interference of our accelerators is mostly connected by their scalability when memory transactions target the same Memory Node, shown during the previous subsection, rather than from the accelerator that runs in parallel.

However, PC benchmark shows an irregular behaviour regardless of the collocated accelerator, which is attributed to two main factors. First, the position of the accelerator on the network can increase the latency of data transmission, as messages cross a larger number of nodes until find their destination. Second, the large workload on a Memory Node also increases the response latency, which negatively affects the performance of latency sensitive applications. This can be observed when PC runs with a Face Detection accelerator, where the interference is larger than 27%.

Finally, we expand our previous results by collocating three accelerators. We sample among all possible combinations and present four interesting scenarios, based on the results occurred by the previous experiments. The results strengthen our previous statements that accelerators are mostly affected by their scalability trend, when they are collocated with other accelerators and share the FPGA resources. An exception is observed with AES accelerator as its interference is increased to 32% and 40%, due to the high workload on the Memory Node. Similar behavior to a lesser extent is also reported with PC accelerator, where its interference exceeds 20%, regardless of the scenario.

To this end, we show that the utilization of a network on chip in VenOS architecture is proved beneficial, as memory requests can be dynamically and fairly served, even by a single Memory Node. When a single accelerator occupies the VenOS architecture, our system provides it the maximum possible resources to achieve high performance. Otherwise, the interference of an accelerator is connected to its scalability trend, as VenOS does not introduce extra performance overheads when FPGA resources are shared.

# 5   Conclusions

In this paper, we present VenOS, a virtualization framework for multiple tenant accommodation on reconfigurable platform. VenOS provides a flexible, scalable and efficient architecture to dynamically share the available resources of a FPGA platform. VenOS provides protection layers both on software and hardware to allow tenants to securely access and manage their accelerators, preventing malicious users to interfere with their execution. Finally, VenOS abstracts from developers all the hardware details of the architecture as well the I/Os operations. Furthermore, VenOS enhances ease of deployment, as developers can utilize already existing well known development tools.

Our results show that VenOS is a resource efficient befitting platform for real-world applications, which benefits their performance from 1.15× to 2×. Furthermore, the use of a NoC for multiplexing multiple tenants on a single FPGA platform is proved beneficial, as our system scale by up to 3.79× when four accelerators are mapped on *User Nodes*. Finally, the resource overhead of VenOS is 11%, leaving the largest part of FPGA fabric to users, while its architecture provides dynamic, fair and secure share of FPGA resources, without introducing extra performance penalties.

**Acknowledgments.** This work was supported in part by the European Union's Horizon 2020 research and innovation programme under grant agreement 955739, project OPTIMA. The authors would like to thank Xilinx for their donation of the Alveo FPGA boards used in this work.

# References

1. Alibaba cloud services. compute optimized instance families with fpgas. https://www.alibabacloud.com/help/en/doc-detail/108504.htm
2. Amazon web services, inc. amazon ec2 f1 instances. https://aws.amazon.com/ec2/instance-types/f1/
3. Deploy ml models to fpgas - azure machine learning. https://docs.microsoft.com/en-us/azure/machine-learning/how-to-deploy-fpga-web-service
4. Hls cryptography accelerator. https://github.com/doctor3w/HLS-Cryptography-Accelerator
5. Khawaja, A., et al.: Sharing, protection, and compatibility for reconfigurable fabric with amorphos. In: Proceedings of the 13th USENIX Conference on Operating Systems Design and Implementation, OSDI 2018, pp. 107–127 (2018)
6. Brodersen, R., Tkachenko, A., So, H.K.H.: A unified hardware/software runtime environment for fpga-based reconfigurable computers using borph. In: Proceedings of the 4th International Conference on Hardware/Software Codesign and System Synthesis (CODES+ISSS 2006), pp. 259–264 (2006)
7. Fei Chen, et. al.: Enabling fpgas in the cloud. In: Proceedings of the 11th ACM Conference on Computing Frontiers, CF 2014 (2014)
8. Fleming, K., Yang, H.J., Adler, M., Emer, J.: The leap fpga operating system. In: 2014 24th International Conference on Field Programmable Logic and Applications (FPL), pp. 1–8 (2014)

9. InAccel: Fpga acceleration lifecyclemade simple. https://inaccel.com/
10. Korolija, D., Roscoe, T., Alonso, G.: Do OS abstractions make sense on FPGAs? In: 14th USENIX Symposium on Operating Systems Design and Implementation (OSDI 2020), pp. 991–1010 (2020)
11. Landgraf, J., Yang, T., Lin, W., Rossbach, C.J., Schkufza, E.: Compiler-driven FPGA virtualization with SYNERGY, pp. 818–831 (2021)
12. Liu, Y., Ma, J., Zhang, Z., Li, L., Qi, Z., Guan, H.: Megatron: software-managed device tlb for shared-memory fpga virtualization. In: 2021 58th ACM/IEEE Design Automation Conference (DAC), pp. 1213–1218 (2021)
13. Lübbers, E., Platzner, M.: Reconos: multithreaded programming for reconfigurable computers. ACM Trans. Embed. Comput. Syst. **9**(1) (2009)
14. Ma, J., et al.: A hypervisor for shared-memory FPGA platforms, pp. 827–844 (2020)
15. Mandebi Mbongue, J., Tchuinkou Kwadjo, D., Bobda, C.: Flexitask: a flexible fpga overlay for efficient multitasking. In: GLSVLSI 2018, pp. 483–486 (2018)
16. Mbongue, J., Hategekimana, F., Tchuinkou Kwadjo, D., Andrews, D., Bobda, C.: Fpgavirt: a novel virtualization framework for fpgas in the cloud. In: 2018 IEEE 11th International Conference on Cloud Computing (CLOUD), pp. 862–865 (2018)
17. Adler, M., et. al.: Leap scratchpads: automatic memory and cache management for reconfigurable logic. In: FPGA 2011, pp. 25–28 (2011)
18. Minhas, U.I., Woods, R., Nikolopoulos, D.S., Karakonstantis, G.: Efficient, dynamic multi-task execution on fpga-based computing systems. IEEE Trans. Parallel Distrib. Syst. **33**(3), 710–722 (2022)
19. Peck, W., Anderson, E., Agron, J., Stevens, J., Baijot, F., Andrews, D.: Hthreads: a computational model for reconfigurable devices. In: 2006 International Conference on Field Programmable Logic and Applications, pp. 1–4 (2006)
20. Quraishi, M.H., Tavakoli, E.B., Ren, F.: A survey of system architectures and techniques for fpga virtualization. IEEE Trans. Parallel Distrib. Syst. **32**, 2216–2230 (2021)
21. So, H.K.h., Brodersen, R.W.: Improving usability of fpga-based reconfigurable computers through operating system support. In: 2006 International Conference on Field Programmable Logic and Applications, pp. 1–6 (2006)
22. Vatsolakis, C., Pnevmatikatos, D.: Racos: Transparent access and virtualization of reconfigurable hardware accelerators. In: 2017 International Conference on Embedded Computer Systems: Architectures, Modeling, and Simulation (SAMOS), pp. 11–19 (2017)
23. Wulf, C., Willig, M., Göhringer, D.: A survey on hypervisor-based virtualization of embedded reconfigurable systems. In: 2021 31st International Conference on Field-Programmable Logic and Applications (FPL), pp. 249–256 (2021)
24. Xilinx: Vitis unified software platform documentation: Application acceleration development. https://docs.xilinx.com/r/en-US/ug1393-vitis-application-acceleration
25. Zhou, Y., et. al.: Rosetta: a realistic high-level synthesis benchmark suite for software programmable fpgas. In: FPGA 2018, pp. 269–278 (2018)
26. Zha, Y., Li, J.: Virtualizing FPGAs in the cloud, pp. 845–858 (2020)
27. Zha, Y., Li, J.: Hetero-vital: a virtualization stack for heterogeneous fpga clusters. In: 2021 ACM/IEEE 48th Annual International Symposium on Computer Architecture (ISCA), pp. 470–483 (2021)

# Author Index

Aklah, Zeyad 32
Alsharari, Majed 103
Andrews, David 32

Burke, Ray 103

Coutinho, Jose G. F. 118

Danilowicz, Michal 166
Deng, Quan 17
Duan, Xiaohui 17

Engels, Stefan Andersson 103

Fang, Li 62
Fu, Haohuan 17

Gaitonde, Dinesh 1
Gan, Lin 17
Guangwen, Yang 62
Guo, Ce 150

Huang, Miaoqing 32
Hung, Eddie 1

Jiang, Peiyong 150

Kabir, Ehsan 32
Koch, Andreas 134
Kong, Minxuan 72
Koziris, Nectarios 181
Kryjak, Tomasz 166
Kwan, Bowen P. Y. 150

Laserna, Javier 47
Liu, Qiang 17
Luk, Wayne 118, 150

Mai, Son T. 103
Miliadis, Panagiotis 181

Niemitz, Lorenzo 103
Nunez-Yanez, Jose Luis 72

Omidian, Hossein 1
Otero, Andrés 47

Papaphilippou, Philippos 87
Pnevmatikatos, Dionisios N. 181
Poudel, Arpan 32

Que, Zhiqiang 118

Reaño, Carlos 103
Rognlien, Markus 118

Shah, Myrtle 87
Sorensen, Simon 103
Spang, Christoph 134

Theodoropoulos, Dimitris 181
Torre, Eduardo de la 47

Volz, David 134

Woods, Roger 103

Xiang, He 62
Xiang, Shengye 17
Xuesen, Chu 62

Yang, Guangwen 17
Yang, Jinzhe 17
Yuan, Ming 17

Zhao, Liu 62

Printed in the United States
by Baker & Taylor Publisher Services

Printed in the United States
by Baker & Taylor Publisher Services